MW00965617

Government by Polemic

Lori Anne Ferrell

GOVERNMENT BY POLEMIC

James I, the King's Preachers, and the Rhetorics of Conformity, 1603-1625

STANFORD UNIVERSITY PRESS
STANFORD, CALIFORNIA

Stanford University Press
Stanford, California
© 1998 by the Board of Trustees of the
Leland Stanford Junior University
Printed in the United States of America

CIP data appear at the end of the book

For Kevin

Acknowledgments

For me, this book has been a long time coming. It had its written inception in my doctoral thesis, but I knew I wanted to work on the topic when I was an undergraduate. Along the way I have incurred so many debts that it is a pleasure finally to acknowledge the following libraries, grant-giving institutions, and persons.

First, I would like to thank the librarians and staff of the libraries and record offices where I spent so much time: the British Library, London; the Public Record Office, London; the Bodleian Library, Oxford, England; the Cambridge University Library, Cambridge, England; the Huntington Library, San Marino, California; the Honnold Library, Claremont, California; and, finally, those cathedrals of learning commonly known as the Sterling Memorial Library and the Beinecke Rare Book Library, Yale University.

The following institutions made it possible for me to complete my research with generous grants: The United States–United Kingdom Fulbright Commission; Yale University; the Whiting Foundation; the Huntington Library, and the British Academy. I am fortunate to work for an enlightened institution that awards its junior faculty a full year of sabbatical leave. This I spent very congenially at Wolfson College, Cambridge University, as a Visiting Scholar. Many thanks, then, are due to President Robert Edgar and Dean Marjorie Suchocki of the Claremont School of Theology; and to Dr. Gordon Johnson and the Fellows of Wolfson College.

I would also like to thank my editors at Stanford University Press, Norris Pope, John Feneron, and Jan Spauschus Johnson, for their support, encouragement, and timely e-mail interventions. Peter Dreyer was a careful, discerning, and saintly copyeditor, for which I am truly grateful. My student Garth Reese helped with the indexing.

Chapter 5 is a revised version of an essay published in Donna Hamilton and Richard Strier, eds., *Religion, Literature and Politics in Post-Reformation England, 1540–1688* (Cambridge University Press, 1995). Permission to use this material is gratefully acknowledged. I have read earlier versions of chapters of this book at meetings of the American Historical Association; National, Northeast, and Pacific Coast Conferences on British Studies, and at the British History seminars held at the Institute of Historical Research, University of London; Cambridge University; and the Huntington Library. Many thanks to all who commented. Since 1991, my students at the Claremont Graduate School and the Claremont School of Theology have listened patiently to a lot of these ideas (sometimes when they expected to be analyzing something else entirely); I thank them for forbearance and insight. Peter McCullough generously allowed me to read his manuscript on Elizabethan and Jacobean court sermons and has offered much excellent conversation on this topic we both love. In addition, the following persons have read part or all of the manuscript and have made many helpful corrections and suggestions: Patrick Collinson, Conal Condren, David Cressy, Constance Jordan, Peter Lake, John Morrill, Michael Questier, Conrad Russell, Michael Schoenfeldt, Paul Seaver, and Kevin Sharpe. What errors and infelicities remain are of course my own.

Finally, I have several profound debts to acknowledge, in areas both professional and personal. I would not have become an historian without the early support and longtime encouragement of my first undergraduate professor in British History, Conrad Russell. David Underdown provided me with excellent advice and non-negotiable deadlines as my doctoral advisor at Yale. Peter Lake oversaw my doctoral research in London and has read many drafts since with patience and good humor: his exacting and subtle critiques of this work have been invaluable.

Last, my neighbor and sometime collaborator David Cressy introduced me to the West Coast academic world and has offered friendship along with erudition, fine gifts indeed.

I would like to thank my best editor and critic, Eric Denton, who over many years has tried his hardest to teach me the fundamentals of prose styling and word processing. Along the way he has learned more about religion and politics in early modern England than any scholar of German literature should have to know, and has not yet called in the debt and expected me to master the writings of the young Goethe. This shows generosity of both intellect and spirit and, undoubtedly, common sense.

I end with a brief tribute to my son, Kevin. He has grown up with a mother constantly at university, and so has endured academic penury, dislocation in the name of historical research, and tough competition when he needed the kitchen table in order to do *his* homework. He is the reason why I had the semblance of a normal life throughout my late pursuit of higher education. And it is precisely because he never typed my manuscripts, read a chapter draft, or showed the least interest in Jacobean preachers that I love him as fiercely as I do. I offer him the dedication to this book, my second-best effort thus far in this life.

L.A.F.

Contents

A Note on the Text

Throughout this text, spelling is modernized in all citations, although the original spelling is preserved in titles of works published in the sixteenth and seventeenth centuries. As much as possible, I have tried to preserve original punctuation and capitalization; I have noted where this is not possible, or where I have emphasized words or phrases in the citations. In the text, dates are Old Style, but the year is taken to begin on 1 January.

Government by Polemic

CHAPTER ONE

Government by Polemic

This is a book about words: not in context, but as context. It traces the history of the immoderate language that characterized the governmental style of a king dedicated to the ideal of moderation. It is based on the often complementary, often adversarial, always interdependent published works of James I and his court preachers as they set about the task of ruling England by polemic. It will, therefore, privilege discourse over action in the political arena, for the remarkable transformation of religious categories that permanently altered the political landscape of Jacobean England was almost solely a discursive phenomenon. This rhetorical upheaval had turned the Church of England inside out by the 1620's, making anti-Calvinists into defenders of the faith and Calvinists into "Puritans." Whether the rhetoric of Jacobean policy was supported in the localities by a coordinated episcopal campaign against something called "Puritanism" therefore poses an intriguing but often inconsequential historical problem. What these words alone accomplished was both real and substantial.

Faced with an overwhelming mass of words and an underwhelming number of deeds, how does the historian assess the significance of political language? The turn to literary or religious studies can prove unhelpful. All Anglican apologists and almost as many literary critics have misread the relationship between doctrine, politics, and language in early Stuart Britain. Lancelot Andrewes, the hero of the *Anglo-Catholic Library*, and John Donne, the hero of Eng. Lit. 101, have consistently been touted as characteristic preachers of the Jacobean age.[1] Recent scholarship, however, questions their place in the Anglican pantheon. If the early-seventeenth-century English Church can no longer be seen primarily as the purveyor of some golden mean, an inspiration for the Newmanesque neo-Gothic, or a creative storehouse for metaphysical poets, this is owing to the work of historians who claim that James I's religious establishment was dominated by men that professed moderate Calvinist doctrinal opinions and espoused pragmatic attitudes on liturgical matters. In these revised standard versions of the English Church, Andrewes and Donne have come to occupy a more interesting space, one where their stylish opinions on liturgy and theology were somehow both important and at the same time relegated to the ecclesiastical fringe. This description might most accurately capture the essence of their roles as members of a religious literati; however, as a way of understanding early Stuart cultural and political history, it remains unsatisfying.[2]

Thus new studies of politics and religion in early Stuart England can confirm but might also lead us to question the force and focus of a recent trend in English historiography. This overturned a view, held since the Restoration, that early Stuart England was a state racked by political grievance, headed resolutely on a "high road to civil war" in the name of parliamentary liberty and—sometimes—, Puritan revolution. Recently, revisionist historians such as Conrad Russell and Kevin Sharpe have drawn a very different portrait, presenting us with a culture in fundamental agreement on basic principles of political moderation and cooperation. For these scholars, the English Civil War was no mighty clash of ideologies, but rather the dreary and dispiriting result of short-term conflicts catalyzed by the "structural weaknesses of the Stuart monarchy."[3]

Political revisionism led, naturally, to new ways of looking at religion in early modern England. Whereas traditional "Whig" chroniclers of early Stuart history praised the triumph of a unique English-style liberty over absolutism,[4] traditional Anglican historiography often trumpeted the ascendancy of a unique English-style Protestantism that enshrined the principle of something known as the *via media*—the "middle way"—over the tyrannical pretensions of continental popery and domestic Puritanism. Revisionist accounts of religion now offer a more complicated scenario, one in which a theologically Calvinist Church flourished from the later reign of Elizabeth I until the death of James I. According to this report, James's son Charles I either knowingly or unknowingly allowed a small set of anti-Calvinist ecclesiastics under the leadership of William Laud, archbishop of Canterbury, to dominate the doctrinal politics of the Church of England in the 1620's and 1630's. The Laudians' increasingly provocative actions provoked a "counterrevolution" by once-comfortable Calvinists now forced into a reactive, protective opposition.[5] The Elizabethan and Jacobean center—a so-called Calvinist consensus—could not hold. And as things fell apart with remarkable alacrity, "England's wars of religion" unleashed a Puritan revolutionary force as short-lived as that of Laud's clerical shock troops had been.[6]

Political revisionists were swift to recognize the benefits of this line of argumentation. Ecclesiastical revisionism offered new support for their theories of Jacobean consensus shattered by Caroline innovation; better still, it kept the Civil War from dwindling into an uninspiring conflict over unlofty issues like finance. More significant, this new scholarship questioned the power— even, sometimes, the existence—of Puritanism in a reign characterized by Calvinist moderation, thereby providing the final blow to an older "Puritan revolution" thesis that had been central to some Whig accounts of the triumph of parliaments.[7]

Little wonder, then, that the past two decades have witnessed an unprecedented number of studies of religion in early Stuart England. These immaculately researched works do make a compelling case for Jacobean consensus and moderation. For, if like Nicholas Tyacke, we focus on theological writings from this period, we find that James ruled over a more doctrinally united Church than did either his predecessor or successor.[8] Turning with Kenneth Fincham and Peter Lake to documented matters of ecclesiastical enforcement, we see that James ruled over a country both better conformed and less contentious on many issues of conformity than it had been under Elizabeth or was to be under Charles.[9] And when with Patrick Collinson we examine the cultural assumptions held by most Elizabethan and Jacobean men and women, we learn that a love of good preaching and an overwhelming detestation of popery united Puritans and conformists alike.[10] The passion that distinguishes their commonly held views, however, suggests that "moderation" did not actually figure in their spiritual ambitions: it would have been deemed "lukewarm," Laodicean. This intolerant disparity between social ideals and religious convictions led to the self-contradictory politics of the Jacobean era.

In the early seventeenth century, the religio-political campaign for that thing identified as "moderation" was anything but moderate. So while I accept and begin with Collinson's commanding view of Puritanism as a reforming force *within* the English Church, Tyacke's paradigm-shifting insights about the revolutionary rise of Arminianism in the 1620's, and Fincham and Lake's influential thesis on the distinctive style of anti-extremism in the ecclesiastical policies of James I, my conclusions differ markedly from theirs.[11] In moving away from Tyacke's almost exclusive focus on theological conflict, I challenge Collinson's finding of a secure place for Jacobean Puritans within the religious settlement. And in my analysis of the polemical strategy undergirding the Jacobean claim to "moderation," I return the powerful force of anti-Puritanism (and with that, its necessary corollary, Puritanism) to its rightful place in early modern religious politics.

To be sure, scholars like Ken Fincham and, especially, Peter Lake have not ignored the anti-Puritanism that we cannot seem to revise out of early Stuart religious history, but they have identified its Jacobean style (following Lake's lead) as avant-garde, the province of a few distinctive but marginalized ecclesiastics at court.[12] This does not go nearly far enough. These voices were always central to James's government by polemic, and new, frighteningly hybrid forms of "Puritanism" developed in polemical works published by royal command during the suppos-

edly quiescent period stretching between the Elizabethan episcopal suppression of the presbyterian Puritan movement and the
Caroline episcopal campaign against "Puritan doctrine." The
power of such works in one reign would reverberate into the
next, articulating a Caroline anti-Calvinist movement that did
back up its words with episcopal action and royal preferment.
Perhaps even more significant, Jacobean official rhetoric provided the Laudians with the long-standing narrative "tradition"
of anti-evangelicalism that has sustained Anglican histories of
the Church since the Restoration.

In the deceptive lull caused by James's disinclination to persecute Puritans by means of persistent episcopal conformity campaigns, the problem of Puritanism was taken up instead in print
debate. Studying the abundant evidence, we see that two notions
of "moderation" were primarily at issue. One was proposed by
conformable Puritans, who reckoned "moderation" meant royal
and episcopal toleration of some kinds of conscientious nonconformity. These were usually liturgical and practical issues upon
which the Bible was silent, and in this silence the less-conforming
found a sanction for their scruples. The other view of moderation
was put forth by those who believed that "moderation" meant
sacramental conformity as an act of loyalty to the royal supremacy. By the end of James's reign, this last polemic dominated the
articulation of governmental policy, finally taking on a daring
doctrinal gloss that ensured that the alliance of moderate Puritans with secular conformists (those who believed sacramental
conformity was itself an *adiaphoric* notion) would be broken. To
be sure, this audacious and official theological shift can be dated
from the 1620's, but in actuality a reign's worth of seemingly less
controversial governmental language had built it an excellent
and nearly airtight case.

Thus carefully crafted rhetorics—aimed at unifying the
Church by promoting "moderation"—in actuality constructed
the stereotype of "Puritanism" that destroyed the political cohe-
sion of the early Stuart Church. This alone ought to tempt us to
cast yet another long backward glance and reconsider the cul-

tural origins of the English Civil War. When recast as conflict-ridden, Jacobean religious politics can no longer stand alone: they are the integral strand that connects the hotly contested Elizabethan ecclesiastical settlement of 1559 to the religious conflict of Caroline Britain. Descried in this context, James's England emerges, not as a haven for religious consensus, but as the rhetorical laboratory for the development of an increasingly powerful and strident anti-Reformation politics.

The conflict of the reign of James VI and I in England, spanning the years 1603 to 1625, has to be grasped if we are to elucidate what exactly "England's wars of religion" were *about*: the last piece of the puzzle, so to speak. But if that conflict is to be understood aright, historians cannot privilege "real" facts over early Stuart polemical discourse. We do not need a fresh view of the evidence; we do need an expanded sense of how evidence actually works to document cultural conflict. We need an account that, in "reexamining the relationship of words to events," does so by considering how words in this period could operate in lieu of action, contradict current, verifiable events, and eventually rescript the assumptions of religio-political culture in such a way as to transform it entirely.[13]

To talk about conflict may appear to move against a tide of revisionist scholarship, but it is actually the logical outcome to those same studies that have permanently restructured our view of Tudor-Stuart religious history. This book signals no return to Whig history; instead, it recasts the narrative offered by revisionists and recognizes the part rhetoric plays in designing it. After all, despite its claims to science, history is built almost entirely from and upon words. Revisionism replaced generations of uncritical parliamentary and Anglican puffery, but the famous archival industry and accuracy of the revisionists has not prevented them from presenting governmental polemic with a similar naïveté; where previous historians forwarded Puritan complaints against governmental repression or Anglican tub-thumping about the uniqueness of the English Church, revisionists have been just as beguiled by early modern monarchical spokesmen who claimed that moderation was their king's intent and a *via media* his policy.[14] The truth is, of course, more complicated when we take a critical look at governmental polemic. We may find no sustained or few effectively repressive religious campaigns under James I, but we should be equally hard-pressed to explain what was actually "moderate" about the language (and by extension, the broadcast intentions) of his government.

Governments invariably do the things they do in the name of "moderation," and it is true that under James the English Church included many different views along a Protestant spectrum, just as it had under Elizabeth and would under Charles. But what counts here is which religious position was aired most successfully, influentially, and persistently in this age. The particular genius of Jacobean governmental polemic was its skill in repackaging an anti-Calvinist, sacramentalist minority ecclesiastical position, not merely as mainstream orthodoxy, which would be interesting enough, but as mainstream orthodoxy under attack, which was a much more effective undertaking. The *via media* touted by these supposedly avant-garde spokesmen for James I was a splendid rhetorical caricature, a powerful and ultimately successful propagandistic strategy aimed at silencing the moderate Puritan voice within the Church, not the extreme sectarian voices outside it. This constant, increasingly shrill court campaign against evangelical Calvinism called into question royal commitment to England's Protestant reformation and the king's relation to the churchmen serving him. It thus broadened the cultural divide opened between Puritans and the opponents of further evangelical reform in the reign of Elizabeth I, with devastating political consequences.

The title of this book, *Government by Polemic*, takes as a starting point the thesis argued by Maurice Lee, Jr., that James's preferred method of ruling his native country, Scotland, after 1603 was "by pen."[15] This attitude was not confined to James's *in absentia* government of his northern kingdom, however, but reflects an overriding policy, influenced by the king's native Calvinism, that recognized the remarkable power of the word, whether discharged by pen or print. From any perspective, religious or secular, James's rule in England was splendidly logocentric. And in view of its power, intentionality, and print longevity, the deliberately contentious political discourse of Jacobean government, expressed in the Chapel Royal, broadcast from the great outdoor pulpit at Paul's Cross, and published in the writings of the king and his religious polemicists, may well be the most tangible proof historians have that the conflicts of the Caroline age arose from long-standing religious divisions with roots in the peculiarly incomplete nature of England's Protestant Reformation.[16]

This argument, therefore, necessarily builds on the revisionist focus on the court as the primary locus of political activity and, related to this, on revisionism's appraisal of the character and rule of James I. The luster of James's self-portrait as "Great Britain's Solomon," the wise and religious champion of peace, has been undergoing restoration in recent years. This is a welcome change from earlier views that, at worst, stressed the "essential littleness" of the man and, at best, condescended to him as a crude and slobbery pedant-king with unnatural appetites, little charm, and less skill in the art of governing. New scholarship convincingly demonstrates James's real strengths in the art of government: his theological erudition, his talent as a writer, his ability to manipulate court factions to his own benefit, his farsighted distaste for war, his native understanding of his northern kingdom, and—most outstanding in this age of religious discontent—his ability to keep his English Church firmly under control.[17]

James I's ruling image was propped up by a politic, if flimsy, religious settlement constructed of equal parts reformed doctrine and unreformed ecclesiology.[18] This fundamentally unbalanced strategy has inspired more theological than political analysis overall. Recent studies have established the doctrinal unity of the English Church in the first two decades of the seventeenth century. But the seemingly endless preoccupation with whether or not there was a theological agreement based on Calvinist doctrine in late Elizabethan and Jacobean England has too precisely fixed the religious cause of the Civil War on the rise of Arminianism in the 1620's.[19] This narrow focus overlooks more significant and longer-running controversies: the issues of religious practice that dominated contemporary print debate from the first years of James's reign. An extra-theological discourse provides us with Jacobean mile-markers along a direct path leading to the religious conflicts of the 1630's. The intemperate propaganda that characterized James I's campaign for political and ecclesiastical order went largely unenforced, but it bequeathed an alternative tradition, a dangerous religious stereotype, and a language of unparalleled intolerance and denunciation, all of which would later support a set of disastrous Caroline ecclesiastical policies.

Without question, James I managed a religious settlement that was remarkable in its age for theological consensus and nonconfrontational policy. But it is also true that he did so while allowing and often encouraging a virulent polemic of denunciation of those who sought any further reform of the English Church. The *Short-Title Catalogue* provides a wealth of evidence that religious controversy thrived in the highly polarized polemical atmosphere characterizing this "moderate" reign. The revisionist admiration of James's maintenance of domestic peace in an age punctuated by religious war has been achieved by conveniently overlooking or carefully explaining away the remarkable contentiousness of these discourses, many of which issued directly from the Jacobean court. The schizophrenic character of this promotion of religious stability manifested itself in two ways: in a language of government that idealized the notion of "moderation" in a rhetoric of extremity, and in the sociocultural tension that is created by juxtaposing de facto toleration and public condemnation. The results were far-reaching. In the powerful discursive arena of the Jacobean court, conforming Puritanism— the force that defined the Elizabethan religious establishment, the last vestige of politically viable, evangelically reformist Protestantism left in England—was belittled, discredited, and finally sidelined.

Credit for this polemical feat must be given primarily to the king and his ecclesiastical spokesmen. The king, who enjoyed a reputation as a learned controversialist in his own right, maintained religious uniformity by barking vigorously rather than by biting. His views were preserved for posterity in the form of speeches and treatises, of which there are an unprecedented number of pages. James stands alone in the history of English monarchs as a prolific author. He regarded his books as self-explanatory, both in the usual sense of their clarity or transparency and in the more literal sense of the service these works did in explaining not only his policies but himself. He was unique in his obsessive attention to the task of literary self-promotion and description, a characteristic reflecting his unenviable position as a foreign king in England. Having spent a good portion of his Scottish reign campaigning for another throne, after 1603, James continued to regard his English subjects, his continental allies, and his enemies, foreign and domestic, as subjects for persuasion—in other words, as a reading audience.[20]

Given his talent for writing, his knowledge of theology, and his love of religious debate, it is not surprising that James I turned to his bishops and court preachers for assistance in this task of governing by polemic. Sermons, not masques, were the major organs of political self-expression at the Jacobean court. Their audience extended well beyond Whitehall. These works provide an insiders' perspective on central government, voiced in the influential language of religion by men adept at the powerful arts of rhetoric. The religious underpinning of civil authority and the Erastian nature of the Protestant state are their *topoi*, commonplaces that reflect the practical concerns of patronage. James's controversialists served both the king and the Church of England, as privy councilors, bishops, deans, and chaplains. The throne commanded their obedience; the pulpit was their métier. Court sermons were recognized as important indices of royal opinion, but court preachers could also draw upon the prerogatives of the pastoral role and their extensive education in the art of rhetoric to advise or even admonish the king. As we shall see, this capacity to persuade the king gave some determined court preachers the power to transform the political and religious status quo while appearing to promote it.

But James also knew how to use his spokesmen to further his own ends, and many of his cues to them came from his own speeches and written works. James's writings have been the subject of several recent studies, but the many sermons preached to him at court and the sermons preached to broadcast the king's policies from the outdoor pulpit at St. Paul's, and their relationship to James's own opinions, have received considerably less attention from historians.[21] This seems particularly unfortunate when we consider the centrality of preaching to the ideological world of Tudor-Stuart England. The ubiquity of sermons in Jacobean culture testifies to their broad appeal. In post-Reformation Britain, public appetite for both print and preaching was phenomenal. Moreover, published sermons issuing from the court pulpit offered something extra—they promised the kind of overt political message that guaranteed a sizable and influential audience. People read these sermons not only because they found them spiritually, intellectually, and aesthetically compelling— and, not incidentally, entertaining—but also to decipher what the king believed. This combination of attractions made for a very persuasive message. Court sermons and the collected sermons of court preachers constitute a large percentage of the sermons published in the early seventeenth century, and they had the built-in market advantage of a singular and powerful identity. Read by privy councilors, court hangers-on, continental observers, university scholars, and British clerics, these sermons were arguably the most influential printed political works available to an early modern audience.

"Sermons have tended to fall between the disciplines in the construction of our sense of the seventeenth century," Jeanne Shami observes.[22] This methodological slipperiness accounts for a certain degree of scholarly neglect. This is especially true of court and St. Paul's conformist sermons, in which political, religious, literary, rhetorical, and theological aims are so admixed that they defy specialized or sustained analysis. Reflecting the secularization of the academy, perhaps, sermons are almost completely ignored in the studies of political language that abound for this period; ironically, this disdain also characterizes theological and Church historical scholarship. Designed to present a politic view of "official" belief, political sermons were rarely if ever explicit in their theology. With so much recent religio-historiographical methodology steadfastly fixed upon the political significance of Calvinism and anti-Calvinism, they have been overlooked as significant contributions to the religious culture of this period. The place of the sermon in literary studies is too often limited to the contexts of Donne's metaphysical poetry. Worse still, the sermons of such court preachers as Lancelot Andrewes and Joseph Hall have been the object of fawning, uncritical attention by some lovers of English devotional literature.[23]

In particular, the excess of attention paid to Andrewes has unbalanced our notion of how different religious styles interacted to produce Jacobean political culture. While he was a prominent preacher and an undisputed court favorite, Andrewes's anti-Calvinist theology and liturgical obsessions cut against the religious grain of Jacobean England. The king enjoyed his elegant, scholarly, and (deceptively) obsequious sermons, but in them Andrewes's less acceptable opinions were kept under wraps, disguised in sophisticated rhetoric. Even so, the king's printer published more sermons by Andrewes than by any other court preacher during the years 1603 to 1625, and the complete Andrewes oeuvre, boosted by the posthumous publication of his *Ninety-Six Sermons* in 1629, constitutes more than half of all the court sermons preached to the first Stuart king of England that were published. We cannot overlook this commanding voice, which forces us to contemplate the influence of a distinctive, culturally challenging polemical style on the mainstream of English religious thought.[24] Lancelot Andrewes's impact upon religious and political ideas in this period must be

viewed, then, from a different angle, and so our questions become: what was the thing contended for most in this period, if
not theology? and, most important, by what marvelous mecha-
nism could an avant-garde ecclesiastic become the much-
vaunted spokesman for the Church of England's "middle
way"?[25]

To understand how a preaching style had such potential to influence political content, it is important to move away from theology to the larger and more contentious world of Jacobean ecclesiology. Doctrinal unity may have been the great achievement
of James's reign, but in this period, the conflict between royal
supremacy and Christian liberty was conducted upon a ceremonial battlefield. Outside the "Calvinist consensus," there were a
multitude of religious practices—kneeling at public prayer and
making the sign of the cross in baptism, to name two—described
in the Book of Common Prayer as *adiaphora*, extra-scriptural
matters under the authority of the monarch that were "not to be
esteemed equal with God's law." In theory, this meant that these
were established by political authority; they were integral only to
the maintenance of religious uniformity and order and had no
direct soteriological significance. In Elizabeth's reign, churchmen
who might have found the unreformed ceremonies of the English Church disturbing in the spiritual sense could tolerate the
same as adiaphora and hope for their eventual reform. Between
1603 and 1625, however, the notion of adiaphora underwent a
slow, serious revision. The Elizabethan defense of conformity—
the claim that it was merely a matter of decorum—broke down
under attack from both nonconformists and sacramentalists, each
forced to state under increasing political duress that the act of reforming or retaining ceremonies was not at all adiaphoric, but "a
substantial part of the gospel."[26]

So-called "matters indifferent" were the central issues of Jacobean religious identity, an identity that was forged in the Elizabethan battle against the popish anti-Christ and the presbyterian
Martin Marprelate, but refined in subsequent skirmishes between doctrinal brethren. This potentially internecine conflict

began, ironically, with the Calvinist consensus and the alliances it made possible within the religious settlement. Conformists, who accepted the Book of Common Prayer, the canons, and episcopacy for order and uniformity's sake, represented majority opinion in James's English Church. But conformists could make common cause with "moderate Puritans," those who were unhappy about ceremonies, yet capable of a limited cooperation in these matters in view of the doctrinal purity of the national Church. The membership of the Jacobean Church consisted of both conformists and many nonconformists, a fact that reflects the unifying strength of their shared Calvinism. Calvinist doctrine also made a bond possible between sectarians unable to conform in any way to the established Church and the moderate Puritans who shared their feelings about, if not their approach to, the unreformed state of the Church. Many conformists could admire, if not emulate, the uncompromising piety of the sectarians. Just as it is possible to align different Jacobean churchmen along a spectrum of Calvinist belief, then, it is also possible to line these groups up along a spectrum of attitudes to ecclesiological issues.[27]

The king might have tolerated a range of ceremonial opinions in his Church, but he had no tolerance whatsoever for those he called "Puritans." (It is important to remember that the term *moderate Puritan*, although a very useful modern construct, would have been oxymoronic nonsense in the seventeenth century.) James's definition of the "Puritan" was shaped by his Scottish experience, which led him at first to define the phenomenon in a very specific and narrow manner. His frequently humiliating exchanges with the republican presbyterians who raised him accounts for the king's easily roused antipathy to anyone who challenged royal authority and his willingness to denounce such persons as "sectarians" and "Brownists." Still, as Patrick Collinson has written, in Scotland he had been "obliged to respect" the power of the Kirk.[28] And, more interesting, it would appear that James's early experience of Scottish-style Protestantism made him sympathetic to a less formalist Church ecclesiology and eager to strengthen the preaching ministry in England.

James came to his new country with a familiarity with and a genuine liking for an ecclesiastical style that had been considered unacceptable by an important few of his English bishops and churchmen. These clerics waged a polemical war against a different kind of "Puritanism" than that which exercised their new king. Like James, English sacramentalist conformists hated sectarianism and confrontative presbyterianism; unlike James, they also despised nonconformity and distrusted both Calvinism and the preaching-centeredness of reformed Calvinist Protestantism. Their task, then—which they took very seriously and performed with consummate skill—was to influence the king in the direction of their own prejudices and inculcate in him their vision for the English Church. That these preachers were able to attain such success and prominence in James's reign despite the real differences between the king's religious instincts and their own testifies to the brilliant paradox that lay at the heart of Jacobean government by polemic. The preaching culture established in England by a Scottish king was eventually dominated at its center by a remarkable minority of Jacobean churchmen, who used the bully pulpit of the court to denigrate pulpit-based Protestantism.

In their style of conformist rhetoric, the Puritan was a stock character, with a gradual progression of guises from "Presbyterian" to "Calvinist," a transformation that was almost entirely accomplished in the official printed sermon polemic of the Jacobean era. Between 1603 and 1625, therefore, governmental displeasure with radical sectarianism metamorphosed into a condemnation of "Puritanism" that expanded to include those we would now call moderate Puritans. This paved the way for a definition of "Puritan" in the 1630's that included even those stalwart defenders of the Jacobean Church and faith, Calvinist conformists. The significance of this polemical shift cannot be overestimated; until now, it has been overlooked. To understand how "Calvinists" became "Puritans" and "Puritans" became outlaws in Caroline England, therefore, we must first look to the way Jacobean polemic could design and redesign acceptable categories of religious affiliation.

To begin with, it must be remembered that the word *Puritan* was in the period both the emptiest and the most powerful religio-political signifier to appear in print discourse. The designation itself, while perhaps embraced as a point of pride by some outspoken hot Protestants, was unequivocally a term of abuse when broadcast from the official pulpits of Jacobean England. The word had such a volatile valency that it was open to any skillful manipulation of its meaning. For that reason, when wielded by the king or his court preachers, the epithet had the power to indict even conformable, moderate Puritans in the Church of England as potential or actual sectaries. The process by which an increasing number of people in this period became classified as "Puritan"—and hence as alienable from the established Church—thus needs to be subjected to an extended rhetorical analysis.

The brunt of this reclassification was borne by less-conforming but loyal clergy and laity, who were actually given a great deal of latitude by local parish leaders, a majority of Jacobean bishops, and—in practice if not in theory—the king himself. They were, therefore, the most vulnerable members of a religious settlement poised at the most significant crossroads of its post-Reformation history. The hard work of Protestantizing the English Church had been accomplished only recently, in the later years of Elizabeth's reign. At the accession of James I, the Church had to decide whether to continue the work of continentally inclined religious reform or to be satisfied with doctrinal purity but not the liturgical reformation demanded by the hotter sort of Protestant. Moderate Puritans, conformable but irritatingly clamorous for change, became the object of intense negative scrutiny in this religio-political inquiry, the articulation of which was primarily conducted from the court pulpit.

In the rhetorical sense, "Puritanism" was a constructed category. The broad range of views on liturgy and doctrine held by the Jacobean clergy thus gave rise to an ontological paradox.

Although all preachers agreed on the existence of something "Puritan," no two could settle on a common set of traits that would objectively define that enigma. The king's preachers deployed an astonishing array of indiscriminate anti-Puritan language as they searched for terms that would capture the ear of the king. A Calvinist conformist bishop indicting "Puritans" from the Jacobean court pulpit condemned radical separatists in England; the anti-Calvinist cleric preaching against "Puritans" in the same forum indicted the moderate Puritan cleric or, more pointedly, the Calvinist conformist bishop who winked at nonconformity in his diocese (and who had preached at court just the week before condemning those separatists). Both spokesmen would have preached with the confidence born of the knowledge that "Puritans" were real people and not just a figment of the political imagination. Their king would have agreed, but his definition of what was "Puritan" often took on a Scottish aspect.

To concentrate on the taut logic of theology, or to take religious language at face value, therefore, is to ignore the flexibility of seventeenth-century religious polemic. The Jacobean age may be distinctive for its discourse of moderation, but the history of conflict in early Stuart Britain and our understanding of the political and intentional nature of rhetoric demand that we look more critically at Jacobean language to discover its apprehension of cultural crisis. Claims of "moderation" and issues reckoned as "indifferent" were the basic controversial elements of court-sermon rhetoric; punctuated by the accusation of "Puritanism," these categories were arguably the most contested received ideas issuing from the pulpit. Historians must learn to be sensitive to the nuances of Jacobean discourse—after all, Jacobean audiences were. We cannot simply be satisfied with reading along the surface of these religious texts.

Generally speaking, historians must do more than "contextualize" seventeenth-century language—if that means, as it too often does, merely uncovering what "really happened" simultaneously with the writing of something. Contextualization is the opening up of texts to their historical meaning, not the crude locating of texts in the past. We need, then, to realize that texts play active roles, not supporting ones, in the course of history. First, we must recognize the intentionality inherent in the enterprise of preaching. Jacobean religious polemicists were exhaustively schooled—not only in theology and scriptural exegesis, but also in the classical discipline of rhetoric. Assiduous scholars of Quintilian and Cicero, James's court preachers were well aware that the practice of rhetoric was the force that transformed words into action. Moreover, the sermons examined here went on to a life in print. Little in an early Stuart polemical text got there by accident: seemingly insignificant words and phrases represent a considered application of the art of persuasion.

The cultural force of rhetoric thus depends upon the familiarity of its basic notions. Polemic capitalizes on the received ideas of a society. These are the "hooks" that make a new argument, a transformed idea, unthreatening or compelling. We need to recognize the skillful amalgam of the familiar and the transformatory in polemic, to uncover, not only what writers expected their audiences to think, but also at what points their audiences would be receptive to new concepts. But scholars cannot be literary Dr. Frankensteins, extracting and recombining bits of various writings in proof-text style. To disengage phrases or ideas from their original moorings and redeploy them in new configurations to illustrate a point too often creates a false support for a historical argument. These fragments have a context within the larger text, and they often cannot be properly understood outside it.

Interdisciplinarity has energized the study of printed texts for this period, but it has also made it necessary for scholars to reexamine the boundaries that both divide disciplines and make the creative tension that exists between them more compelling. My methodology is best described as a hybrid of disciplinary approaches that, true to my training as a historian, still gives precedence to close reading and often depends on empirical analysis. Informed by early modern rhetorical studies, it parallels the examinations of political discourse undertaken lately by cultural historians, who in turn have been influenced by the work of literary scholars and "contextualist" early modern political theorists.

Yet we can never merely identify rhetorical tropes or discursive contexts and hope to make a simple case for their importance. Historians must show the significance of such strategies; they must uncover the origins of politics in rhetoric. The study of early-seventeenth-century printed sermons demands an approach that recognizes that—in an era that appears to be resistant to the Habermasian search for the discursive activity of a secularly defined "public sphere"—religious texts had a broader reach and a potential for wider dissemination (through their distillation in diocesan initiatives and local pulpit interpretation) than did strictly secular political-theoretical texts. In this study of sermon polemic, then, we must rediscover something James and his preachers knew instinctively: the unique ability of religious language to shape political action.

This book thus traces interconnected narratives: one rhetorical, one historical. Its purpose is to mark the progress and significance of anti-Puritan rhetoric at the court of James I. This I do first by examining sermons preached at court and at Paul's Cross on the three major political holidays of James's reign, Accession Day, Gunpowder Treason Day, and the commemoration of the king's escape from the conspiracy of the Gowries. The chronology of these Jacobean political events is also a chronology of the public representation of Puritanism.

I confine my analysis for the most part, therefore, to sermons not only preached at court (often before the king) and from the outdoor pulpit at St. Paul's by the king's preachers, but also printed during his reign. This is not to argue that there was some kind of absolute privilege for print in this period that outweighed the influence of the court auditory or circulating manuscript text. Keeping in mind the Jacobean print history of Jacobean court sermons, however, permits consideration as to the broadcast intentions of James's government. It also rescues Jacobean court sermon rhetoric from the overwhelming posthumous influence of Lancelot Andrewes, most of whose court sermons were not published until William Laud and John Buckeridge compiled and edited them in the reign of Charles I.

Second, I examine the two central typologies in Jacobean religious polemic: the image of James as the new Constantine and the imagery of his subjects' religious decorum as expressed in the act of kneeling in worship. Within the parameters of these discursive images, as a relatively moderate concept of Puritan nonconformity gave way to the culturally explosive concept of "doctrinal Puritanism," court preachers produced a transformable typology of the "Puritan." Historical context, therefore, figures interactively with polemical imagery in this analysis of religio-political rhetoric. What emerges is proof, not only of the effect of events upon language, but also of the effect of language upon other language, and, finally, of the reciprocal relationship of language and event.

From 1603 to 1624, England enjoyed a period of unprecedented peace, both at home and with foreign powers. The king, after an uneventful accession and with a guaranteed succession, gloried in the epithet *Rex Pacificus*. War with Spain was an Elizabethan memory. The Gunpowder Plot, although serious, sparked no untoward crisis: in fact, its most significant legacy may well have been the formulation of a royal political theory that recognized the existence of loyal English Catholics.[29] The Puritan faction that had once brandished admonitions had become, to a great degree, reconciled to a Church wherein they were accounted theological brethren. Enforcement of ecclesiastical canons was marked by flexibility and compromise on the part of both bishops and less-conforming clergy. It is in the religious polemic of the period that we find evidence of a cultural fissure that undermined this deceptively consentient society.

Language played a central role in the politics of religion. Recent research has shown that James's method for preserving domestic peace was to isolate what he considered to be extremism at either end of the religious spectrum, a policy that was almost entirely executed by means of official rhetoric. The courtier

Non-conformists

Dudley Carleton reported to Sir Thomas Edmondes in 1610: "The court sermons have been well and exactly hitherto discharged ... [t]he sword cuts even now betwixt papist and Puritan; prohibitions are beaten down with a club, yet rise like Hydra's heads, and prove the worse for preaching against."[30]

Carleton's analysis acknowledges the dissimilar effect that anti-papist and anti-Puritan polemic would have had upon a Jacobean audience. The purpose of "even"-handed criticism could not have been the equitable distribution of governmental condemnation, considering the very different threats papists and Puritans posed to the government in an age of doctrinal consensus. To subject both to similar critique did not so much isolate extremism on both sides as create it on one side by treating disparate offenses as equal. The much-touted *via media* was, in effect, a sophisticated rhetorical strategy aimed at the creation of an increasingly marginalized identity for Puritanism.

The narrative of this transformation begins with the problem posed by the accession of a Scottish king to the throne of England (the subject of Chapter 2, "Two Churches or One?"). The peaceful "union of the crowns" and the religious unity of two Protestant nations were prominent themes in sermons preached at the accession of James I. But James's scheme for more complete political union with Scotland did not succeed with either his new and Scots-wary Parliament nor his suspicious and uneasily hybrid court. While it is customary for historians to applaud the relative ease with which the English throne passed from Elizabeth to James, it must be noted that the uncontested accession nonetheless ushered in a transitional period remarkable for its length, volatility, and turbulence. This was in great part owing to the fact that James VI and I initiated his English reign with an entirely unpopular governmental campaign; we can trace the prolongation of transitional governmental politics by the length of time it took for James to abandon the union scheme. Its failure did not, however, dissuade the king from pursuing a less ambitious, but equally daunting, project: partially to conform his Scottish Kirk to the liturgical standards of his English Church, a

task he broadcast through the medium of English court sermons.[31]

The overwhelmingly negative image of Scotland thus provided the first brush strokes in the new Jacobean portrait of the
Puritan. The quick failure of James's political program and the
persistent problems caused by his long-term religious program
ensured that anti-Scottish rhetoric had an early and definitional
effect upon the anti-Puritan rhetoric of court sermons. Accession
Day became a forum for preachers to compare the king's two
churches. To James, a Calvinist king well-acquainted with Scottish clergymen's contumacious behavior toward monarchs, a Puritan was an enemy not to right doctrine but to royal authority.
The Kirk's resistance to episcopacy was labeled "Puritanism,"
the denunciation of which spilled over to implicate those English
Protestants whose "Puritanism" consisted only in the desire to
see the English Church more perfectly reformed of its popish
remnants of ceremony and liturgy. English moderate Puritanism
became associated with the excesses of Scottish presbyterianism.[32]

In the unsettled period that followed England's transition
from an Elizabethan to a Stuart state, it would take a Catholic
plot to give this portrait a more dangerous coloration (the subject
of Chapter 3 of this book, "Rewriting the Plot"). On the anniversary of the Gunpowder Plot, court preachers had to speak on the
topic of a violent threat to royal authority. Outraged at Catholic
treachery, many were dismayed by James's post-Plot realpolitik.
They were especially concerned about the king's tolerant attitude
to loyal English Catholics and his continued diplomatic ties with
Spain. Court preachers observed the king's political mandate,
however, balancing denunciations of Catholicism with what
Dudley Carleton might have called "evenhanded" rhetoric denouncing Puritans. Some even created a genre of anti-Puritan
sermons that derived increased rhetorical force from the dangers
exemplified by a treasonous plot. The king's promotion of an
oath of allegiance to identify loyal Catholics only added to this
picture of alienated Puritanism, as arguments meant for an in-

ternational papist readership were powerfully redeployed at home against English Catholics and nonconformists.

In order to complete the transformation of "Puritanism," however, the portrayal of the "Church" needed revising as well. In his determination to avoid war with papist European powers, James invoked the principles of ecumenical Catholicism to justify his pacifist policies. Court preachers cited the tradition of Constantine to present the king as the leader of a new Christendom united by broad doctrinal tenets and ceremonial uniformity. (The significance of this imagery is discussed in Chapter 4, "Great Britain's Constantine.") Canny court preachers recognized the anti-Puritan potential of this royal campaign. The comparison of James to Constantine led inevitably to discussions of the nature of the Church he governed at home. Was it to be so specifically defined as Calvinist, reformed on the continental model, or as part of a larger ecclesiastical universe that included non-Roman Catholicism? Here we see, as we saw previously in the campaigns to conform the Scots and in the Oath of Allegiance controversy, that the arguments the king used in an international or British context could be used at home to attack the domestic phenomenon of moderate Puritanism.

By the last years of James's reign, then, all that was left to halt the assimilation of moderate Puritanism altogether was a radically new view of liturgical conformity (the subject of Chapter 5, "Kneeling and the Body Politic").[33] The second half of James's reign found the king increasingly under fire for his pro-Spanish foreign policy and his determination to keep out of the war in Bohemia. Against this backdrop, his language of conciliation began to sound to many like the language of capitulation to popery. James needed a strong voice to counter a vociferous "Calvinist party" in Parliament that opposed his less confessionally influenced foreign policy. Court preachers responded to James's political dilemma by associating political obedience with a notion of the "beauty of holiness," elevating liturgical concerns beyond the realm of the adiaphoric. James's sacramentalist clergy, whose devotion to the scenic apparatus of religion had always been more widely broadcast than their doctrinal beliefs, seized the polemical moment. They denounced nonconformity as an offense, not only against the authority of royal supremacy, but also against God. In this atmosphere, not only the style, but also the ideological content of Lancelot Andrewes's sermons took center stage. This language would have a limited impact in the waning days of James's reign, but it established the rhetorical mode by which anti-Puritanism became anti-Calvinism in the reign of James's successor.

These sermons provide a dramatic example of how polemic is transformed by the process of its application to political crisis. But they also demonstrate how historical events are influenced by the power of words. Put simply, in the mid 1620's, all Calvinists became Puritans, at least according to the official rhetoric of this logocentric age. Once conformity had been identified as essential doctrine, it needed only a succession, a new archbishop, and a well-documented alternative rhetorical tradition to be associated with essential doctrine: anti-Calvinist liturgical theology now presented in court sermons as both "true and ancient." The sermons of the Jacobean court provide early evidence of the disastrous limitations of the Calvinist consensus in early Stuart England.

PART I

Sermons on Political Occasions

Two Churches or One? The Accession of James VI and I

"Much hath been said, and more hath been written, of . . . union," preached Robert Wakeman before James I in April 1605 in what might appear to be congratulatory mode.[1] After a century of religious upheaval with each Tudor succession, the confessionally uneventful accession of the Protestant James VI of Scotland to the throne of England in 1603 should have been as welcome as it was unprecedented. A contentious issue, however, undermined the peaceful transition to Stuart government. The king arrived in his southern kingdom with some unwelcome excess baggage: Scottish advisers, Scottish cronies, and Scottish clergy. (Left to be determined, of course, was the question of how Scottish the king himself was.) Worse still, James came with a plan to make over his two kingdoms into one politically united island nation. Wakeman might just as well have been bemoaning the fact that, in the first years of James's reign, the only way for an ambitious man to get ahead quickly was to be a Scot or to promote the king's union scheme.

The evidence of such industry abounds: representations of Anglo-Scottish union dominated the cultural landscape of early Jacobean London. The triumphal arches that heralded James's first entry there were marvels of imperial imagery; printed works about the union poured from presses; court masques and marriages were swift to exploit its metaphoric possibilities.[2] It was an auspicious time to kick off a campaign. "[T]he benefits that do arise of that Union which is made in my blood . . . do redound to the whole Island," James told his first English parliament,[3] and on that note of anticipatory self-affirmation, he announced his intention to secure a complete political union of his

native and adopted countries. The king's optimism was prema-
ture. His scheme for formal union was a failure, abandoned as
hopeless within five years. James was left in 1608 much as he
had started, with a union of crowns alone, two nations united
only "in [his] blood."

The relatively scant historical interest in the formal campaign
of 1603–8 terminates altogether with the end of James's more
ambitious plan. By this I do not imply that historians of England
have ignored the history of Anglo-Scottish relations under the
early Stuarts; on the contrary, the topic has received a great deal
of attention in recent years. On one side of the interdisciplinary
divide, literary critics have found the personal union to be a perfect example of the "embodiment" of new principles of British
nationalism. And on the other, historians of the revisionist stripe
have found in the skittish chronicle of Anglo-Scottish relations
enough confusion to support their claim that the civil wars of the
1640's had their origins in the inherent weaknesses of early Stuart bureaucracy. Yet historians rarely, if ever, go farther back
than the Scots rebellion of 1637 or Charles's general ineptitude in
ruling his father's native kingdom.[4]

Historians of Jacobean England once saw James's scheme as a
personal foible, soon abandoned; now revisionists present it either as an act of political acumen that was ahead of its time or as
a harbinger of future problems of multiple rule. But the influence
of Scotland (or, for that matter, Ireland) on English religious debates prior to 1637 has attracted little detailed attention.[5] An
amendment to this state of historiographical affairs has been offered by Kenneth Fincham and Peter Lake, who in a timely revision of a 1985 article on the ecclesiastical policy of James I now
state, not only that "Caroline policies and priorities make sense
only in the ideological and political policy of James I's reign,"
but also that "the origins of Jacobean policy towards English Puritans and Catholics clearly lie in Scotland."[6] Their analysis is
welcome but sketchy: although it briefly relates the narrative of
James's dealings with Scottish presbyterians and Catholics prior
to his accession to the English throne, it does not address at all

the problematic *ideological* example demonstrated for England by
Scotland after 1603. Even historians who have acknowledged the
importance of the king's Scottishness to an understanding of Jacobean ecclesiastical policy have neglected the influence of union
on the politics of discourse that most often shaped that policy.

Like the Tudors before him, James I recognized the importance of official propaganda; he preferred government by polemic to visual imagery, however, which set him apart from his
predecessors. It is high time, then, to dissect the language of union and analyze its particular impact on English political discourse. This chapter focuses on the representation of Anglo-
Scottish union in the intertwining languages of treatises on union, royal speeches and other writings on the union, and, especially, the union-inspired sermons of the king's preachers, of
whom at least two (John Gordon and John Thornborough) also
wrote union tracts.[7] In doing so, it reconstructs an early-seventeenth-century union lexicon that had its most powerful and
longest-lasting influence on English religious politics. The
scheme for political union inspired a contemporary debate about
how united James's two kingdoms were in matters of religion.
This debate allowed English court preachers to interrogate the
assumption that such a unity would naturally exist between two
nations conjoined by a single monarchy and a shared Calvinist
theology. But England and Scotland most assuredly did *not*
agree on the adiaphoric issues of ceremony and Church government, and therein lay an insurmountable difficulty.[8] The accession of a Scottish king to the English throne brought the example
of Genevan-style reform disturbingly close to home. The Kirk of
Scotland proved the first and greatest challenge to England's
commitment to pan-Protestantism in the seventeenth century; as
we shall see, court polemic on the subject exposed the inherent
weakness of the Calvinist consensus, not only between James's
two kingdoms, but also within James's new Church.

Campaigns for Anglo-Scottish religious unity predated
James's accession scheme, and they demonstrate the powerful effect that the idea of Protestant unity had on the debate over the

extent of reform in the late sixteenth century. These particular campaigns had their origins both in European pan-Protestantism and in the religious settlements of Elizabeth I and James VI. England's reformation appeared to be stalled at the extra-doctrinal stage, however, and the optimism of Elizabeth's more continentally inspired Protestants in 1559 began to fade. Both bishops and the trappings of their office remained firmly in place. In Scotland, James was determined to retain a modified, limited episcopal structure in the Kirk despite the power of his presbyterian ministers and their success in instituting liturgical reforms on the example set by Geneva.[9] These two very different settlements shared one trait beyond a curiously cobbled-together quality: this was the desire of James and Elizabeth, two monarchs with slightly shaky claims to authority in their separate kingdoms, to take and keep control over their potentially over-mighty Protestant churches.[10]

English Puritans looked for support to their more reformed neighbors to the north on the ultimately misguided assumption that Elizabeth might be persuaded to reform her religious settlement to continental specifications. Conversely, the beleaguered archbishop of St. Andrews, Patrick Adamson, also sought advice from his English counterpart, John Whitgift, on the equally mistaken notion that the queen would have some interest in combating the presbyterian affront to a royal supremacy. But in this period, ironically, English Puritans and Scottish presbyterians enjoyed more mutual conversation than did their episcopal enemies—the archbishops needed Elizabeth's permission to confabulate and she, having no interest in pursuing a closer relationship with the Kirk, refused to grant it. The Scots' lively concern for the continued reformation of the Church of England guaranteed, however, that English Puritans could continue to look north to find the support and solidarity that was precluded at home by their own queen's hostility to the cause of further reform.[11]

The Kirk's interest in reforming the English Church was as strong, then, as the queen's interest in Scottish religious matters was weak. By the death of Elizabeth in 1603, this unbalanced state of affairs made many in the English episcopate concerned about the undue influence of a mainly presbyterian Kirk on both English nonconformists and their new Scottish king. James VI's accession called up old fears of presbyterianism in England, despite the virtual cessation of such agitation by the 1590's. At this time, the Puritans of England looked primarily for relief from the burden of ceremonial conformity. They posed little or no threat to the episcopate and were for the most part included in the English Church, wherein they accounted themselves doctrinal brethren.

In addition, James arrived in his new kingdom with a Scottish preaching retinue (the size of which varied according to rumor) at a time when England's bishops, court chaplains, and aspiring court preachers needed to secure preferment under a new regime.[12] Fear and favor-seeking led English court preachers to develop a skillful union rhetoric that was simultaneously critical and complimentary, as well as chauvinistically pro-English. Many court sermons in the early years of James's English reign turned the union project into a campaign to educate the king in English conformist attitudes by defining "Puritanism" as "radicalism," associating that radicalism with Scottish presbyterianism, and, finally, implying that the moderate Puritan desire for further ceremonial reform was merely a dangerous variant of what James had been working to subdue in his northern Kirk. Eventually, union became a key support for what English Puritans found most disheartening, the idea of ceremonial uniformity. Whether or not James "anglicanized" his multiple kingdoms, his preachers did all in their power to "anglicize" the king.[13]

The Argument for Union, 1603–4

One thing had augured well for James's ambitious accession project—the perception that confessional unity already existed between his two kingdoms.[14] Protestant alliance was by far the most compelling justification for the idea of Anglo-Scottish union. From 1603 to 1605, writers both English and Scottish produced an impressive array of pro-union propaganda. Many of these sermons, tracts, and treatises argued that an exemplary model for union could already be found in Anglo-Scottish confessional affinity.

These writings present their case so convincingly that they have managed to lull most scholars of the period into a false sense of interpretive security.[15] Satisfied with reading the lines rather than between them, historians have declined the opportunity to interrogate the protestations of confessional unity that tract writers employed as a rhetorical strategy.[16] As a result, they find relatively little to interest them in the early history of Anglo-Scottish religious union, preferring to trace to its Caroline or Laudian origins the breakdown of ecclesiastical relations that led to the Civil War. When viewed in the religious context, however, the writings of 1603–5 should inspire the very skepticism they were intended to dispel. They provide the essential background to the divisions that characterize the contentious history of Anglo-Scottish relations in the 1630's.

Highlighting doctrinal consensus merely served to underline the disparity between these two very different Protestant cultures. In 1604, the Scottish presbyterian writer Robert Pont betrayed the anxieties that undermined any discussion of religious union between James's two kingdoms. His tract *De Unione Britanniae*, published in London and Edinburgh, vehemently denied that any substantial problem existed between British Protestants. Church and Kirk enjoyed doctrinal unity: granted, they did not enjoy "equality and like perfection" in polity and liturgy (one assumes that Pont recognized more "perfection" in the Kirk's polity), but this was no obstacle to "ecclesiastical unity."[17] There is, however, an ecclesiological snake lurking in this Edenic vision. In his treatise, Pont condemns as "Puritan" the kind of nonconformity that led to sectarianism. But he also disapproved of overly rigorous polemical campaigns for conformity, claiming that "many worthy, reverent, and learned men" in England had been "injuriously" identified as "Puritans" as a result.[18] Here Pont grapples with a problem both substantive and semantic. He defines "Puritanism" as an unjustifiable separation from the established Church over matters that should have been "indifferent," but his concern that nonseparatist critics of liturgy and polity not be libeled qualifies his condemnation. His contradictory statements illustrate that the promotion of union could break down in the simple attempt to define either adiaphora or "Puritanism" in a manner acceptable and comprehensible in both Scotland and England.[19]

De Unione Britanniae begs a question: how politically astute was it even in this period to dismiss so pointedly the differences in ecclesiastical practices that distinguished the Scottish Kirk from the English Church? When the king asked Francis Bacon to draw up a set of articles outlining arguments for union based upon precedent, Bacon was less disingenuous than Pont. Carefully (and, as it turned out, presciently), he observed that while religion was indeed "a point of union," it could not be considered a decisive point. It had, in fact, "some scruple or rather grain of separation enwrapped and included in it."[20] With a fine skepticism about Calvinist consensus, Bacon highlighted the problem of England and Scotland's very different attitudes to church government and ritual practice. No principles of "moderation" applied here: Bacon sensed that such theologically "indifferent" matters were nonetheless potentially divisive. They formed the secret heart of unavoidable religious and cultural incompatibility.[21]

The rhetorical campaign for full political union serves as a starting place for the argument of this chapter. Nervous affirmations of writers with a desire to please a new king notwithstanding, in 1603, Anglo-Scottish unity was neither self-evident nor uncontested, particularly in the case of religion. This becomes clear when we consider the view from the court pulpit between that year and 1608. Sermons preached to the king in the opening years of his reign concentrated, often uneasily, on James's accession as a symbol of the unification of Scotland and England. Unlike union tracts, in which confessional issues were glossed over, these sermons were overwhelmingly concerned with the present extent and future significance of Anglo-Scottish religious unity. Their presentation of these ideas was markedly ambivalent. James's precocious scheme showed all the distressing symptoms of failure to thrive, and the language of Calvinist consensus proved unequal to the task of reviving it.[22] The language of religious unity, however, found a new nondoctrinal focus, with far-reaching implications for the English Church.

While it is doubtful whether any of James's court preachers believed he would allow a presbyterian polity in the Church of England, they were not above implying that presbyterianism could logically be associated with a relaxing of ecclesiastical conformity. This they were able to do by pointing out that the Scots had marshaled a doctrinal argument, not only for the presbytery, but also for what the English would regard as nonconformity. The Kirk regarded the reformation of liturgical practice as scripturally inscribed and commanded: a "substantial part of the gospel." In contrast, most apologists for the Church of England in 1603 argued that those ceremonies still observed by the English Church had not been forbidden by Scripture.[23] All parties in the English Church, from moderate Puritan to enthusiastic ceremonialist, agreed that certain practices could be classed as adiaphoric; what they did not agree upon was which these were.[24] The prayer book stated clearly that common worship ensured "discipline and order" when performed in uniformity, but acts of worship in themselves were "not to be esteemed equal with God's law."[25] This concept of "indifference" made it possible for English moderate Puritans to stay within the Church, although they tended to be a clamorously unsatisfied minority. The practical aim of the tenet was to allow Puritans to conform by persuading them that their scruples were misguided. Practices not expressly forbidden in Scripture could be performed without danger to the conscience; in fact, order and uniformity, insofar as these reflected the will of the monarch, demanded a secular obedience, commanded by God.

Now, however, the aspirations of English moderate Puritans could be expressed by mainstream practice in Scotland, and so their calls for further reform surely reflect, not only the usual renewal of hope inspired by the accession of a new monarch, but also new hopes kindled by the example of James's ceremonially austere northern Kirk. After all, the Book of Common Prayer also supported a clear argument for further reform. Its *dicta* on ceremonies support diversity of practice among national churches, stating that monarchs can "upon just causes" alter or eliminate practices as well as keep them. While these statements were obviously designed to allay concern about (or undue comparison with) the varied styles of worship embraced by Protestant churches on the Continent, it is easy to see that they could also be read as mandates for monarchs to reform as well as retain ceremonies. Theoretically, then, many ceremonies could be altered, most logically when nations underwent transformative change. The unprecedented experience of Anglo-Scottish union, and with that, the potential to create a new unified national Church, provided just that reforming moment for England.

Certainly, James's own words could have been interpreted as a call for an adjustment of attitude on the topic of Puritanism. Robert Pont may well have taken his concern about the semantic problem of "Puritanism" and the unjust libeling of precise churchmen from James's own BASILIKON DORON, the first edition of which was printed in Edinburgh in 1599. A revised edition of the king's book was published in England at the accession, wherein Puritans would have found much to encourage their hopes of further reform. In the revised preface to his work, the king compared moderate Puritanism in England and Scotland by equating politically loyal nonconformity in the former with politically loyal presbyterianism in the latter, and went on to confess that he personally considered both "opinions" adiaphoric, so long as they did not lead to sectarianism.[26] The king invited those of contrary opinion in these matters to press their case "by patience and well grounded reasons"; for his part, James would keep an open mind, since any display of acrimony in this dispute would only give encouragement to papists waiting to exploit disunity in the Protestant Church.[27]

The rebuke at the heart of this statement of solicitude can

hardly be more obvious, and it shows the apparent open-mindedness of the king's remarks in a much subtler light. While Protestant disputes over ceremonies were respectable "old controvers[ies]," upon which James proclaimed himself loathe to "pronounce . . . [a light] sentence," they were, after all, conducted over "things indifferent," and therefore should not be allowed to challenge the king's right to order the Church as he saw fit. The accession edition of BASILIKON DORON had conflicting English and Scottish contexts, therefore, which set the tone for the schizophrenic discussions of ceremonial conformity that characterize James's early English reign. It endorsed the pan-Protestant Erastian ideology behind prayer-book language on ceremonies, which supported the separate and self-regulatory natures of the king's two churches; however, by conflating the very different challenges posed by English nonconformists and Scottish presbyterians, and naming both adiaphoric, it appeared to assert that Church and Kirk were overseen by one single-minded royal supremacy.[28]

No matter the singularity of the royal supremacy, and no matter how broadly the king constructed his ecclesiology, James faced such different challenges from his two churches that to subject them to a unilateral policy would have been impossible. To collapse the issues of polity and liturgy together and make both subject to his authority did not address the fact that the issues raised separate and characteristic problems for each kingdom, and, to be fair, the king was far too intelligent to rule as if this were actually the case. He wrote and spoke as if it were, however, because the language of pan-Protestant unity was a useful and effective rhetoric with which to confront his churches' internal dissensions as well as their external incompatibilities.[29]

Here the conflationary effect of the king's bilateral governmental policy—one in which he found it necessary to govern his northern kingdom not only by his pen, but also by the pens of his English preachers—may be seen. The immediate context for a disproportionate percentage of the court sermons published in England during James's reign was ecclesiastical resistance from

Scotland, a fact that surely reflects the ongoing significance of union and the centrality, to court preachers, of James's continuing identification with his native country. It also means that rhetoric designed to teach recalcitrant Scots ministers the proper meaning of *adiaphora* has to be understood in its English context, where it would have had different consequences.

An analysis of sermons preached at court at the time of James's accession and on celebration of Accession Day throughout the reign will show that this strategy was as singular on the part of the king's spokesmen as it was bifocal on the part of the king. Jacobean court preachers, forced to tout a union that threatened them, invariably supported the idea of Anglo-Scottish unity by endorsing, in the strongest language possible, ceremonial uniformity—in England. Here those seemingly "indifferent" matters of ecclesiastical practice played a leading and highly contentious role. Strident sermon language against Scottish practices, heard in court or read in London, would have condemned by conflation a domestic nonconformity that, while it resembled the Scots variety, was a distinct and separate phenomenon. To censure the Kirk was therefore to vilify English moderate Puritans, not merely by associating them with the radical (if outdated) political threat posed by presbyterianism, but also by making it clear that their anticipation of further ceremonial reform—a desire encouraged by the language of adiaphoric theory and now exemplified in the practice of a Genevan-style church in the "neighborhood"—was futile and increasingly inappropriate. To trace the progress of union rhetoric before, during, and after the failure of James's formal scheme for Anglo-Scottish union is to understand the powerful way the example of the king's native kingdom shaped a new political identity for Puritanism and eventually altered the ideological justification for Erastian Protestantism in England.

Creating New Alliances, 1603–8

The religious context of the Anglo-Scottish union can be located in the rhetorical space between a royal speech and a court

wedding sermon. James I's trenchant remark to his 1604 parliament, "[W]hat God hath conjoined then, let no man separate. . . .
I hope therefore no man will be so unreasonable as to think that I
that am a Christian King under the Gospel, should be a Polyga-
mist and husband to two wives, . . . that being the Shepherd to so
fair a flock, should have my flock parted in two,"[30] is usually interpreted as an expression of the king's plans for full political
union, but it had an equally recognizable religious import. In its
evocation of the responsibilities of the godly prince, this speech
presents a statement of intent to the churches of England and
Scotland. These churches, as we have seen, would have heard
the king's words in entirely different ways, and both with not a
little anxiety. Here James faced the challenge of being not one
husband to two wives, but two husbands to the One True
Church.[31] This bigamous arrangement required more tact and
subtle delicacy, perhaps, than the governing of a united kingdom.

    The language of the king's maiden speech made a noticeable
impact upon the print discourse of the union project. It enjoyed
an apogee of elaboration at the court wedding of Lord and Lady
Hay on Twelfth Night, 1607 (an affair in which it is tempting to
see a domestic secular prototype of James's preference for con-
ducting foreign policy by means of multi-confessional marriage
alliances).[32] The sermon, preached by Robert Wilkinson, was
based on Proverbs 31:14: "She is like a merchant ship, she
bringeth her food from afar." The occasion provided a nonpareil
opportunity to explore the metaphoric connections between marriage and the union of two kingdoms, and, as with any sermon at
which the king was present, the thing signified to which nearly
every sign pointed was James himself.[33] The sermon is a remarkable one, since the complexities of the event lend themselves to a
corresponding richness of fourfold interpretation. The metaphors
of ship and merchant, initially applied to the bride, were also
employed to describe and compliment the king. The image of
marriage called up, not only evocations of political union (Wilkinson called the couple the "little image of this great intended

union"), but also the religious implications of the Church as the bride of Christ. In the atmosphere created by this court wedding, redolent with a heady mixture of religion, politics, and *hymen*, it is not surprising to find that—here as in the masque that crowned the festivities—even analogies could change partners and continue to dance.

Recognizing this, we can detect a tacit theme in this sermon, that of the king's relationship to his Church. Following the rhetorical lead of the language of the king's speech, Wilkinson referred throughout his sermon to marriage as a metaphor for union, and at one point made an intriguing observation:

But as the saying is in the schools, *similitudo non currit quatuor pedibus*: many things may be like, yet nothing like in all things: Therefore though a woman in many things be like a ship, yet in some things she must be unlike, and some qualities of a ship she must not have. As for example, one ship may belong to many merchants, and one merchant may be owner in many ships, yet neither may one woman divide her love to many men nor one man divide himself to many women . . . for wives admit no plurality when they be construed with one husband, because (as the prophet saith) though God at the first had abundance of spirit, yet he made but one, but one woman of one rib.[34]

The final phrase transforms this paean to marital fidelity into a statement with profound political and religious implications. The reference to the indivisibility of a woman's love is reminiscent of the king's 1604 speech and so refers to his project for the union of his kingdoms. To extend this into a statement about James's project for his supremacy over a unified Church/Kirk, it is necessary to recognize that Wilkinson's sermon is based in part on the traditional exegetical strategy that transformed scriptural references to conjugal love into a metaphor for the relationship between Christ and his Church. As the sermon's secular centerpiece, James is a type of Christ: as God's vicegerent upon earth, he is the bridegroom to a faithful and undivided Church.

It is equally important, however, simply to consider the date of this sermon's publication. Wilkinson concludes with an address to the king that locates both the text and the setting in its

political context: "[Y]our majesty is to us indeed a royal merchant, not only for the union of holy marriage, which yokes and
couples one sex with another, but as merchants do by intercourse
of traffic, for knitting and combining one kingdom with another.
And I will not say it is kingly, but divine and heavenly to unite
into one things of divided nature."[35] Wilkinson's sanctification of
the personal union was a consolation prize of sorts, for by the
time of the Hay wedding, the scheme for complete political union was effectively dead in the water, leaving only the union of
crowns and a polemic of religious unity lingering in its wake.[36]
The rhetoric of this sermon interweaves actual event, the failed
politics of the union project, and ongoing expectations for both
kingdoms, with the result that each context provides commen-
tary on the others, and all lead to an inescapable conclusion.
England and Scotland had now to acknowledge the benefits of
their own continuing alliance, a makeshift marriage of conven-
ience, perhaps, but then marriage had always offered a safe haven against what the preacher described as "the contentions and
unquietness of them that live among us, the sharp assaults and
oppositions of them that hate us, but chiefly the unfaithfulness
and treachery of them that seem to love us."[37] Given this sermon's multivocal qualities, it is easy to see beyond this encomium on the protective benefits of conjugal alliance. If we apply
the analogy to its religious context, we find a call for inter-
Protestant unity in the face of Catholic aggression: "them that
hate us." But it would appear that the division Wilkinson feared
was not between Church and Kirk. His reference to English Puritanism, here characterized as intestine "treachery," suggests
that what *was* divided was the Church of England.

To understand how the rhetoric of marriage could be recon-
figured into sturdy, native, English-variety anti-Puritanism, we
must look back and note that one of the distinctive features of
the union of Scotland and England was the fact that the bridegroom was the one to lose his maiden name. James proclaimed
himself "king of Great Britain" in 1604, carefully delineating the
power signified by the title as personal only.[38] The king's will-

ingness to enact by prerogative what Parliament failed to grant legislatively provoked controversy about the extent of the king's arbitrary power, thereby extending the polemical life of the language of union and expanding its rhetorical implications and possibilities.[39] Such an act had significant religious consequences as well. The king and his propagandists insisted that the king's personal style would implant a constant awareness of Anglo-Scottish unity in both the "hearts and heads" of his subjects, thereby transforming the union into a social, if not political, reality. This interpretation of union had its "spiritual and eternal" analogue in the kingdom of God on earth; preaching in front of James at his coronation, Thomas Bilson had suggested that the titles of sovereigns could signify Christ's endorsement of the royal supremacy.[40] The Scottish context discloses a further religious dimension to the king's new style of "Great Britain." James had reintroduced episcopacy to a loudly protesting presbyterian Kirk in part by royal proclamation, and it seemed certain to many that he planned to impose some form of royal supremacy on his northern Church.[41] If we deny ourselves the benefit of historical hindsight, we can see just how unsettling the year 1604 would have been, both for the Kirk and for the Church of England. Did the "king of Great Britain" intend to become the head of a "church of Great Britain" as well? And how was this Church to be defined, as pan-Protestant or as anglocentric? And where, exactly, did the example of Scotland fit into either vision?[42]

At the time, the answers to these questions depended in part on who was doing the talking and what use they made of history. Like the union scheme, the king's new style required a defense based on precedent in order to make James's proclamation appear to be a revival of ancient tradition, rather than an intolerable and arbitrary novelty. It inspired some interpretations that exceeded their brief: perhaps the most intriguing formulation can be found in the court sermon celebrating the proclamation itself, which was preached before James and the Lord Mayor of London on 28 October 1604 and later printed as an instruction manual for the commissioners on the union project.[43] John Gordon, a Scottish preacher who had accompanied James south after the accession, and who had previously distinguished himself by writing a panegyric on the union, claimed that the origin of the name "Britannia" was to be found in the earliest records of biblical history. To find it, however, took some concerted and imaginative effort:

[T]his name of *Brittania*, or *Brettania* cometh from the name of such a one of the posterity of Japhet [Gen. 10], that did first divide the Isles of the Gentiles, unto whom by lot this Island did fall. Therefore it is most certain that as the rest of the names of the kingdoms of Europe, did take their original name from the sons of Japhet: even so we must seek the etymology of Brittania, out of the Hebrew language, which is Brit-an-iah, and doth consist of three words. BRIT signifieth, *foedus*, a covenant; AN, *ibi*, there; IAH, *Dei*, of God. Which three being conjoined in one, do signify, that THERE IS THE COVENANT OF GOD, that is, in this Island the covenant of God was to be established.[44]

Locating both the past and future of the island in an expanded European context, Gordon portrays union as a long-awaited act with apocalyptic consequences. His cabalistic etymological survey raises James's dual kingdom above other Protestant nations by demonstrating the special covenant encoded in the name of Britain. The allusion is transparent: the confederation of Scotland and England would confer the leadership of the battle against the popish Antichrist on James VI and I. "Let all men remember by the foresaid examples," Gordon declared, "that the union of kingdoms hath always been the furtherance of true religion, but division of kingdoms hath been the overthrow of true religion, and advancing of idolatry."[45] Gordon's celebratory sermon thereby transforms the king's proclamation of his "personal" title, a declaration that could have been interpreted by the cynically minded as the first admission of the failure of his political program, into something "prophetical"—the first clarion call to a divinely ordained crusade.[46]

This apocalyptic strain of polemic has most often been associated with Gordon, other Scottish preachers, and the predilection of the Scots for religious covenanting altogether, but scholars have not previously considered how this rhetoric would contribute to the English discursive atmosphere of the years 1603–5, when these union-related writings were printed.[47] Gordon's sermon exemplifies how this kind of "international Calvinist," anti-Catholic sentiment could be touted as one of the important forces uniting Church and Kirk.[48] James himself had deployed just such a language in BASILIKON DORON when he invoked anti-popery as a common cause to persuade nonconformists to submit to his authority in inessential ecclesiological matters. Union-inspired anti-Catholicism could, however, call forth a more determined campaign for nonconformity that eschewed all ceremonial forms tainted by popery. With careful examination, we can detect hopeful longing for this type of reform even among some dutiful and loyal preachers at the Jacobean court.[49]

For churchmen weaned on the Cranmerian notion that things adiaphoric could be further reformed, and imbued with the Elizabethan spirit of war against the popish Antichrist, the idea of intimate relations with the Kirk held out the hope of assistance in the task of moving the Church of England closer to two related and cherished ideals of Protestant purity.[50] In this passage from a 1604 court sermon, John Hopkins cites the union of Israel and Judah as a paradigm for Anglo-Scottish union, invoking a striking image to portray the benefits of religious alliance: "For now the two pieces of wood so long disjoined, mentioned in the 37th [chapter] of Ezekiel we might also say, are made one in the hand of our sovereign: Now is that made one in government, which nature had made one in situation: now the two brethren Joab and Abishai may help one another."[51]

Hopkins's appropriation of the prophetic voice, punctuated by his own repetitive and importunate use of the word *now*, anticipates—indeed calls for by anticipatory syntax—a new opportunity for cooperation between Kirk and Church.[52] In view of this, his brief reference to the sons of Zeruiah reveals his more specific socio-religious intentions. In 2 Samuel 2, after the death of Saul and David's consecration as king of Judah, Joab and Abishai fight together against a faction opposed to David's rule in Israel. The narrative of Hopkins's argument unfolds to associate this Israelite faction with Catholic recusants in England. For Hopkins, the elimination of stubborn popery began with the extirpation of popish practices in the Church of England and ended with stricter laws enforced by the magistrate. Since he had called for the cooperation and help of Scotland in this venture, it is clear that Hopkins intended this brotherly assistance to be marshaled first toward the further reformation of the Church.

Hopkins welcomed the accession of James as a chance to repair the spiritual state of England, which he described in the euphonious phrase "sound doctrine, sick manners; good religion, evil practice."[53] The characterization points up a discrepancy between profession and action, demonstrating the gulf not only between the Church's teachings and society's behavior, but also between the Church's reformed teachings and its unreformed ceremonies. The sermon text allows Hopkins to forge a link connecting these two interpretations. His sermon is based on Ezra 7:26–27: "And whosoever will not do the law of thy God, and the law of the king, let judgment be executed speedily upon him . . . blessed be the Lord God of our fathers, which hath put such a thing as this in the king's heart, to beautify the house of the Lord," words that appear equally suited to endorse a Puritan-style campaign to clean up the streets or a proto-Laudian-style campaign to decorate the Church. Instead, Hopkins's approach adapts the language of the former, applying it to the circumstances of the latter to novel effect. He defines "beautification" as purification, a purging of those things "corrupted with the uncleanness of men's traditions." (His proposals for what should be set up in their place reads like the work of a Puritan petitioner: godly evangel and conversation, government support of a "pure" ministry, doctrines and practice based on Scripture.) The contention that unclean practices in the Church were attributable to corrupt human tradition employs a coded rhetorical condemnation of the "superstitious" practices still used by the Church.[54]

An unusual and emotive concluding plea on behalf of James's third church, the Church in Ireland, provides the rhetorical link between Hopkins's socio-religious reform program and his concerns about domestic Catholicism: "This point of beautifying the church maketh me call to mind the miserable state of that poor kingdom of Ireland, of whom we may say as it is in Solomon's song, We have a little sister, and she hath no breasts; what shall we do for our sister, when shall she be spoken for? . . . their souls [are] poisoned with idolatry and error."[55] This image of Ireland as sister complements and recalls Hopkins's use of the biblical imagery of 2 Samuel to portray Scotland as brother. Identifying the popish threat in the Irish Church and pinpointing the inspiration for reformation in the Scottish Kirk, Hopkins reconfigures the image of the union of Britain as a macrocosm of ecclesiastical problems and theological strengths. He can then locate a logical counterpoint to popery in Scottish ecclesiological style and apply the remedy to the Church of England.

Hopkins's strategy demonstrates how multiple kingdoms offer metaphoric advantage: they gave voice to the many apprehensions raised by James's early English reign. In England, the accession had raised hopes of further reform in those who had considered the king's rigorous Calvinist upbringing and his careful conciliation of moderate elements in the Kirk as an encouraging sign. Catholic subjects were just as hopeful about the king's relation to Mary Queen of Scots and his years of careful conciliation of powerful Catholic nobles. Rather than hewing to a circumspect "middle way" by eschewing either of these positions as potentially radical, Hopkins offers moderate Puritan reforms inspired by union with Scotland to counteract the heresy of Catholicism. Hopkins's sermon represents only one way to advise the king on the matter of further reform, however, and we shall see that, at court at least, it became an increasingly uncommon one.

The Call to Judgment

Early in his reign, James was presented in court sermons as a kind of cipher: an empty peg on which different factions might hang their hopes for the future. Sermons preached to James during these first years often appear designed to sound out the boundaries of the king's religious attitudes—something that reflects more the anxious clerical observation of a new king's preferences than it does any truly broad range of opinion. Court sermons printed in this period thus offer an intriguing official counterpoint to the Catholic and Puritan petitions sent to James after his accession.[56] But the bishops, deans, and important local clerics who preached at court were more than spectators; they also played a part in episcopal deliberations, at Convocation, and in the pulpit in developing and inculcating the new religious settlement expected at the accession of a monarch. Their awareness of their important supporting roles accounts for the remarkable predominance of one theme in early Jacobean court sermons, that of the Solomonic duty of the king to show wise judgment and solicit advice.[57]

Court preachers presented themselves not merely as important advisers to the king but as his co-authors in publicizing the work of religious settlement to a larger, influential audience. In 1604, James's chaplain Richard Field rather grandly declared that the writing and printing of sermons and other religious polemics convened "a greater and more general council than either Constantine, Theodosius, or any of the Roman emperors either did or could do."[58] Preaching to James on 30 April 1605, Robert Wakeman advised the king on religious matters in a firm and somewhat hectoring tone. His concluding application of the text was punctuated by the staccato, rhymed anaphoric construction *let . . . yet* ("Let bloody tyrants delight to grieve all by wrong and oppression; yet godly princes must seek to content all by executing justice and judgment"), which syntactically balanced the king's power against that of the papacy.[59] James's polemicists aimed beyond the royal audience, moreover; in print, the flashy and persuasive rhetoric they used before the king had its hearing (or reading) outside the court. And while court preachers frequently employed the theme of wisdom in judgment to demonstrate the need for the king to remain firm against "fawn[ing] and flatter[ing]" appeals by English "followers and favorites" of

Rome (Wakeman again, in a dazzling display of deliberate alliteration),[60] what should also be explored is how this language could be used against the moderate Puritans who so far had managed to remain within the English Church.

The influence of the Hampton Court conference called by James to assess the arguments of moderate Puritan nonconformists can be felt in the court sermons preached in the waning of the union project.[61] Held in January 1604, the Hampton Court conference could easily have stood for all that staunch conformist bishops feared about the declaration of James VI that he would grant a hearing to nonconformists who were willing to argue their cases with "well-grounded reasons."[62] The conference turned out to be quite another kind of forum, however, as James allowed the moderate spokesmen, who had been handpicked to represent the "Puritan" view, to be stymied at every turn, their inoffensively stated arguments denounced as impertinent, impious, and downright dangerous by Bishop Richard Bancroft.[63] In his star performance at Hampton Court, Bancroft returned to themes he had made his own before the accession, in the 1580's and 1590's. On 9 February 1588, for example, Bancroft had preached at Paul's Cross against the *classis* movement in England. The preacher cited James VI's problems with the Kirk as an example of the insolence an English presbytery would show toward monarchical authority and went on to warn his audiences not to be influenced by the Scottish dismay at the state of the English Church. His remarks indicted by association both the Church of England's Scottish critics and their English Puritan allies: "*Inimici hominis domestici eius*: our friends are turned to be our enemies. And you know the old saying, *Fratrum odia acerbissima*, when brethren fall out, they grow to great extremities. The papists did never deal with more eagerness against us than these men do now."[64] Bancroft's comparison of Puritanism first to presbyterianism and then to popery was a rhetorical strategy that would define court rhetoric on the subject throughout James's reign, in part because the king's accession and the union offered this type of critique an unparalleled power of context. In his astute characterization of the nature of fraternal strife (a theme later reworked by Robert Wilkinson in *The Merchant Royall*), the bishop drew an analogy between the substance of England's internecine religious battles and the polemical style that expressed them.[65]

Here at Hampton Court, as in 1588 and 1593, Bancroft raised the specter of a king under attack by the presbytery, only this time he had both king and moderate Puritans in his immediate audience. Apparently sympathetic to his bishop's overwrought rhetoric and loathe to appear weak in the face of potentially over-mighty subjects, the king made few concessions to his moderate Puritans and flatly refused to satisfy them on any contested issue of ceremonial conformity, citing the overriding importance of domestic religious peace and the preservation of his own authority. James's famous monitory outburst to the Puritan representatives, "no bishop, no king," made it clear that the king's association of English nonconformists with Scottish presbyterians was not as benign as it may have seemed in 1603. The ingratiating tack he had taken in BASILIKON DORON, wherein the king presented himself as eager to debate these adiaphoric issues with loyal churchmen of different views, was now replaced with an angry warning that presbyterianism was so intolerable that English nonconformists would do best to avoid any imputation of the same by dropping their resistance to the ceremonies. His lot thrown in with ultraconformists like the bishop of London, James now took the Bancroftian line on the similarity of nonconformity to presbyterian polity in order to quash the reformist hopes of English moderate Puritans.[66]

Not all bishops were such hammers of the Puritans as was Bancroft. Those clerics more sympathetic to the plight of Puritans in their dioceses scrambled to make sense of the events at Hampton Court. Preaching before James at Whitehall in May 1604, one such bishop, Anthony Rudd of St. David's, described the events at Hampton Court in the language of the union project. In his sermon, the king, here identified with Solomon, had to decide between what appeared to be equally persuasive claims

presented by two plaintiffs. In Rudd's text, Solomon's prayer after his anointing is to be given the ability to "discern between
good and bad";[67] this he desires above wealth or power. Solomon
then demonstrates his god-given gift, deciding against a plaintiff
who loses her case with, literally, divisive tactics: "If two women
strive before Solomon, about the living child, and the case prove
difficult upon the pleadings on both sides, he will at length ad-
judge the child to her in whom he findeth a motherly affection,
which cannot abide to hear that bloody speech of partition: *Nec
mihi nec tibi, sed dividatur.*"[68]

The point of this passage is straightforward enough: religious
division is a bad thing; and in the aftermath of Hampton Court,
its point could hardly have been more obvious. What lends
Rudd's rhetoric such a remarkable quality of complexity, however, is the preacher's own role at the conference. Rudd was an
Elizabethan bishop sympathetic to nonconformity, and his moderate Puritan stance had been firmly in place at the Hampton
Court conference, which he attended. The rejection of the Puritan
case for nonconformity there did not entirely daunt Rudd; indeed, rather than see him as a turncoat to some good old cause in
this sermon, we should read it as an attempt to remind the king
of his own commitment to the notion of union. This would account for the representation of time in this sermon: the case
"proves difficult," the judge decides "at length." The king's
words on the issue of the union could be converted into paro-
nyms for another idea of unity, a unity based not upon uniformity but on tolerance for domestic doctrinal brethren.[69]

Rudd's sermon demonstrates how contextual suggestion
could link by implication the issues raised by Anglo-Scottish
union to the ones raised by the Hampton Court conference. It derives no small part of its power from the striking evocation of a
violently divided body, constructed by the preacher in language
strongly reminiscent of the images of division that characterized
James's accession speech. Here, then, we also see that Rudd's
words were designed to mediate between two audiences. The
representation of disunity used in arguments to remind the king

of the doctrinal unity of his church(es) could also explain to Puritans why the case for nonconformity had failed at Hampton
Court. In the interest of unity, the Puritans had been heard. Their
arguments failed in the interest of the greater good of a Church
unity defined by ceremonial uniformity. Rudd's moderate Puritan sympathies thus had to take a back seat, perhaps temporar-
ily, to his mandate to defend the Church on a basis determined
by the king at this time. While his sermon praises the king as a
wise and clement judge, it also explains to nonconformists why
they have been rebuffed. Rudd proposes a methodology for
thinking about adiaphora that allows for two possibilities: either
the Puritans could put aside their differences with the established Church or the king could keep an open mind on the issue
of conformity after thinking about this case "at length."

At this time, we can detect in the multivalency of Rudd's language (and of his king's, for that matter) that the very notion of
"consensus" was undergoing an intense polemical scrutiny. As
this received idea shifted at court between doctrinal and ceremonial bottom lines, surely both ultraconformists and moderate
Puritans believed that they had a case that would be heard. The
volatility of the ecclesiastical situation can be seen in the fact
that, a few months later, in Convocation, Rudd could be found
pleading for leniency for nonconformists on the grounds that
they subscribed to the Calvinist doctrinal unity that was the
standard of the English Church. The call for judgment and wisdom, therefore, refers almost tautologically to court preachers
themselves, who walked a polemical tightrope at this time. They
had to balance their political and religious interests with those of
their new sovereign, whose enthusiasm for union both dominated and confused domestic religious issues.[70]

Soon after the Hampton Court conference, however, it became
apparent that James's desire for political union would have to be
tempered. As early as October 1605, the Venetian ambassador to
the English court had not only predicted the failure of the political union scheme but also claimed that James was already aware
that it was a lost cause.[71] In one sense, then, the waning fortunes

of English nonconformity bore a distinct similarity to the political eclipse of the king's union project. Like the Puritans, James was forced to modify innovative plans for which accession was supposed to have made the decisive argument. And as at the Hampton Court conference, the union of England and Scotland had to take a back seat to what was presented as pressing religious danger. The issue was scheduled for debate in the English Parliament in 1605, at a November session that was disrupted, spectacularly, by the discovery of the Gunpowder Plot. If the Hampton Court conference signaled the end of Puritan hopes of further reform by raising the specter of Scottish presbyterianism, the plot marked the end of James's ambitions for Great Britain in somewhat the same way. The plot may have been conceived in Catholic grievance, but the plotters' rhetoric justifying their action traded on the lexicon of union. Their motive, they claimed, was the influx of Scots into England; they were "against," they insisted, "all strangers."[72]

The Gunpowder Plot provides evidence of the confidence with which Catholic traitors felt they could exploit anti-union and anti-Scottish sentiment in England. (The reaction of the Scots who offered to protect their king against further attacks by Englishmen did little to lessen continuing Anglo-Scottish tensions.) In the anti-Scottish context, therefore, we might be forgiven for seeing the Gunpowder Plot itself primarily as an idea ripe for rhetorical exploitation, a notion whose time had arrived. Here the nervous monitorings—of the union project by Scots and English; of James's attitude to the border inhabitants of the religious settlement by Puritan and papist; and of the new monarchy by members of the Elizabethan religious and political establishment—all came together to form a highly volatile mix on the verge of combustion.

The discovery of the Gunpowder Plot may have thwarted the Catholic plotters' confessional agenda, but it furthered their stated opposition to formal Anglo-Scottish unity. While the program for union effectively went missing amid the distractions of the plot, certain rhetorics of union pertinent to the English context remained: the person of the king, his claim to the title of "Britain," and his periodic disagreements with intransigent elements in the Kirk. The failure of political union returned James to the status of dual monarch, however, which turned his campaign for the conformity of the Scottish Church into an enterprise with dual consequences.[73] English court preachers were pressed into service in these holy wars between king and Kirk, ensuring that the problem of Scotland initiated and underpinned much of the rhetoric of ceremonial conformity that issued from the court pulpit for the remainder of the reign. James's various and bitter disputes with unruly factions in the Kirk over the extent of his authority—to call or dismiss general assemblies, to impose new articles of conformity, possibly to initiate proceedings for a Scottish prayer book—were all part of a campaign to establish royal supremacy in Scotland.[74] Elaborated from the English court pulpit and by London and Oxford presses, however, that campaign complemented the promotion of royal supremacy in England, making an indelible mark on the public presentation of English nonconformity. Dual-directional polemical engines of the ecclesiastical policy of James I, court sermons redrew the picture of a Puritan based on the ecclesiastical policy of James VI.

Intimations of Failure, 1606–8

In 1606, one of the most obstinate of James's Scottish ministers, James Melville, complained that the thinking of English court preachers was, doctrinally speaking, flawed: they condemned presbyterians and papists in the same breath, "as though the ane had beine joynit in the same judgment with the uthir."[75] As a piece of rhetorical analysis, Melville's observation was apt if a bit succinct: court sermons did chastise Catholics and Puritans evenhandedly in order to imply that resistance to the king was an act laden with politically universal implications. The Jacobean Church's claim to be a *via media* increasingly rested, not on some quality of doctrinal or ceremonial latitude, but on this Bancroftian polemical strategy that spoke of all treasons as equal.

When compelled to illustrate their political critique by the condemnation of specific religious actions, however, court apologists had to recognize that some treasons were actually more
equal than others and strategize their way around the real disparity between papist and Puritan religious resistance. One sure
way to maintain a rhetorical *via media*, a vantage point from
which it was possible to condemn in equally successful fashion
the extremes of popery and Puritanism, was to use the example
of Scotland to magnify the perception that English Puritanism
was still a very dangerous thing indeed.

That in mind, it is hardly surprising to find that the first bold,
explicit, and sustained polemical attack on Scotland by a preacher at court was in 1606, on the first Accession Day after the Gunpowder Plot. Anthony Maxey preached in front of James on the
second chapter of the Song of Solomon: "[S]tir not up, nor waken
my love, until he please," employing the traditional conjugal interpretation of this Old Testament text and providing us with yet
another demonstration of the prevalence of the marriage theme
in the polemic of the accession and the union. Maxey applied this
interpretation of Scripture to the state of religion under James's
rule. From the idyllic setting of the Song of Solomon, the preacher constructs a paradox. Until James's accession, the Church had
suffered much "schism, contention, and heresies." The reign of
this peaceable "Salomon" and the promise of a Protestant succession had offered the Church a respite.[76] After sketching this
brief and attractive picture of what the accession should have
ushered in, Maxey abruptly changes rhetorical gears, warning
his royal audience about actual and potential disturbers of the
"church's sleep" in language that moves from soothing and congratulatory to strident and condemnatory.

Preached as it was in the aftermath of the Gunpowder Plot—a
golden age of English pulpit anti-popery if ever there was one—,
it is striking that Maxey did not use this opportunity to lambaste
the pope, the Jesuits, or English recusants. (In fact, there is only
the barest mention of the plotters, and that in a short ironic aside
in the conclusion.) Instead, on Accession Day, Maxey chose to

single out English Puritans with a bitter invective that both re-
prised and refocused Bancroft's "our friends are turned out our
enemies" sermon of 1588: "*inimici nominus domestici eius*, our *own
calling and countrymen* are our most unkinde and cruel enemies."
Maxey accused these domestic provocateurs of refusing to provide public support for the doctrinal solidarity of the English
Church. They incessantly clamored "about such points as make
not to the furtherance of the people in good life and devotion";
they also castigated and ridiculed the liturgy prescribed by the
prayer book:

> If when we celebrate the Lord's Supper, we play (as they say) a pageant
> of their own, and make poor silly souls believe they have an English
> mass; if churchmen affirm, that our church hath in it still, so many black
> marks that the natural children of the church cannot discern it? What
> hope can there be that the blessed spouse can ever attain unto any set-
> tled and joyful rest?[77]

We can detect the heart of Maxey's critique in a brief phrase
contained within a common complaint. First he presents a typical
Puritan argument for further reform: that theologically unsophisticated people would be misled by the "English mass," and
that adiaphoric ceremonies ought then to be excised for the sake
of these people. The request for further reform of the ritual actions of the liturgy had been advanced for this very reason at the
Hampton Court conference and had been firmly dismissed by
James himself, who had reinterpreted the Puritans' plea on behalf of simple folk into an intolerable critique of the state of the
Church under his rule—a challenge to his royal supremacy. The
example of recent events, therefore, underpinned Maxey's presentation; he reports the Puritan viewpoint in order to refute it.
The reproduction of a protagonists' argument is a sophisticated
but risky rhetorical strategy. In terms of polemic, it works like a
dream: here Maxey transforms his reproduction of the points of
an argument by repetition of the same word to begin a series of
clauses. The word he chooses, *if*, turns the Puritan argument into
a subjunctive query and allows him to answer the Puritan argu-

ment rather than merely parrot it. The language of concern for uneducated souls, in Maxey's opinion, was a smokescreen to disguise a politically destabilizing Puritan agenda. His strategy places that agenda—rather than its rationale—center-stage. He recasts the case for nonconformity to prove that the Puritan clergy, far from being the noble victims of their own conscientious objection, were instead courting "popularity," thus making them self-important and politically dangerous.

A closer look suggests, however, that Maxey could ventriloquize his opponents' arguments for the simple reason that he himself sympathized with them. A tireless and not entirely successful campaigner for royal preferment, Maxey was an old-school, Elizabethan-style Calvinist whose Jacobean court sermons paid explicit attention to theological matters. This sermon testifies to a crisis of conscience called forth by these early debates over adiaphoric issues of conformity, and it was a crisis of this Calvinist conformist's conscience every bit as much as it was a crisis of the Puritan. The precise hair-splitting "churchmen" to whom Maxey refers were men his audience would have recognized as the clergy placed in opposition to the Church after the publication of the 1604 canons. He identifies these objectors to the English liturgy as allied to the Church's "natural children," apparently in order to challenge their claim to be the true defenders of Protestantism. At this point, however, it seems possible to admit another meaning in the language that Maxey chose in condemning by association his nonconforming counterparts. By speaking of "natural children," Maxey suggests notions both of illegitimacy and consanguinity, as if to highlight the contentious familial relation of Puritans and their followers to the established Church.[78]

In terms of the still-settling state of the Jacobean religious settlement, Maxey's strategy reflects, perhaps, a necessary ambivalence. The polemical atmosphere generated by the Hampton Court conference and the picture of the Church—not to mention the actual deprivation of the clergy—that emerged from the publication of the 1604 canons adds a poignant weight to Maxey's charge.[79] The deprivations had inspired a flurry of writings in defense of nonconforming ministers that constituted a public debate over the inclusiveness of the English Church. Just how far did the Calvinist consensus extend to unite the English Church during a conformity drive, even if that drive was more rhetorical than actual? Here we have proof of Maxey's dilemma: in denouncing his doctrinal brethren, his language veers between repudiation and a kind of backhanded acknowledgment that the case for nonconformity had respectable Protestant antecedents. Reporting with dismay the public assumption that "the reformed though they lose their livings, yet they will keep a good conscience, but the formalists will ever be of the same religion the king is of,"[80] Maxey had to defend recent events by distancing the Church from the quasi-familial claims of its nonconformists. This led him to make distinctions between types of reformation and types of reformers, which he did in part through a recasting of recent religious history and a re-situating of Scotland in England's Protestant narrative.

In short, Maxey disavowed the intimate claims of Calvinist consensus by associating English nonconformity with Scottish ecclesiastical practices. First, Maxey drew upon the lessons of recent history to denounce "divers personages of great credit and countenance," who in the 1580's "had cr[ied] out for the Geneva discipline, and Scottish reformation in the church." This remarkable use of the term "Scottish" as an adjective modifying the noun "reformation" distinguishes Kirk practices from the English style of reform. Furthermore, the reference to "Geneva discipline" emphasizes the cultural distance between the English Church and its northern neighbor, allying Scottish to continental reformation in a distinctly negative comparison.[81] Maxey sustains the image of the Continent long enough to praise those English bishops who, upon return from Marian exile, also reverted to an English practice of religion and employed the "form of service and order of ceremonies" established under Edward and Elizabeth. He compares these English reformers, Jewel, Grindal, and Barlow, to those he calls their "stirring and strange" Puritan opponents, who are represented in the 1606 and 1614 printed editions of this sermon by a marginal roll call of the worthies of the Scottish Reformation: "Knox to the commonality folio 49," "Buchanan *de Jure Regni* page 61," and "Scottish presbytery in prison at this day."[82] Here is a carefully drawn, uncompromising picture of "Scottish reformation," which emphasizes both its dangerous polity and its antipathy to liturgy, while portraying those characteristics as un-English and allied through the anti-ceremonialist firebrand Knox to Geneva. In terms of text and context, however, it is more important to observe that Maxey has opposed this vision of the Kirk to the continentally inspired churchmanship of Elizabeth's reign, in which at least one representative, Archbishop Grindal, can be classed as a moderate Puritan and a role model of conscientious objection in his own right.[83] The comparison highlights just how focused the basis of Maxey's critique was on issues of ritual and liturgy—evidence that the English critique of Scottish presbyterianism ultimately aimed at English moderate Puritanism, not radical sectarians.

The language of union was finally transformed into a malleable critique of Scottish presbyterianism that could be shoehorned into purely domestic concerns over ceremonial conformity.[84] The transmogrification of Scotland was accomplished in court-sermon polemic. From 1603 to 1607, court preachers had labored to create two separable Scotlands: one associated with Geneva and one associated with England. The Genevan Scotland, which made its boldest appearance in Maxey's 1606 sermon, became an evil twin whose bad example could be employed against any campaign for further reformation in England in order to silence it. To construct the English Scotland, preachers commandeered the imagery of union to support domestic religious unity. After the failure of the formal union project, any notion of Scotland as distinct or influential—for good or ill—is impossible to detect. Preachers continued to talk about "union," but by that they meant something vague and abstracted—a way to comment upon the king's authority over a "uniform" English Church. We might hail Maxey's sermon as the first sign that

James, in failing to secure a formal political union, had finally become an honorary Englishman.

Union and Uniformity After 1607

After Wilkinson's sermon of 1607, direct references to the union are mostly to be found in Accession Day sermons. Two by Lancelot Andrewes show that the language of union was not dead, even if the project that inspired that language was. In the hands of the most politically resourceful and rhetorically sophisticated preacher at the Jacobean court, however, the idea of union served only to represent the need for a royal supremacy. Andrewes preached on Accession Day in 1607 on the text of Judges 17:6, "[I]n those days, there was no King in Israel, but every man did that which was good in his own eyes." Andrewes's exegesis of the text centered on the story of Micah, who in the absence of monarchical authority set up a thriving household religion with his mother, contracting with an itinerant priest to perform the services for (as the preacher humorously phrased it) "ten shekels and a suit, or because now the world is harder, ten pounds."[85] Andrewes's retelling of the story of Micah and his mother makes them over into the likeness of contemporary recusants, but his overall strategy aims at a more general authority, and this leads him to remind his audience that a king was set over them to suppress more than one form of evil religion: "One would think . . . we were free enough from Micah. We are not. Even to this day do men still cast images or imaginations (all is one) and up they set them, at least for their own households to adore."[86] Andrewes's condemnation of "imagination" may be a reference to Puritanism, not only because the syntax of his sentence has set up an obvious polarity, one that was common at court, but also because the phrase evokes ideas of "novelty," the private judgment that shrugs off the restraints of legitimate tradition and authorized public religion. By equating such "imagination" with the papist "image" in the deceptively casual parenthetical "all is one," Andrewes suggests a court commonplace—the equating of

Puritan and papist—that sets up a brief discussion of James's union of kingdoms.[87]

The religious representation of union forms the centerpiece of Andrewes's encomium on James's accession. He makes an explicit comparison between the kind of religious disorder that marked the time of Micah, when Israel was divided, and the division of England and Scotland: "The like imperfection was it, even the dividing this island under two sovereigns. The reducing of both those under one, was promised Israel as a high favor. The same to us performed can be no less, even that now there is a king indeed. Rex, one king; one and no more, absolute entire king over all the tribes, over all Israel."[88] Having vividly evoked the confusion of a world torn by a multiplicity of kingdoms and a variety of private religions, Andrewes's strikingly repetitious invocation of James's kingship channels religious chaos into the jurisdiction of a single authority: "one," "entire," "absolute," king. James's political self had been, in a sense, redivided by the failure of the union project. Andrewes offers instead a substitution rhetoric touting the king's ability to "reduce" two national Protestant churches into a singular entity.

This strategy was given an even more detailed treatment in 1611, when Andrewes again preached to the king at court on Accession Day. The assigned text was Psalm 118:22, "The stone which the builders refused, the same stone is become the Head of the corner," a verse he interprets by means of an elegant architectonic metaphor.[89] Andrewes stressed that the Psalm referred specifically to the head of a "corner," *in caput anguli*. This corner was created by adjacent planes meeting in a single line, a paradigm, Andrewes suggested, for the union of two nations. While the two planes represent separate entities, they intersect along a single line that culminates at a point represented by a "headstone."[90] We have, therefore, a transparent allusion to the union of Scotland and England and to James VI and I. This meticulously detailed illustration provides a substantial geometric imagery with which to express the significance of James's accession. This is integral to Andrewes's overall strategy, which is to distinguish the nature of a congruent, or dual, "kingship" from the nature of a singular "headship":

"Head," and "of the corner," that is, as some interpret it, of Judah and Israel. But that is thought somewhat hard. For those two were not two kingdoms, nor ever so reckoned, until Rehoboam's time. And what, if David had not happened to have been first King of one tribe, and after of all, should he have lost his name then? . . . Shall no King be *caput anguli*, if he have but one entire Kingdom? Shall not Solomon as well as David? No question but he shall.[91]

Moving between metaphors of singularity and duality, Andrewes asks a provocative question: what significance does the relation of England and Scotland have for the nature of the royal supremacy? Was James the head of two churches or one? (The answers are, in order, "none" and "one.") Andrewes differentiates between the union of crowns, which placed the king over dual nations, and religious unity, which made that king head of the one common thread between them. In lieu of a united kingdom, Andrewes offers his sovereign the vision of presiding over a united Church. But by downplaying the importance of Scotland within that union, he has also signaled that the Protestant unity over which James was to preside would not be defined by what Maxey called "Scottish reformation." This very different polemical vision of James's authority in the context of a newly united Christendom was to become one of the most significant leitmotifs of the Jacobean reign.[92]

From the accession of James VI to the Gunpowder Plot of November 1605, court discourse owed much of its rhetorical strategies to the idea of union. What I have traced here is a chronicle of the way in which court preachers, court writers, and the king himself dealt with the representation and significance of Scotland. It is basically a literary narrative anchored by a generic form and a shared lexicon of overarching, repetitively familiar— and familial—themes: marriage, Solomon, Israel; biblical citations: Song of Solomon, 2 Samuel, Micah; and catch-phrases: "I

am (he is, your majesty is) the husband . . . ," "let no man separate . . . ," "the union of kingdoms hath ever been. . . ." The fortunes of political union soon waned. But the representation of
union expanded to articulate a more important, long-lasting debate over the meaning of Protestant unity—first as it existed
between Scotland and England, and then, most significant, as it
worked within the English Church itself. This language was
powerful enough to challenge the notion of Calvinist consensus
at a time when doctrinal unity was the proudest achievement of
the Church of England, the idea that made the center hold. It is
here we begin to see the remarkable impact that the accession of
a Scottish king had on the cultural definition of Puritanism at a
crucial period in post-Reformation England.

James inherited one Church at the crossroads of reformation—
far enough along to be comfortable in its Protestant doctrine, yet
with too many extra-theological issues left unresolved. He
brought with him the experience of governing a Church that had
often moved too fast and too far from the control of the monarch,
where matters, as he put it "were inordinately done by a popular
tumult and rebellion, of such as blindly were doing the work of
God." James saw that reformation as "extraordinarily wrought
by God," however, and there is much evidence to indicate that
he had a lingering affection for some aspects of Scottish Protestantism.[93] A recent analysis of what James VI and I intended for
his churches argues persuasively that the king never aimed at an
actual uniformity of Church and Kirk, but for "congruity."[94] At
best, James wanted to "raise each church in the estimation of the
other," by strengthening preaching standards in England and the
episcopate in Scotland. In other words, James aimed at a general
ecclesiastical authority with expressions of royal supremacy
geared to the individual characteristics of each institution. Neither was in danger of losing its distinctiveness under a blanket
ecclesiastical policy. This may well be true, but it is not a conclusion we can draw from reading court sermons, wherein the subtle judgment that the king actually applied to the art of governing his churches was articulated in one-sided, unsubtle polemic.

In part, this gulf between word and deed existed because the language of religion did not admit nuance, but it is also indicative of a significant court-pulpit dynamic. James's English preachers brought their own concerns to bear on the issues important to the king, which meant that even when they used the king's words, they transformed them. These concerns, reflective of the many hopes that accession called forth, were as diverse as the polemic they used was single-minded.

While it was an encouraging sign to moderate Puritan clerics and laity who awaited a further reformation of the Church, the new king's initially Scottish perspective on religious matters raised the fears of many other English ecclesiastics. James came to the English throne with a personal definition of "Puritan" based upon his experience with the altogether more problematic presbyterian Kirk of Scotland, in which issues of ministerial insolence and disobedience loomed large, and nonconformity hardly at all. (James's rapid acculturation to the beauties of English liturgical holiness is a subject for a later chapter.) Threatening to many in his English episcopate, therefore, was James's sympathy toward the evangelical style, if not the presbyterian content, of Scottish Protestantism.[95] English conformist clerics with no love for Puritans could worry—given James's background, his carefully ambiguous remarks in BASILIKON DORON, and his enthusiasm for a preaching ministry—about what the king's familiarity with the Scottish style in religious matters would presage for the Church of England. Their language betrays concern about what was now to be a fixed point of ecclesiological comparison and an ongoing neighborly rebuke to the less reformed Church of England.

Despite the quick failure of the actual union project, the representation of union survived to make a significant and long-lasting impact upon the campaign conducted from the court pulpit against domestic nonconformity. The ultraconformists' pursuit of a "moderate" course was at its heart a rhetorical strategy aimed at eliminating the Puritans' own claim to moderation. These clerics had to convince their new king that there was no such thing as "moderate" nonconformity, by focusing first on what Bancroft had called "Scottish Genevating," then worse, "English Scotticizing," and finally on what Maxey would denounce as the enemies within their "own calling." Presbyterianism posed no "real" problem in 1603 in either Scotland or England, if by "real" we mean some kind of substantial, sustained affront or challenge to James's authority.[96] In England, however, "Presbyterian" was still the most powerful name with which to conjure up anti-Puritan sentiment. Given his own experience with resistance to his authority in Scotland, the king was open to suggestions that presbyterianism and nonconformity were just two sides of the same anti-monarchical coin.

This was, however, a strategy that depended on the actual possibility of Anglo-Scottish political union for its greatest power. With the issue of union safely ended for the moment, court preachers would need a new and dangerous paradigm to impute to Puritanism. Paradoxically, this was supplied by the example of Catholic treason in the Gunpowder Plot of 1605. It is to this next phase of court-pulpit anti-Puritanism that we now turn.

CHAPTER THREE

Rewriting the Plot: The Fifth of November and the Image of Puritanism

In a sermon at Paul's Cross celebrating the fourth anniversary of England's miraculous deliverance from the Gunpowder Plot, Robert Tynely memorably described 5 November 1605 as the "birth-day of our Nation." Tynely did not say—and it has been overlooked by subsequent commentators—that it also marked the coming of age of James I, as the event that catalyzed the Scottish king's transformation into an English monarch in a manner more dramatic and convincing than accession had been able to achieve. During the early years of James's reign in England, the king was often a stranger, not only to the public view, but even to the court itself. As the scheme for union grew increasingly unpopular, and the clamorings of disgruntled Puritans and papists flooded bookstalls and filled the hands of street hawkers, the discovery of Gunpowder Treason presented the king with an unparalleled opportunity to redesign his image. So well timed was it, so precisely did it suit this rancorous and unsettled domestic climate, that we might well be forgiven for suspecting that Gunpowder Plot was solely a creation of words, fashioned from monarchical paranoia, governmental cunning, and propagandistic enterprise.[1]

The Gunpowder Plot captured the collective imaginations of James I and his subjects not least because it was, and remains to this day, a genuine forensic mystery. Questions about its authenticity remain. The best recent account of the plot concludes that the idea of Gunpowder Treason "kept itself alive" during James's reign because the government was never able convincingly to explain it, although it never stopped trying.[2] Today, its convoluted, whodunit-style narrative no longer wields the same fascination it had for an earlier generation of historians, and confessional politics do not spark the same level of acrimonious debate about its significance. Still, there is no disputing the power of Gunpowder Plot to captivate the minds of Jacobean Britons, for whom the contemplation of large-scale attempted murder at the hands of papist rebels was no parlor game.[3] Recent historians have prudently abandoned the cold trail of the authentic plot, therefore, and have concentrated instead on its central place in the mental world of English anti-popery or the new Protestant calendar.[4]

But Gunpowder Plot did not exactly "keep itself alive" in this reign; James and his spokesmen worked assiduously from the outset to rewrite its narrative. Thus it drew a distinctive discursive power from the politics of rhetoric that is the outstanding feature of the reign of Great Britain's Solomon. As competing religious views constructed and reconstructed the unstable foundations of Jacobean "moderation," the ecclesiastical policies of James I required that the plot be manipulated into uniquely nuanced and intricate presentations. The unexecuted, unresolved plot was adaptable to any part of James's broadly designed program, and with constant airing and exercise on a newly proclaimed national holiday, it became a superbly flexible and well-toned rhetorical commonplace. Jacobean religious stability may have kept the worst of the plot's negative energies at bay, but this stability worked best at preventing a indiscriminate pogrom against Roman Catholics.[5] This is not to ignore Gunpowder Plot's singular contribution to the politics and language of anti-popery in the years preceding the civil wars. But historians have overlooked its other, more immediately incendiary use: as a vehicle for the development of the politics and language of anti-Puritanism.

This chapter explores the conundrum of this assertion, tracing the development of a peculiar and characteristic Jacobean anti-Puritanism in sermons preached at court and from the London outdoor pulpit of St. Paul's, where on national holidays court chaplains were chosen to preach by the bishop of London.[6] There are two important dimensions to this examination. First, it also includes sermons preached on the anniversary of another thwarted plot aimed at James, the infamous "Gowry conspiracy" of 5 August 1600. James had imported this personal holiday to England with his accession, but like his other Scottish innovations, it was met with a certain degree of skepticism, even by his loyal preachers.[7] Now Gunpowder Treason made Gowry treason credible; Gowry Conspiracy gave Gunpowder Plot a uniquely Jamesian twist. The king had at last found an exemplar of Anglo-Scottish union with potential for polemical success. Gowry and Gunpowder sermons from these two pulpits were printed in almost equal numbers during James's reign, with Gowry sermons usually offering preachers a second chance to talk about the treason dearer to their hearts, Gunpowder Plot. These are reasons enough to include both sets of sermons in one generic subset of Jacobean rhetoric, that of the "plot" sermon.

With this mention of printed sermons, I come to the second and most important dimension of this chapter. Paradoxically, perhaps, I want to rescue the Jacobean Gunpowder Plot lexicon from the overwhelming influence of Lancelot Andrewes. His contribution to Gunpowder and Gowry sermon rhetoric is immense, but of the nineteen sermons that Andrewes prepared and delivered *coram rege* on these days, only three were actually printed between 1605 and 1625, and those for a specific and official polemical purpose that is the subject of this chapter.[8] Andrewes's anti-Puritan leanings are well documented, but they are, risking redundancy, best described as "Andrewesian": elaborately coded and often kept to a minimum of public exposure.[9] While Andrewes's would indeed be a powerful voice in support of this chapter's argument, it would, in effect, be too powerful: to rely overmuch on the massive amount of evidence his sermons alone provide for these two holidays is to unbalance the operations and typecast the language of anti-Puritanism as it developed in the rhetoric of Gunpowder Plot.[10]

The Politics of Aftermath: The King's Speech, 9 November 1605

Gunpowder Plot garnered its most dramatic effects from the convenient fact of its nonoccurrence.[11] The failure of the plotters to realize their ambitions meant that the narrative of the plot was appropriated by James and his government and stage-managed in an impressively organized fashion. This began with a theatrical flourish worthy of Shakespearian treatment: a few days before the opening of the second session of James's first Parliament, Robert Cecil delivered to the king a ominously cryptic letter supplied by the Catholic Lord Mounteagle, whereupon James, to the amazement of his court audience, cracked the code of a secret plan to blow up Parliament, his family, and himself. (The only truly terrified person in the room may well have been James, whose anticipation of and apprehensions about personal danger had been forged in the fiery furnace of sixteenth-century Scottish politics.)[12] After this dramatic prologue, the government's actions appear to have been better rehearsed than those of the unfortunate plotters, who were rounded up, tortured, and publicly executed within the space of a few months. During this time, the king and his spokesmen instituted a media blitz of speeches, royal pronouncements, and official news reports. The volumes of print issuing so swiftly after the plot's discovery is evidence of a diverse and well-coordinated campaign aimed at constructing an authoritative public interpretation of the meaning of "Gunpowder Treason."[13]

Governmental efforts to control the terms of this debate moved into place with impressive dispatch. Befitting the case that the plot itself had no material existence (it produced no action in itself, but merely expressed the "will to act," in the words of Lancelot Andrewes), it had unpredictable polemical consequences in the chaotic early years of James's reign. Astoundingly, the discovery of the plot first stimulated a conciliatory royal rhetoric on Catholicism.[14] This untoward reaction makes sense if the larger political context is considered: James I did not want Gunpowder Plot simply to provide a broad conduit for the channeling of English anti-papist energies, as this would have had serious consequences both at home and abroad. In 1605, James was determined to avoid precipitate dealings with Catholic governments—especially Spain, with which he had recently concluded a peace treaty.[15] He needed to claim that he did not persecute for reasons of religion; he therefore had to insist, however disingenuously, that his domestic policies had not driven the plotters to such desperate measures.[16] An unwelcome alliance between a continental Catholic power and a disaffected Catholic minority at home would have given any Protestant monarch in this age reason for pause, but for this king, hardly settled and still perceived as foreign himself, the odds were too uncertain to come out swinging in only one direction. James I's most delicate and pressing task, then, was how to speak forcefully against Catholic treason in the face of the small but intractable problem of English recusancy and the large and undeniable fact of continental popery.

Thanks to James's ambivalent attitude toward confessional issues in the first years of his reign, the spectrum of articulate Catholic opinion in England was almost as broad at this time as that of the Protestant. James's practical assessment nonetheless appears to have been that Catholicism posed little threat to a country that had enjoyed nearly fifty years of Protestant government.[17] The actual population of committed English Catholics was small, and of these there were none who were too dangerous. But there persisted within England a core of obstinate and clamorous recusants, some very powerful, as well as many questionably observant subjects nicely identified as "church papists."[18] The king had to denounce the crimes of the guilty without alienating these two constituencies. A close examination of subsequent official responses to the plot reveals, however, an even more complicated political agenda. James was acutely aware not only of disaffected Catholic opinion, but also of nonconformist and anti-unionist feeling in England. He was determined to use this gift from God—his delivery from treason—as a position from which to launch a tripartite defense of his authority.

The multivocality of James's intentions is well documented in the text of his speech to a Parliament hastily reassembled on 9 November, four days after the discovery of the plot.[19] A large part of this speech was devoted to a carefully nuanced discussion of the difference between secular treason and conscientious objection in matters of religion, and at its center was a remarkably subtle and humane pronouncement on English Catholicism. The king announced his determination to confine the guilt of treason to the actual conspirators and not to indulge in a blanket condemnation of papists. While the gunpowder plotters were "parricides," it was not logical to assume that all Catholics were, by reason of their religion alone, traitors. James planned, therefore, to investigate the plot with "caution and wariness," not aggression. Marshaling a incisively compelling emotional argument, he reminded his parliamentary audience that their forefathers had all been papists; how could they possibly now believe that entire generations had been condemned for eternity?[20] And with this powerful caveat against undiscriminating anti-popery, the king suddenly and savagely turned on those familiar purveyors of a hotter sort of Protestantism, describing himself as "detesting in that point, and thinking the cruelty of Puritans worthy of fire, that will admit no salvation to any papist."[21]

The sting in the tail of this passage deserves closer examination. To begin, by the time James condemned those he called "Puritans," he had set in motion a substantially qualified definition with logical political implications. He identifies "Puritans" in extreme terms, as unfeeling tyrants who would deny salvation to their papist forefathers. Their opinions thus become diametrically opposed to James's stated policy: this king is not a religious persecutor, but "Puritans" would peremptorily consign their own ancestors to hellfire. (James's accusation also condemns, by a sly form of hyperbolic suggestion, Puritan disdain for ecclesiological traditions.) In the king's intertwined patriarchal and incendiary metaphors, the resemblance of Puritans to plotters is made plain. James could now suggest, with credible logic, that treasonous papists and overvigilant precisians intersected on at least one political plane. What united them was a quality opposed not only to his style of kingship, but to what that style represented: the exercise of a legitimate authority to define and enforce a principle of "moderation" in church and state.

James's speech demonstrates one method for the articulation of this "moderation." Inspired by specific events, a variety of religious positions would be staked out in official presentation; out of these, a typology of extremes would emerge by inference and allusion, and all would be set against the king's reasonably tolerant ecclesiastical policies. This discursive phenomenon has been convincingly outlined elsewhere, but its specific operations remain to be described and analyzed in detail here, where its apparent broadmindedness will be subjected to more skeptical scrutiny.[22] The much-vaunted "middle way" of Jacobean speech and sermon can appear as a rational path cutting through a thicket of theological hairsplitting, pretended reformation, and sociocultural unrest; but the *via media* was no less a polemical construct than those iniquitous twins the "Puritan" and the "papist." In other words, "moderation" was not exactly the reasonable alternative to provocations undertaken in the name of religion that it appeared to be. It was a received idea, so strongly allied to the political process that almost any extreme course could be justified in its defense. The rhetoric of the Gunpowder Plot yields abundant evidence for two important strands of this kind of "moderate" language. Here the Jacobean discourse of moderation enjoys one of its finest hours, as "Puritans" are castigated in a language that locates its critique in the notion of Catholic treason.

James's willingness to condemn precisians alongside papists had polemical antecedents that had originated in a dispute dividing the English episcopate over the need for further reformation. Most notable on one side was Richard Bancroft, future archbishop of Canterbury and doughty despiser of all things Puritanical, who had long been writing tracts that condemned Pu-

ritans and Catholics as equal threats to monarchical authority.
Long before the Hampton Court conference, as we saw in Chapter 2, the emergence of a presbyterian challenge to the Elizabethan religious settlement had led Bancroft to voice his own version of the admirably succinct religio-political admonition "no
bishop, no king." His was a doubly brilliant polemical campaign
in the late sixteenth century. Motivated by a hatred of Scottish
reformation and grounded in the real fact of militant Spanish
Catholicism, it could manipulate powerful fears of popery to re-
bound against the very people who felt they had done the most
to repudiate it. The end of the *classis* movement in the 1590's
meant that the godly thereafter took a relatively benign course,
calling for alteration of ceremonies and the prayer book. (The
eventuality of reform in these areas was something of a commonplace in the Protestant outlook of moderate reforming bishops.) But this did not did not lead to a relaxing of Bancroft's
rhetoric against overheated Protestantism in the early seventeenth century. He continued to attack this new "paper tiger" as
he once had Martin Marprelate, with all the vitriolic anxiety of
an aging and embittered company man resisting a demand for
his early retirement.[23]

Compelling and influential rhetoric does not spring, like
Athena from the brow of Zeus, fully grown from the imaginings
of skilled polemicists; it is the product of observation and experience. No matter how cleverly he retailored it to suit the English
climate—and no matter how well it rode the coattails of certain
vested (or vestiarian) interests in his new kingdom—, James's
language of the "Puritan-papist" threat was not grounded in the
intricate process of discursive logic, or even in the internecine
battles of an inherited Elizabethan episcopate, but in his actual
dealings with over-mighty subjects in Scotland. After all, this
was not the first time the royal person had been threatened. On 5
August 1600, James VI had been assaulted and imprisoned tem-
porarily by Scottish nobles of such impeccable Protestant cre-
dentials that Calvin's successor at Geneva, Theodore Beza, was
said to have wept over the execution of one of them.[24] The so-

called "conspiracy of the Gowries" had done much to teach James that treason was not the exclusive undertaking of popery. More significant, perhaps, the Gowry affair—in which James conveniently got rid of some importunate aristocratic creditors (to consider a less respectful version of the event)—proved the utility of treason-accusation as a means for royal rehabilitation, whether financial or reputational. This new delivery from danger gave the king the chance to revise once again the narrative of his own political experience.

The commemoration of James's delivery from the conspiracy of the Gowries had not previously impressed his English subjects, who displayed the same cynical disinterest as had Scottish critics about the king's account of his escape and continuing interest in celebrating it. Now James made rhetorical capital out of the similarities between these attempted treasons: "I may justly compare these two great and fearful Domes-days, wherewith God threateneth to destroy me and all you of this little world that have interest in me . . . it pleased God to grant me two notable deliveries upon one day of the week, which was Tuesday, and likewise one day of the month, which was the fifth; thereby to teach me, that as it was the same devil that still persecuted me, so it was one and the same God that still mightily delivered me."[25] Extraordinary chronological coincidence demonstrated the singular relation between Gunpowder Treason and Gowry Conspiracy, an affinity that found expression in the sermons James ordered to be preached on 5 August and 5 November for the rest of his reign. The language employed on these occasions, wherein the narrative of James's delivery by divine means underpinned the narrative of God's providential care for a chosen nation, played an integral role in shaping English religious and national identity.

But James's reference to "all you of this little world that have interest in me" is also a reminder of the Scottish dimension of a speech that was only partly concerned with Gunpowder Treason. The king now turned to the matter so violently disrupted by the discovery of the plot, stating that he had only planned to attend the opening days of this parliamentary session because his presence was essential to its business, which was the "delivering the articles agreed upon by the commissioners of the union." The Gunpowder Plot set back a process already crippled by public suspicion and parliamentary reluctance.[26] Recalling them for the coming January, the king reminded members of Parliament to arrive ready to turn their attention to the question of union when their abortive session reconvened. James mentioned his own patience in waiting for the matter to be worked out, reminding his audience that the union of crowns already in place was merely a starting point for the great work that lay ahead.[27] It is obvious that, at this time, the king was not willing to postpone the further union of his two kingdoms—something he considered a simple and self-evident political necessity—for fear of a few barrels of gunpowder. We can, therefore, infer a second domestic context for James's warning against an overenthusiastic investigation of Gunpowder Plot: it would disrupt progress on the union, if indeed so notorious a nonstarter could be said to have been at risk of disruption. The king's instructions to Parliament betray his awareness and frustration that Parliament had little interest in agreeing on terms for Anglo-Scottish unity and a great deal of interest in deploring the 1604 canons and airing fears that popery was on the rise in England. Not even his bishops could be counted on to provide support for a program that might lead to a closer relationship with a church whose polity they abhorred and whose lack of ceremonial they despised.[28]

If 5 November indeed marked the "birth-day" of James I's reign, therefore, it came as a surprise party, one planned for years by the plotters, yet organized and orchestrated in a matter of weeks by his own government. It did succeed in wiping the project for the union off the parliamentary slate; however, this allowed James gradually to apply his considerable rhetorical energy and enthusiasm to new religio-political projects. The images supplied by the forces of gunpowder, treason, and plot were both striking and multivocally allusive. The king could manipulate them to offer his English subjects a chance to identify with him, or to condemn the wrong kind of traitorous Catholics without offending the right kind (whether they were traitorous or not), or to warn off the hotter sort of Protestant from using the notion of the dangerous increase of papists in the land to justify their resistance to ecclesiastical conformity. Indeed, he could do all these things simultaneously.

Within weeks, the king's speech to Parliament and the official reports of the interrogations, trials, and confessions of the plotters were bound together and sold as a package publication.[29] James's speech to Parliament struck a keynote for plot sermons, in which court spokesmen parroted the king's phraseology and restated his concerns. The king's own willingness to borrow the forms and language of their religious discourse made this a reciprocal act of ventriloquism. James had designed his remarks on the plot in 1605 to evoke the idea of a sermon, from his opening citation of Psalm 145:9 ("The mercy of God is over all his works") through his utilization of homiletic-style text divisions. He concluded this section of his speech with an unambiguous declaration of polemical strategy:

[I]f I have spoken more like a Divine than would seem to belong to this place the matter itself must plead for mine excuse. For being here come to thank God for a divine work of his Mercy, how can I speak of this deliverance of us from so hellish a practice, so well as in the language of Divinity, which is the direct opposite to so damnable an intention?[30]

When the king claims the privilege of a divine in a secular setting, it is hardly surprising to find divines using the words of the king in the pulpit. This passage demonstrates the crucial role religious rhetoric played in the operations of Jacobean government. James's admission that only the "language" of religion could adequately express and in some way counteract the "intention" of treason not only apologizes for his borrowed style, but also announces that the official response to Gunpowder Plot will be developed through the medium of homiletics. There is an inherent tension signaled here—not only between the king's words and his government's actions, but also between the king's words and their mode of influence. James's eloquent evocation of the inseparability of the languages of politics and religion undercuts and renders incredible the central assertion in his speech—that the difference between recusancy and treason would be self-evident to his audience, or indeed to any future audience. This raises the issue of how the king's mouthpieces would respond to such a difficult mandate. Their re-presentation of the king's original message exposes the complexity and ambivalence of the relation between the language of the king and the sermons of his preachers.

Sermonic Variations, 1605–7

The first official sermon to be printed after the discovery of the plot was preached at Paul's Cross on Sunday, 10 November, by William Barlow, bishop of Rochester. Barlow had been a chaplain to Queen Elizabeth and, more recently, had secured a reputation as a court reporter of sorts by writing *The Summe and Substance of the conference, which, it pleased his Majesty to have with the lords, bishops and other clergie at Hampton Court*.[31] In this official, and thus seemingly definitive, account of the conference, Barlow managed both to tout the episcopal agenda at Hampton Court and to represent it as a one-sided victory by the king over Puritanism. The technique proved to be useful in his next work, *The Sermon Preached . . . the Next Sunday After the Discoverie of This Late Horrible Treason*, which presents a homiletic version of this hot-off-the-press, "official" reporting style. Rather than suppress the natural infelicities of a live performance, editorial intervention at the print stage highlighted the imperfections of Barlow's prose. That this was a deliberate strategy is clear from the remarkable preface that introduces the sermon. Ostentatiously excusing its hasty construction, breathless delivery, and precipitate printing, it sets up the expectation of a thrillingly immediate and raggedly emotional performance.

And in these stylistic particulars, Barlow does not disappoint. The preface recounts the circumstances of the sermon's inspira-

tion and construction in meticulously overwrought detail. Barlow had known all along that he was to preach at the Cross on
this first Sunday of the new parliamentary session, but the discovery of the Gunpowder Plot on the eve of its opening had
forced him to scrap his original text and undertake a hasty revision. In his anxiety, he had found it nearly impossible to find
words fit to comment on the astounding news: only the king's
speech of the day before and "divers circumstances sensibly received and imparted . . . overnight, by the Earl of Salisbury" had
given him the inspiration to write a new sermon. Such was the
preface's subtle acknowledgment of the fact that the eminent
personages mentioned had exercised control over his sermon by
providing him with a goodly portion of the actual prose—a
script for speaking to the situation at hand.[32]

Calling the plot "tragi-comical—tragic in the dreadful intention; comical in the happy and timely detection thereof," Barlow's preface admits the essential theatricality of the politics of
the plot.[33] As we shall see, it is a theatricality that defines the
rhetorical style of all Gunpowder Plot sermons.[34] This must be
attributed, at least in part, to the preacher's need to fill in or flesh
out what might have happened in the subjunctive space created
between the conceiving of a "dreadful intention" and its abortion
through "timely detection." In explaining what might have happened, but did not, Gunpowder Day preachers turned to imagi-
natively lurid reconstructions, which in turn often led to the expedient of role-playing. Given time and a bit of distance, this
technique led to a remarkable rhetoric of soul-searching that
speculated about the mind-set and desires of those strangers in
England's midst, its recusant minority. But here, and more immediately, role-playing serves to instruct the audience in the official version of the plot. The preacher takes the part of his audience: both are shaken from the usual patterns of their lives by
this inconceivably terrifying situation, and both must turn to the
king's words to negotiate potential social chaos.

While it would be foolish to dismiss what must have been the
very real sense of fear that pervaded London and Westminster at

this time, it would be naïve to assume that Barlow's sermon simply reflected this public concern. Rather, the sermon derives its pathopoeic energy from that disorientation, by presenting Barlow's confusion as the basis for a rhetorical style. His voice is emotional, shrill, and distracted (although it must be admitted that this frazzled tone would have been familiar to readers of Barlow's previous works, all of which are masterpieces of the polemical art of pathopoeia).[35] In several places the text breaks off, and a marginal addition instructs the reader that here or there Barlow interrupted his sermon to read out either Lord Mounteagle's letter disclosing the plans of the plotters, or the governmental reports of their examinations and confessions. These techniques lend credibility to Barlow's account of the plot, which was nonetheless an expression of governmental policy in a time of crisis—not some value-neutral news report. Moreover, this official rhetoric was refracted through the bifocal lens of the early Jacobean episcopate's characteristic political and religious biases. There is another agenda at work here, therefore, which can be traced in the oblique variations Barlow plays on themes inspired by the king.

Preaching on Psalm 18:50, "Great deliverances giveth he unto his king, and showeth mercy to his anointed David, and to his seed forever," Barlow represented James's delivery from the treachery of popery as a microcosmic demonstration of God's care for England. The assertion implied rebuke to those who put undue trust in foreign policy to guarantee domestic safety. Compared to England's experience of divine providence, mere "worldly" alliances were as nothing. Foreign powers, warned Barlow, might offer assistance in time of trouble, but their help came at too high a cost:

Their deliverances are not without some annoyance, even the very *salvere* of the tongue, like the saliva thereof, hath some venom in it . . . they speak friendly to their neighbors, but imagine mischief in their hearts. But their real deliverances [are] much more noxious. . . . Ask their help in distress they will grant it; but . . . either they exact a tribute, which exhausteth the Treasury, or impose Conditions, which infringe the Liberty, or require a future aid, which weakeneth the Power, or betray upon an advantage, which redoubles the Misery, or upbraids the benefit, which exulcerates the mind.[36]

Barlow grounds his rhetoric in the king's delivery of an accession promise: peace. Indeed, since this peace (and the conciliatory negotiations both foreign and domestic that had preceded it) accounted for James's ambiguous policy toward English Catholics, on one level, this passage could merely question how far the dictates of foreign policy should temper the response to Gunpowder Plot. Since the religious context afforded him a paradigm that could not offend, Barlow could express these concerns without challenging James's speech. But by fitting the narrative of the plot into the scheme of a providential national myth by evoking the Elizabethan, anti-Spanish fears that designed it, he also presents by allusion the case against a new Jacobean peace.[37]

Thus intersecting meanings signpost a busy intersection of issues. By citing divine intervention in the plot as definitive proof of James's "anointing," Barlow asserts that his right to be king comes from the will of God and not from the disputable politics of accession. The sermon testifies to the fact that accession politics were still kicking up a cloud of dust two years on, contributing to a profoundly unsettled state that Gunpowder Plot exemplified in spectacular fashion. The passage is a reminder that one of the unenviable jobs of the official pulpit in these early years after accession was to praise the king's unique position as a Scottish king to renegotiate treaties on the Continent. Here the plot gives Barlow a chance to vent his own unhappy feelings about foreign alliances—but not only because he had a persistent, native Elizabethan aversion to Spain. To praise the king as peacemaker also had the unfortunate effect of highlighting the king's Scottishness, which, as I have suggested, reminded the English episcopate of their persistent, native Elizabethan aversion to Puritan Scotland.

No matter what its effect up north, government by pen in the king's adopted country had several drawbacks. In spite of his willingness to speak publicly, write letters, and publish books explaining his position on everything from the obedience due to a king to the kind of table manners princes should use, the Scottish king James VI seems to have been a cipher to his new English bishops. The signals he sent through speeches, treatises, and preferment were astoundingly complex, and in the early years after his accession in England, we find a confused and irritated court exhausted from the effort of taking the royal pulse on the issues of the day. In his tireless and wide-ranging campaign for Elizabeth's throne, James had tried to please all of his domestic constituencies, drawing the same kind of ingratiating distinctions between dangerous and loyal Puritans in BASILIKON DORON that he had drawn between dangerous and loyal papists well before his speech of 9 November 1605. The unsurprising result was that he had succeeded in displeasing Puritans, papists, and anybody else who was unconvinced by his equivocating approach to religious policy. Add to this the widespread hateful distrust of Scots expressed by everyone, including Guy Fawkes and many lords spiritual, and far from disdaining Barlow's cribbing of the king's speech to Parliament, we begin to marvel that he found any words in it at all with which to indict actual and potential enemies of the crown.[38]

And at this point in the sermon, in fact, Barlow pointedly glances off the complicated issue he has raised.[39] An explanation of the operations of anointing appears to be so integral to the sermon's argument that it comes as an initial disappointment to be told that the preacher has run out of time to discuss it. Nonetheless, Barlow pleads the hourglass: "So would I liked to have handled this word *Anointed*, which makes a king a sacred person, to have showed unto you that this practice of murthering princes is made an axiom of theology among the romanists." Barlow tersely defines this Catholic regicidal theology as "positive divinity ... whereof, were there no other, the word "anointed" is an unanswerable confutation. Touch not mine anointed, saith the Prophet, Psalm 105:15 ... and yet, those who make religion the stalking-horse for treasons pretend the Catholic cause (as those conspirators now did) to murther the Lord's Anointed."[40]

In so abruptly ending his examination of the confessional motives of the plotters, Barlow dismisses their religious grievances—an important thing to do, given James's insistence that he was no oppressor of loyal Catholics and had no intention of becoming one. Barlow can then attribute this threat to the king as one solely perpetrated by political motives.

But Barlow's attempt to prove the plot was motivated by treasonous impulse masquerading as religious conviction also allows for a significant shift in his attack. Claiming to be unable further to discuss the Catholic theology he has so tantalizingly suggested, and with all the power of his succinct and therefore unspecified description still open to use, he changes focus to implicate particular members of his outdoor auditory:

> Against [the conspirators] I would in this case (if the time had served) have been more bitter, but that I remember there are some amongst us, who challenge unto themselves the *quintessence* of anointing: as he [said in] Isaiah 65, Come not near me for I am holier than thou, yet [they] come very near to the same dangerous position: not to speak of Knox and Buchanan, the two fiery spirits of that Church and nation where they lived, what means that speech of some of our own country, extant in print, in the late Queen's time of blessed memory? that if their reformation not be yielded unto there would be shortly a bloody day in England?[41]

Barlow maintains the style of urgency initiated with the preface. His reference to time running out places a heightened emphasis on the danger of treasonous Catholicism by the simple expedient of deliberately declining to discuss it.[42] Barlow then shifts the urgent emphasis invoked by the deliberate overlooking of dangerous papist disaffection onto this new—and for Barlow, more compelling—topic. Although the words used to effect it seem blustery and blunt, rhetorically this transfer is sophisticated—and, indeed, brilliantly underhanded.

It is important to note the ascending quality of Barlow's anti-Puritan critique here, for, despite its careful qualification, anti-

Puritan rant this most certainly is. The opening allusion to persons who consider themselves "holier than thou" may end in the very specific denunciation of Scottish presbyterians, but the progressive syntax of the passage leaves no question that the preacher sees such religious snobbery as bearing an uncomfortably close affinity to more dangerous positions. Barlow's polemical reputation had been built on his talent for blistering anti-Puritan invective, and in his manipulation of the rhetorical art of paralipsis an audience would have detected—perhaps even applauded—his stealthy, eventually triumphant return to his métier. The reference to speeches "extant in print" announces that this sermon would not only provide one of the first official comments on Gunpowder Plot, but would also contribute to an ongoing print debate between episcopal defenders of ecclesiastical conformity and godly nonconformists in England.

It is here, then, that Barlow signals a perceptible departure from the agenda set by the king's speech, wherein James identified as "Puritans" those in his audience opposed to his moderation on the issue of Catholicism. Refracted through the lens of the above passage, Barlow's earlier vague remarks about "nations" and "neighbors" come into sharper focus. His earlier isolationist remarks now appear as a *caveat* against establishing too close an alliance with Scotland to counter a Catholic threat. (The remarks about exhausting the treasury, for example, seem to be aimed directly north.) The warning demonstrates Barlow's particular conflict with English nonconformists, who could now point to the more completely reformed Kirk as a model for further reformation south of the Tweed. Barlow's mention of Knox and Buchanan relocates the anti-"Puritan" language of the king's speech of 9 November, therefore, by recalling another recent event when anti-Puritan bishops discredited English nonconformist demands by tarring them with the brush of Scottish presbyterian politics.[43] In effect, Barlow's Paul's Cross sermon of 1605 contextualizes Gunpowder Plot in the language of the Hampton Court conference; it bears, therefore, as much affinity to his *Summe and Substance* as it does to the king's speech.[44]

Barlow was the very model of an anti-Puritan conformist, and his performance of the duties of official commentator for the years 1605–6 ensured that Gunpowder Plot first emerged as a powerful cautionary image in the campaign for conformity that followed the publication of ecclesiastical canons in 1604.[45] On the plot's first anniversary, he preached before the privy council and law judges while Lancelot Andrewes preached *coram rege*.[46] Andrewes's sermon went unpublished in James's reign, but at the king's request, Barlow's was printed under the title *A Brand, Titio Erepta*. The obvious attraction of this sermon for James would have been its exposition of the interests that united monarchy and government. Citing as his text God's words to the prophet Zechariah, "Is not this a brand snatched out of the fire?" a slightly less agitated Barlow began this year's homily with an exhaustive roll call of those who could claim a personal interest in the near escape of a year ago: "[T]here is none in this church, or in the land, of honor and birth; or office of state, or place of justice, but he may (methinks) give for his impress a brand."[47]

A Brand demonstrates how James's political needs could be furthered alongside those of his bishops, but whether this illustrates a solidarity of purpose rather than a fortuitous intersection of concerns is harder to assert. A scant year after the devastating news of 5 November, Barlow still had relatively little to say about the specific menace of Catholic treason. Instead, in a repeat performance of the noteworthy rhetorical strategy of his 1605 Paul's Cross sermon, he claimed to have no time to condemn the actual perpetrators of Gunpowder Treason: "My duty is to keep me to my text. Of the *incendiarii* . . . not one word, either by way of invective or commemoration. For . . . they come not within my text."[48] What did come within Barlow's text was a long series of complaints sure to find an appreciative audience among the ruling elite to whom he preached. Barlow shamelessly panders to this audience, enlarging the idea of Gunpowder Plot into a metaphor for the treachery of what the preacher describes as "popular" opinion. The allusion allows him to spice his sermon with powerful overtones of personal grievance:

Were I a basket-maker, or a garland-winder, or of any base trade that should make me sweat for the bread I eat . . . no man would malign me, no man would traduce me; but now that I give myself to the study and interpretation of the scriptures, I am a *divine*, a *writer*, a *preacher*, *me oblescis notant*, I am scorched coal black with their oblisques and their obloques.[49]

Taking pride of place in *A Brand* is a long outline of the disadvantages and dangers of the episcopal life, which for Barlow was threatened not so much by explosives as by the slanderous speeches of the hotter sort of Protestant. He explicitly connects this manifestation of "popular opinion" to recent well-known ecclesiastical disputes. Here bishops stand proxy for the king, just as Puritans do for gunpowder plotters:

And certainly so it is, the meanest mechanical tradesman amongst us enjoys his vocation with less envy and regret than the minister doth (for, even to be a priest, is reproach enough itself in our times). Secondly, [if] he is an *high priest*, his superiority and degree draws on the first fire, for thither issueth the fiery blast of Corah and his complices [Numbers 16], "You take too much upon you, Moses and Aaron, ought there not to be a parity in the priesthood? And this fire, as you know and we feel, hath set *rotam nostrae generationis* as St. James speaketh [James 3:6] unto a combustion . . . no sooner had the Apostle, II Corinthians 11:28, declared his Prelacy, . . . [but] Saint Paul must smart, by the scorching calumnies of *false brethren*.[50]

What distinguishes this lengthy passage is its intertwining of incendiary imagery: "drawing first fire," "fiery blast," "combustion," "scorching calumnies," with allusive references to Puritanism: "parity in the priesthood," "false brethren." If the images are somewhat noncommittal, the relation between them is made explicit in the progress of the passage. We glimpse the initial shift to a Jacobean idea of "Puritan," as the provocations of that late Elizabethan mocker of the clergy Martin Marprelate take on a new and darker elaboration. In Barlow's interpretation, the potential treason of Catholic gunpowder plotting is actually made manifest in Puritan contumelies against the episcopate.[51] His reference to James 3:6, "And the tongue is a fire, a world of iniquity:

so is the tongue among our members, that it defileth the whole body," is especially telling: it demonstrates just how seriously Barlow's discursive engagement was with Puritanism, even on a day more appropriately devoted to the discussion of the potential firepower of papists.[52]

Sermons on 5 November continued to display this remarkable bait-and-switch condemnatory tactic as the influence of Barlow, Hampton Court, and the king's initial warnings about overenthusiastic anti-Catholicism infiltrated the discourse of the pulpit. In a Gunpowder Day sermon preached at the Cross and published in 1607, the royal chaplain Martin Fotherby (later bishop of Salisbury) alluded to England's peaceful foreign policy while calling in the same breath for national thanksgivings for its singular relationship to God. With peace in the realm, the Church of England was a haven "in itself" and also a "sanctuary for all the afflicted members of all other churches. ..." As regarded the Continent—England's "new peace with old adversaries" notwithstanding—, there was ample reason to remain vigilant. Fotherby reminded his audience that the word *jubilation* in the Hebrew also meant "military cohortation," and new friends could not always be trusted. Roman Catholic and Protestant countries had to acknowledge that there was a confessional hindrance to their secure alliance: "There cannot be *vera amicitia*, if it be not *Christi Glutino Copulata*."[53] Like Barlow, Fotherby uses this caveat about peace with Catholic powers to shift to a criticism of domestic religious opposition: "For be it, that [England] lacked the fear of all foreign enemies, yet lack we not the danger of domestical and intestine, which are more to be feared." His remark raises a rhetorical antithesis, presenting peace abroad as the ironic counterweight to unrest at home.[54]

In alluding to Catholic recusancy in order to introduce a stinging criticism of Puritanism, Fotherby utilized what had by now become a pulpit commonplace. In addition to papists, he claimed, there were other "secret, undermining enemies" in Church and country intent upon acts just as devastating as those once planned by the plotters. The commemoration of England's delivery from Gunpowder Treason should also celebrate the Church's victory over these hedge-Puritans:

[E]ven in this respect also have we great and just cause to jubilate unto God; who hath most graciously delivered this famous church of ours, not only from those our forenamed enemies, which openly oppugn her, but also from others unnamed too, which secretly undermine her: endeavoring, by a colourable pretense of reformation, to bring it into utter desolation and destruction . . . that whereas now there is heard the voice of holy singing and jubilation, there might be nothing seem[ly], but only the "abomination of desolation."[55]

These words transform the condemnation of nonconformity, hinted at in the king's speech and boldly stated in Barlow's two sermons, into a positive endorsement of ceremony and liturgy. Fotherby's sermon reveals his attachment to the "beauty of holiness." Soon to become notoriously central to a certain episcopal mind-set, such fixations on the scenic apparatus of the Church were neither a 1630's phenomenon nor exclusive in this period to the precocious clerics Lancelot Andrewes and John Buckeridge. A sturdy bedrock of Jacobean sermon polemic defending the liturgy in overwrought language existed for the study and use of later Laudian conformists. Moreover, the works of Fotherby and Barlow demonstrate how the hyped-up hysteria of Gunpowder Day made their attack on nonconformity and defense of ceremonial markedly obsessive and stylistically hyperbolic. The demands of such a rhetoric forced these writers to imply that destruction wrought by gunpowder was no worse than giving in to demands for further reform, a comparison that in its very audaciousness must have been both memorable and effective.

Fotherby and Barlow stridently oppose Puritan contumelies against the episcopate, in expressions that point to both men's self-conscious engagement in the post–Hampton Court print debate with the godly in England and the presbyterians of Scotland. Recalling Barlow's evocation of "tongues of fire," Fotherby also described nonconformity with metaphors of vocality, which in this sermon serves an underpinning imagery of the beauties of the English liturgy: "Neither is there anything in this worthy church of ours, which so greatly needeth to be reformed, as that such filthy and unclean birds be chased out by whom it is defiled, and by whose jarring sounds ... the holy music of our church is greatly disturbed."[56] Fired by an enthusiasm for ceremony, such uncompromising sentiments came easily to Fotherby. He was a tireless hammer of the Puritans in his sermons. Preaching ten days later at court, on 2 Timothy 3:8, "As Jannes and Jambres resisted Moses, so do these men also resist the truth," Fotherby interpreted the twin resisters as Puritans and presbyterians and utilized a marvelous range of invective. This sermon and his Gunpowder Day sermon, along with two others, were bound together and dedicated to none other than Richard Bancroft, whom he identifies as his patron. Appended to the sermons is a waspish defense of the use of the sign of the cross in baptism, originally written to support the publishing of the 1604 canons, and thereby ensuring Fotherby's place in the pantheon of early Jacobean conformists whose minds were fixed on ceremonies.

Paul's Cross often demanded a bold polemical tone from the court servants preaching there on national holidays. In general, sermons at this great outdoor auditory displayed a hotter sort of Protestantism and, related to this, a great deal more unqualified anti-Catholic sentiment than sermons preached at the Jacobean court, which makes the appointment of an outspoken ceremonialist like Fotherby to preach there on this particular day especially revealing. It suggests politic joint decision-making between the bishop of London and King James's council, at a time when it was imperative for both to avoid any appearance of sponsoring an anti-Catholic line that intolerably challenged James's pursuit of continued peace with Spain and secular compromise with English Catholics.[57]

Here Fotherby's—and, earlier, Barlow's—well-known anti-Puritan biases and ceremonial advocacy would have challenged Puritan concerns about the king's pro-Catholic foreign policies, while keeping fears about his domestic policy focused on areas of intervention in which the episcopate was responsible. Neither preacher was particularly soft on recusancy, and both hated militant Catholicism, but, as these sermons illustrate, Barlow and Fotherby unambiguously reserved their greatest fear and loathing for Puritans. With the godly reforming agenda in transition, the image of Puritanism was especially vulnerable to the reshaping operations of their homiletic campaign. Thus the ecclesiastical policies of James I and the biases of his bishops demanded and, literally, constructed this remarkable rhetorical strategy, in which anti-Spanish and anti-Catholic sentiments functioned as polemical facilitators of a carefully qualified but unquestionably forceful anti-Puritanism.[58] This rhetoric, which in operation balanced out opposed extremist views and, in doing so, effaced them, illustrates one methodology for the expression of Jacobean "moderation."

Between 1605 and 1608, then, we must look to the more private forum of the chapel royal to find a subtler rhetoric of religion. But while its polemical edge might appear blunted to the point of dullness, it is anything but anodyne. It is, in fact, even more expressive of the peculiarly provocative quality of Jacobean "moderation." The primary exponent of this sophisticated line was Lancelot Andrewes, who preached before the king or at court on almost every remaining Gunpowder and Gowry day of James's reign, during which time he announced his own characteristic anti-Puritanism in strategies more elegantly nuanced than either Barlow's or Fotherby's. Andrewes was altogether less cagey than other preachers about the king's dealings with continental Catholicism: where they had to balance their intemperate criticisms of foreign policy with crudely unmistakable anti-Puritan ranting, Andrewes simply interpreted the king's policies favorably by stressing James's self-image as *Rex Pacificus*. On 5 November 1607, for example, Andrewes's court sermon was based on Psalm 126, "O Lord, turn again our captivity, as the streams in the south." Andrewes anticipated criticism of James's conciliatory attitude toward continental Catholic powers and his own Catholic subjects; "southern streams," he explained, was a metaphor for the king's policy, signifying that James would respond to Gunpowder Plot in "no violent way, but even only by thawing and melting the hearts of Princes." Peace was paramount abroad; at home, conversion was to be accomplished by example rather than by compulsion.[59] This would have been implicitly disturbing to hotter Protestants calling for a stricter governmental treatment of papists, but these deceptively emollient words went unpublished until 1629. James's need for a rhetoric that punched above the weight of actual governmental policy might account for the peculiar print history of the sermons of his pulpit favorite. The king's politic intent might have been to "thaw" hearts rather than to batter them, but it would seem that the king needed the more crudely obvious polemical tactics of a Barlow or a Fotherby to broadcast by publication his "moderate" religious policy.

A very different sermon by Andrewes, preached on Gowry Day 1606, went into print, however—but not until 1610, along with Andrewes's 5 August sermon for 1610. The only Gowry court sermons to be printed in James's reign,[60] these confirm the rejuvenating but obliterating effect Gunpowder Plot had on the public presentation of James's personal, Scottish holiday. In the exordium to this sermon, Andrewes resorts to Gunpowder Plot imagery to illustrate the significance of the day's commemoration: "He that six years since hath delivered him from the hurtful sword, very lately this year (this very year) hath delivered him from the perilous gunpowder; thus yearly he heaps upon us new deliveries." Perhaps surprisingly—considering the Knoxian aspects of the Gowry conspiracy and Andrewes's ceremonialism—, these two sermons display none of the overt anti-Puritanism of a Barlow or a Fotherby. In fact, they are unique in the Jacobean Andrewes print canon for their studied silence on the topic of nonconformity or presbyterianism and their concentration on the topic of foreign Catholicism, albeit this line of argumentation is precisely qualified. Since these two sermons were most certainly intended to contribute to a developing international print controversy, it is appropriate to treat them as framing devices for another style of plot rhetoric, therefore, one wherein the post–

Hampton Court language of court anti-Puritanism gave way to an equally searing court condemnation of jesuitical Catholicism. These languages overlapped in the pulpit in the year 1606, but they remain almost entirely separate in print, with the rhetoric of anti-jesuitism replacing the rhetoric of anti-Puritanism in court sermons from 1608 to 1610.

The Plot Thickens: Anti-Jesuit Rhetoric at Home, 1606–10

Beyond the general utility of its divine-right sentiments or their attractive packaging in elegant syntax, clever wordplay, and witty rhetorical apparatus, there lies another reason for the 1610 publication by royal command of Andrewes's 1606 Gowry sermon. The sermon was both preached and published in Latin; and while we have reports of other such sermons being delivered at court, this and one other sermon preached before James and the king of Denmark on 27 July 1606 are the only Jacobean court sermons to have been published in Latin.[61] The publication of these two sermons without translation are practical reminders that the king of Denmark would not have understood an English sermon, but beyond this, it also suggests a mode of ideological influence not wholly dependent on content. By the early seventeenth century, most sermons preached in England were published in English, with Latin remaining as the parlance of university disputation and international religious controversy. In the case of Andrewes's sermon, its publication in Latin, strong anti-Jesuit language (both unusual for Andrewes and somewhat inappropriate to a sermon celebrating the comeuppance of Protestant lords in Perth), and the print date of 1610 locate this work primarily in the context of James's literary response to the Gunpowder Plot—in fact, it frames this kingly treatise. In 1606, the pulpit Andrewes played the role of John the Baptist to the king's 1608 work *Triplici nodo, triplex cuneus. Or An Apology for the Oath of Allegiance*, but in 1610, the same sermon, now in print, added voice to that same campaign, now in full swing.[62]

Andrewes's 1606 Gowry treason sermon thus owed its style, its imagery, and, eventually, its publication to the next phase of

the politics of Gunpowder Plot, which began with the international consequences of a domestic campaign. Parliamentary leg-
islation in May 1606 put the king's contentions about secular
loyalty and English Catholicism into practice by requiring recusants to take an oath renouncing the papal deposing power, but
not the pope's spiritual leadership. Despite this reassuring language—or, more likely, because of the obscurantist specificity
that marked its division of secular and sacred authority—, the
pope's response to the Oath of Allegiance was swift, severe, and
uncompromising. Breves issued from the Vatican in 1606 and
1607 forbade English Catholics to take it, and a bevy of international papal apologists, most of them Jesuits, took up the pope's
cause. James needed support for this project outside Britain, and
he counted on Catholic as well as Protestant monarchs to defend
the principles of princely authority against these defenders of
Paul V. The king promptly took up his own literary cudgels to
defend his brainchild, conscripting many of his preaching divines (notably, Andrewes) to write treatises of their own defending the oath against his detractors. In the several incarna-
tions of his *Apology* (it was first published anonymously, although its authorship was hardly a secret, and updated in 1609
to answer criticisms),[63] James sought to reassure his Catholic
readers, in overwhelming detail and with many reasonable arguments, that he would not require papists to confirm his royal
supremacy. He did expect them, however, to renounce the
pope's political authority in England.[64]

Analyzed in this context, Andrewes's Gowry sermon mani-
fests a very specific utility. A sermon issued by royal fiat in the
language of international Christianity and intermonarchical
communications would provide a prop for James's image
abroad, presenting him as the equal of the continental monarchs
whom he was courting against the opposition of the pope. One
of their number, after all, was James's guest at the time the sermon was preached: James's brother-in-law, Christian of Denmark. This fact is proudly trumpeted in the title: *Concio Latine
habita Coram Regia Maiestate quinto Augusti 1606*. Without pro-

gressing beyond the title-page, then, the reader is already presented an image of James as *Rex inter pares*—a king who not only hobnobbed with other kings, but also shared his chapel with them. And indeed, the title alone proclaims that James is the provider, through the sermons of his own churchmen, of religious instruction to continental monarchs.[65]

The publication of this Gowry sermon in Latin by the king's printer in 1610 is a literal demonstration of the problematic duality of the discursive images of international and domestic politics. English secular priests, struggling to counsel their remnant flock, had to decide how much authority to cede to the pope and his Jesuit polemical agents, on the one hand, and to cede to James I and his homiletic spokesmen, on the other. Andrewes's sermon also created an image of James as the pope's equal and rival at home, but the suspicions of English Catholics would have been raised by the atmosphere of polemical schizophrenia that surrounded the subject of their inclusion in the *via media* of their king's religio-political ambitions. The domestic context for *Concio* underscores the inherent conflict between the king's rhetoric insisting that the oath would be used to distinguish between "foreign" (i.e., disloyal) and "English" (i.e., loyal) Catholicism, and his Parliament's enactment of such an oath in a bill entitled "For the Better Detecting and Suppressing of Popish Recusants." This perceptible division between James and his Parliament over matters of religion would have given recusants little cause for security. The controversial and divisive nature of the monarch's claim to a civil authority in matters many of his subjects would have considered spiritual would have been illustrated all too well in the recent contentious history of James's dealings with English Puritans (in and out of Parliament) after Hampton Court. The Oath of Allegiance, like the oath of supremacy, was no instrument of moderation—both were aimed at the ferreting out of conscientious objectors, and both forced the guarantee of loyalty in language that created profound disquiet for papists and Puritans alike.

The domestic rancor and polemical divisiveness that characterized the 1604 campaign for conformity thus provides the practical link connecting this new strand of plot rhetoric to its anti-Puritan counterpart. The king's insistence that the oath was designed to prove the civil loyalty of papists brought Puritan anxieties about domestic popery to the fore. These fears were first concentrated upon the conviction that a promise of mere civil fealty would be insufficient to block the murderous impulses of heretical religion. In February 1605/6, the godly parliamentarian Edward Hoby described the doubts expressed by members about the king's course of action. Hoby complained that an oath of allegiance would provide "insufficient assurance" of the loyalty of papists in "court and chamber."[66] To concede the pope's spiritual authority within England, as the king protested he was willing to do in his *Apology*, was to unhitch secular loyalty from the shared religious premises that made it secure. To depend on the force of language alone to negotiate the gulf yawning between civil and religious loyalty was asking not only the improbable but also the hitherto unimaginable.

In the second phase of Gunpowder Plot investigation, entries in the *Calendar of State Papers, Domestic* clearly articulate the almost paranoiac concern by many in James's government, especially the earl of Salisbury, about the possibility that papists would prevaricate under examination: "Jesuits and priests are now allowed by the pope to deny their profession or to swear and foreswear anything to heretics for their own preservation."[67] While the doctrine of equivocation had a real existence— recusant priests often did counsel English Catholics to exercise some form of mental evasion when taking the oath or undergoing questioning—, it had an exaggerated cultural presence as the foundation of a Protestant monitory myth. The obsession with popish credibility can be found in any number of popular venues, including the theater: the year the Jesuit priest Robert Garnet was executed for his part in the plot, the Porter in *Macbeth* addresses an unearthed relic with, "Faith, here's an equivocator . . . who committed treason enough for God's sake, yet could not equivocate to heaven." Garnet had written a manual on equivocation, and another Jesuit, Robert Parsons, had defended the practice in *A Treatise Tending to Mitigation* in 1607. In it, Parsons suggests that to equivocate under oath was not to perjure oneself but simply to recognize and exploit the fact that any set of words could support more than one signification. This came uncomfortably close to calling equivocation just another rhetorical strategy in an age distinguished by an excess of confessional controversy.

Like so many creations of polemic, the Equivocator was based on emergent anxieties. His star turn as the sneering villain of the oath controversy expresses a prevailing suspicion, not only that words alone would prove ineffective to pledge Catholics to civil obedience, but also that the forces of popery could as easily manipulate the power of words in an evil cause as could the English government in a good one. The court and Paul's Cross sermons for 1608–10 trace the lineaments of this cultural anxiety, and as a result, they display an anti-Catholic rhetoric unparalleled in these pulpits on any other Gunpowder or Gowry day in James's reign. The figure of the Equivocating Jesuit allowed preachers to lambaste the Catholic enemy in plot sermons, counteracting a polemical language that previously had been qualified by James's startlingly conciliatory comments about international Catholicism and overshadowed by Barlow's obsessions with conformity and conferences at Hampton Court.

Andrewes's Gowry sermon for 1606 provides the first preached and best sustained example of this new focus in plot sermons. Like other preachers, Andrewes took the king's lead in order to pull it down new paths. The opening remarks of this sermon recall the king's succinct remarks about the similarities between Gunpowder and Gowry, "as the same devil persecuted me, so the same God mightily delivered me." But here, ascending into baroque realms of biblical and linguistic elaboration, Andrewes sharpens the focus of James's 1605 speech:

[T]o kings, more than others, that malignant one shews himself more malicious. ... He it is, that destroys kings. Namely, the angel of the bottomless pit; of whom the same John speaks, Apocal. 9.11. His name in Hebrew is Abaddon: in Greek Apollyon, that is, "a destroyer." A destroyer: a name directly opposite to God's name. His name is SAVIOR.[68]

Here the repeated emphasis on the word *name* creates an atmosphere of disclosure: Andrewes will dare to accuse the devil that persecutes kings. The nominal opposition of "Savior" to "Destroyer" then sets up a play on words that condemns this enemy in their own words:

[O]ur age brings forth strange children. Strange indeed. A kind of men, which style themselves—of the Society of JESU . . . is not this a strange thing and monster-like, that these, who from Jesus a Savior, have made a name for themselves, are accounted most wicked, even the Ambassadors of Abaddon, traitors to kings, the overthrow of kingdoms in what state soever they get footing?[69]

The description of treason as jesuitical retells Gowry day's essentially domestic and Scottish narrative in the tropes of international conspiracy. This will allow Andrewes to tailor his polemic to the prevailing continental furor over James's response to Gunpowder Plot, but, most significant, it introduces an argument about alienating religious influence at home. Andrewes's remarks about "strange children" and "monsters" follows characteristic Gunpowder Plot stylistics, which most often depend on images of untimely birth to describe the failure of the traitors to accomplish their ends. Here parturient language evokes images both foreign and domestic, while entwining them: it paints a picture of the alien nourished in England's womb. This strategy updates the fears once raised by the discovery of Gunpowder Plot. The fertile minds of the gunpowder plotters may have failed in 1605, but now, in the birth of a sect of "strange children," monsters who have insinuated themselves into the very bowels of a kingdom, England witnesses their eventual triumph.

The image of clandestinity could be connected to the doctrine of equivocation with polemical ease. Transferring its object to "other secret, undermining" enemies, the language of covert conspiracy once so effectively applied to Puritans now took on a new, foreign straw man. Here, for example, Andrewes goes on to describe the distinguishing characteristic of these jesuitical "strange children":

[T]hese [enemies] of ours, are of the same lineage of David: their marks are every way alike, *filii alieni* [strange children] (saith David, Psalm 18:45) *mentiti sunt mihi* [they have lied to me]. Even the same thing which he saith twice in this Psalm. "Their mouth speaketh a lie, their right hand is a right hand of iniquity." And are not these of ours just like them? Also except, what David calls lying, that, they call "equivocation." A diverse title, no different things ... both mouth and right hand (for taking oaths) is estranged from their mind, their mind estranged from God; at least from the true God: For from an *equivocal* God, that is, the God of this world, it is not perchance estranged.[70]

In this passage, Andrewes's image of natal monstrosity—strangeness—is illustrated by the disparity between word and meaningful intention—estrangement—that underpins this Jesuit doctrine. He thereby opens up the somewhat cerebral concept of equivocation to a grosser physical description of its duality. When the open mouth and the upturned right hand are "estranged" from the mind—almost literally, made "strange"—, when outward form so redirects the idea of truth, Andrewes suggests, equivocation is physically monstrous. This brilliant rhetorical strategy, which out of the parturient images of the failure of the plot delivered a literally misshapen image of monstrous new doctrine, was to influence subsequent sermons on the plot, as other preachers at court and Cross joined the print debate surrounding the Oath of Allegiance controversy.

On Gunpowder Day 1608, the archdeacon of Ely, Robert Tynely, preached a vigorously anti-Jesuit sermon at Paul's Cross. Tynely constructed this sermon around the Oath of Allegiance, which had become the literary obsession of a year that also saw the publication of James's *Apology*. Clearly, Tynely saw himself as a major contributor to the king's engagement with foreign controversialists: the published version of this sermon identifies Tynely's object as Robert Parsons, whose attack on James, *The Judgment of a Catholic Gentleman concerning Triplici nodo, Triplex cuneus*, had recently arrived in England. Tynely's self-conscious

identification with the oath controversy accounts for his focus on
the equivocality of the rhetorical enterprise itself, with the Jesuit
enemy first defined by his skillful but mendacious approach to
controversial discourse. In the introduction to his sermon, Tynely
promises that he will unmask the verbal disguises of Parsons
and his band of wily, unscrupulous propagandists. All Jesuits
were adept at arranging "rhetorical flowers" whereby they "gar-
nished and polished" heretical ideas into snares for the religiously unsophisticated.[71] Tynely contrasted this crafty rhetorical
style with his own, an unassuming humble "country manner."

Tynely's modest disclaimer about his own rhetorical skills is
itself a device that not only sets up a contrast between him and
his opponents but also enables him to mount a critique of Jesuit
Catholicism that focuses on their black art of appearances. He
suggests that the "religious craft" of Jesuit polemical style is
merely the literary manifestation of their protean and dangerous
natures. In a passage that links their deceptive rhetoric with their
deceptive practices, he explains:

[H]e which will deceive, must set a good face upon it; and make the
matter seem, at least wise probable; else were they not their craftsmas-
ter: for as the comical poet says . . . guiles are no guile, if deceit cloak
them not . . . no greater mischief than if they be seen. For thereby the
prey is lost, and they go home empty-handed; as fowlers do, when the
birds espy the nest.[72]

Tynely's "country manner," then, also serves to put him in the
place of an innocent observer in a harsh world; through it, he can
claim a kind of comradeship with his audience at the Cross. Such
role-playing points us, once again, to the unparalleled theatricality of plot rhetoric. Tynely's fondness for the language of gulls
and "guiles" locates this outdoor sermon within some of the traditions of another outdoor urban entertainment, the city come-
dies of Jacobean theater. His following complaint could have
been staged as Jonsonian knockabout farce: "What is their drift
in transforming themselves into as many shapes as meet with
objects? now a courtier, then a citizen; here a country gentleman,

there a country swain; sometimes a servingman, a swaggerer, Pot-companion; another while a priest."[73]

Of all the alchemical con men, according to Tynely, none was "so subtle as the Jesuit." Like Andrewes, Tynely recommends their detection through recognition of their distinguishing doctrine: "Of all their wiles, I commend unto you the equivocating shibboleth, the very forge of lying and deceit; which bewrayeth them by their speech."[74] Tynely's admonition reveals his fears about the persistent persuasiveness of the Catholic cause. His description of these masters of disguise, Jesuits who could be all things to all people, exemplifies in vivid fashion his concern that Catholicism would never be extirpated in England, and that a papist "fifth column" would remain ready to be proselytized into violent action.[75]

Tynely's concerns were echoed in court. Preaching to James on 5 November 1608, the future bishop of London, John King, also noted the Jesuit propensity for insinuative shape shifting, a characteristic he promptly described in punning terms:

Their names are diverse according to their natures and manners . . . these changelings, chameleons, these Mattheus Tortos, crooked apostles, torturous Leviathans . . . ambiguous in their answers . . . this serpent, *surrepent* [slithering] generation, with their meandering turnings and windings, their mental reservations, their amphibolous, amphibious prepositions, which live, as those creatures, part in the land, part in the water, so these half in the lips, half in the heart and conscience.[76]

In a letter written 8 November 1608, a courtier, John Chamberlain, told Dudley Carleton that Dean King's Gunpowder sermon was "so well liked that we will shortly have it in print."[77] The popularity and notoriety of this particular court sermon may have had to do with its outspoken, uncompromising stance on Catholicism and its daringly open critique of the king's foreign and domestic policies. Stimulated by the views of the preacher he had just heard three days prior (and with barely disguised pleasure in sharing the latest morsel of juicy court gossip), Chamberlain told Carleton of growing concerns about James's domestic and diplomatic conciliation of Catholics. In his Scottish

reign, Chamberlain feared, the king might have had more contact with the pope than he was now willing to admit. These suspicions had been raised by a certain "Matthaeus Tortus," the
slippery character of the above passage, who in a recent book
had claimed that James had established relations with Pope
Clement VIII in 1599.[78]

John King's homiletic version of the so-called "Balmerino affair" demonstrates the dangerous potential of a routine polemical strategy in plot sermons. Gunpowder and Gowry sermons
characteristically featured a narrative account of their respective
event, wherein court preachers commended to the king the
providential similarity of his two deliveries from treason. As we
have seen, the vacuum at the center of gunpowder narrative led
to sanguinary, imaginative descriptions of what might have
happened had the plot not been discovered. Gowry sermons, on
the other hand, faced a different and trickier problem—the fact
that no one except James much cared about the episode nor actually remembered any version of it except the one wherein the
king behaved pusillanimously. Based invariably on James's
story, the stilted recitals of the infamous tower room episode by
court preachers are masterpieces of unintentional insult. In his
own reprise, while purporting to answer James's papalist contemners, King manages to deliver a set of extraordinary backhanded compliments to the king. His introductory query to this
lengthy passage—"[D]o we bless God for preserving the life of
the king and shall we not bless him for preserving the honor of
our king?"—suggests that James's honor was indeed in rather
too much need of preservation:[79]

It was eight years since, upon the fifth of August last, that the Gowries
conspired against the life of the Lord's anointed, and received their de-
served meed. There have been *oculi nequam* in the world, mistrustful
eyes, that have looked awry upon that fact ever since, and would not
believe it. . . . It were strange to give you a parallel to this, coetaneous
[coterminous], I think, in time, and of the same standing. It was eight
years since likewise, in the days of Clement the eighth, that letters were
sent unto Rome, to the pope and to two cardinals, Aldobrandine and

Bellarmine, wherein *the hand of the king was abused, his heart never could* ... so far is it from him with other kings of the earth to receive the mark of the beast imprinted in his forehead, that he is jealous, impatient, cannot endure that any scratch of a pen, or type of a printer's press should leave the least note of suspicion upon him, as if ever he had but a thought in his heart to fall down and worship that golden calf.[80]

In his zeal to combine narratives with rhetorical logic and skill, King allies the disturbing allegations of "Mattheus Tortus" to the credibility vacuum at the heart of the Gowry conspiracy. He paints a picture of James using the physical imagery of equivocation inspired by Andrewes, but, in doing so, the preacher must then justify the equivocating disparity between the hand and heart of the king. King's subsequent need to explain away the king's act in the subjunctive language of "so far is it from him ... as if ever he had" merely works to highlight the holes in James's story. These are points Chamberlain could hardly have failed to note, as his salacious report to Carleton suggests. Furthermore, considering that this was a Gunpowder Day sermon, King's damaging exercise in *comparatio* only begs the question of James's own accountability and veracity in his policy on popery.[81]

Astonishingly, the sermon was printed by royal command without delay. Risky as it seems, there was method behind the publication of this sermon. At the very least, it signals the fact that this year the king needed a stronger line against popery than he had ever needed before, even one that held up his actions to an unflattering mirror. King had made his polemical reputation by being as rabidly anti-Catholic as Barlow was anti-Puritanical, and he fell to his task with undisguised relish. He denounced "romish, popish, anti-Christian, Catholic, catacatholic cruelty" with a rhetorical energy that distinguishes this work as the harshest sermon on popery to be preached at the Jacobean court on any date, let alone the fifth of November. Taking as his text Psalm 11:2–4, "For loe the wicked bend their bow ... that they might secretly shoot at them that are upright," King described the plot in martial terms, calling it "an armed, enraged, military

sin; it sendeth forth arrows . . . [with] skillful artificial cruelty."
By calling the plot "military," King located the events of 1605
within a general, international Catholic conspiracy. His sermon
reflected the dismay felt in England over the recent conclusion of
a marriage alliance between France and Spain. This new entente
between two previous enemies cast the shadow of a threatening
pan-Catholic European alliance over James's dream of presiding
over a Protestant empire. The king's foreign policy, which depended upon these two great European Catholic powers keeping
each other in check, now appeared ill-advised.[82]

Yet the king's need to signal his displeasure about the underhanded dealings of continental Catholic powers does not explain
why James allowed the printing of this sermon, in which the
preacher's overwhelming animus against popery threatens to
overcome his political judgment, and leads him time and again
to challenge the king's policies and question his decision to allow
a degree of leniency to English papists. The conclusion brings
this approach to its confrontative summit in an astounding address directed to the king, which is worth printing in full. First
King alludes to international religious controversy and Jesuit
slander to vent his fears for the future:

Most gracious sovereign. You are yet a living Lion. And the Lion of the
Tribe of Judah grant you may long and long to be. It may be they fear
the Lion's paw, and dare not as yet break forth. But when you shall be a
dead Lion (as that imperial Lioness now is and Lions must die as well
as worms) these dogs will bark at your manes [too], these egyptical
dead flies will cause the sweet ointment of your precious and glorious
name to stink upon the face of the earth . . . with their leprous, venom-
ous breath and libelous, infamous pamphlets, as they do hers.[83]

Above is a variant on the rhetoric of Elizabethan remembrance,
which was a frequent feature of gunpowder sermons. Here it
qualifies King's daring reference to James's mortality, which, if it
had not been enclosed in this condemnation of James's controversialist opponents, could well have earned the preacher a
harsh reprimand. But when King leaves the past behind, and
concentrates on present tense, domestic affairs, he employs a de-

gree of direct criticism that is, to put it mildly, remarkable:

> It is not this plea: *justus quid fecit?* That can excuse you. I would they
> had juster cause to ask *justus quid facit?* That your Majesty would do
> them right and administer justice upon them, in the timely execution of
> your laws, and necessary castigation, coercion of their unrestrainable
> audaciousness. That your faithful and good servants did not demand
> with groans of heart, *misericors quid facit?* What meaneth his Majesty to
> deal so graciously with them: some justice with mercy and lenity would
> do well. Some frosts with the fire that warmeth the snakes in the bowels
> of your land . . . if justice go on to sleep as it were her dead sleep, the
> tares of disloyalty, treasons and seditions be so thick sown in the field
> of your kingdoms, by these envious men, these seedsmen of Rome, that
> it will be difficulty . . . afterwards to remove them.[84]

What is provocative here is not King's demand that James do
justice to traitorous Jesuits in England, but King's depiction of
the miseries the king's policies caused at home (pointedly and
directly referred to as "your land") and his hardly politic demand that James modify his policies. This kind of rhetoric was
not new to the court pulpit, but its press history certainly is. Recent and similar tactics by John Burges in 1604, when in a court
sermon he criticized the 1604 conformity drive and deplored its
effect on James's subjects, had earned that godly and painful
preacher arrest and imprisonment. An examination of the different circumstances surrounding the preaching of these two sermons reveals why King's sermon was published rather than con-
fiscated in 1608.[85]

To begin with the most basic distinction: King was an aspiring
bishop, Burges an aspiring Puritan minister. This meant that
King enjoyed a certain advantage of intention, confirmed at
Hampton Court, whereby it was assumed that the monarchy and
its chaplains pulled in the same direction. "No bishop, no king,"
in other words, could be read from either perspective. Burges, on
the other hand, represented a minority of clerics who had resisted conformity to the 1604 canons. On disputed issues, the
king could interrogate his Lords spiritual at table, while lesser
men explained themselves from prison. This only explains, how-

ever, why King did not go, like Burges, to the Tower. To say that
Burges's ordeal merely reflects James and his bishops' more immediately censorious attitude to Puritanism is not particularly
revealing in the case of this sermon, given King's own sympathies for moderate Puritanism.[86]

These were sympathies, however, that looked a great deal
more useful in 1608 than they did in 1604 (or were to in 1617, for
example). What made this sermon not only immune from censure but also subject to promotion by publication was the way it
played into the prevailing issue of the period on a day dedicated
to the airing of these concerns. Burges's 1604 sermon fit into the
claustrophobic local context of a domestic conformity campaign
(and resistance to the king's scheme for Anglo-Scottish union),
while King's could be expanded to fit in the larger world of what
might best be called domestic-international controversy. When
Burges warned the king of displeasure with his campaign for
Protestant conformity, therefore, he suggested that James could
not unite his Protestants within one national polity; when King
warned James of domestic Protestant displeasure with foreign
Catholic intrigue, he offered James the chance to prove that he
could unite English Protestants and anti-Jesuit Catholics in an
international cause. To recognize the subtle contextual differences between these two rhetorics is also to recognize the volatility and vulnerability of the shifting relationship between moderate Puritans, nonconformists, and their supporters at the Jacobean court.

This episode points up the complexity of the Jacobean style of
government by polemic. It is a style governed by the king's ambivalent promotion of preaching, which pulled in two directions:

James learned to expect and enjoy the English episcopate's style
of flattery and deference, but he had grown up with, and assigned a great measure of rhetorical as well as evangelical credibility to, a Scottish style of exhortation and admonition. His ap-
preciation of a homiletic discourse that cut against his personal
image, while promoting his political interests, revises and updates the concept of "criticism and compliment" that has domi-

nated our understanding of how words worked at the Jacobean court.[87] James's promotion of a moderation articulated in immoderate terms produced a rhetoric that proved its sincerity by opposition. The process may be revealed in part in the "language of binary opposition" that characterized the religious and political discourse of post-Reformation England, but it is demonstrated at a more immediate level in the competing images presented by a preacher and his king.[88]

Lancelot Andrewes's 1610 Gowry sermon, preached before the king and printed in the same year, both represents the apogee of this sermonic involvement with the king's controversial needs and signals the beginning of the end of its expression by a rhetoric of confrontation aimed at the king. In its printed 1610 edition, this sermon extends to seventy-three quarto pages, which in itself suggests its weighty participation in the great polemical debates of 1608–10. The sermon is based on 1 Chronicles 16:22, *nolite tangere Christos meos*, and while it is aimed at James's pro-papal contemners, in one section Andrewes appears also to have the king's anti-papal supporter John King in mind:

> [B]y an undecent and overfamiliar touch, void of the reverence that is due to them, *laeditur pietas*, duty taketh hurt, and wrong is offered to his anointed. Mary Magdalen was not about to have done our savior any harm, when after his resurrection she offered to touch him; only because she did it as one mortal (where the case was offered now) and not with the high reverence pertaining to his glorified estate, she heard, and heard justly, *noli me tangere*. The touch which in any way impeacheth the high honour of their anointing, *nolite tangere*, takes hold of that too.[89]

Andrewesian subtle ambiguity makes this passage double-voiced. At first glance, it seems merely to echo King's own concern that James not be dishonored by the many tracts and treatises written against him by continental and domestic Catholic critics. But Andrewes's choice of Mary Magdalene's offense as the type of this dishonor, and his exoneration of her purpose in so touching Christ, also makes Andrewes's object equally misguided members of the king's inner circle. The intriguing passive expression "*laeditur pietas*, duty taketh hurt," therefore, with its

recognition of the affinity between piety and duty, better expresses Andrewes's discomfort with the intemperate performance of an episcopal colleague and fellow court preacher than it
does any outrage at the contumelies of foreign propagandists.

Also significant about Andrewes's sermon is its broadcast of
what would increasingly become the leitmotif of ultraconformist
sermons after 1610, the notion of *noli me tangere*. As we shall see,
this language would be used to indict Puritanism as both spiritually and politically presumptuous, by way of a compelling rhetorical methodology that created an image of both Christ and
James being touched by unworthy hands.[90] As telling from a
practical point of view is the fact that never again did King, or any
other anti-Catholic firebrand, preach at court on Gunpowder Day.

Until 1622, Lancelot Andrewes took over the court pulpit on
the fifth of November, and henceforth anti-Jesuit and anti-Catholic polemic cooled down enough to allow the resumption of the
ambivalent language of Jacobean moderation. Andrewes's Gunpowder Day sermon for 1609 thus signals the end of a polemical
era. The text on which Andrewes preached was Luke 9:54–56,
the story of the disciples who asked Jesus to rain down fire and
brimstone on the Samaritans who refused him shelter. Andrewes
began by justifying the text: "For so long as this verse shall stand
in this Gospel it will serve for a resolution to this question:
whether upon pretense of religion, Christ will allow the Jew to
blow up the Samaritan?"[91] The answer was, unsurprisingly, no,
and Andrewes went on to explain to his auditory that the actions
of a few hotheads did not cause Jesus to seek retribution:

This spirit was not then, in all; neither all the disciples or all the Samaritans. Some there were on both sides, more moderately affected.
The disciples, I doubt not, did all of them—the other ten too—much
dislike this discourse offered Christ, yet all cried not for fire, two only,
these two only of the twelve. On the other side, the Samaritans neither,
all were not thus inhuman.[92]

Andrewes condemns violent action "upon pretense of religion,"
in what would appear at first glance to be a reference to Catholic

plots that aimed at ridding the world of English "heretics." But in emphasizing the moderate tendencies of both the disciples and the Samaritans, Andrewes suggests as well that all extreme actions are antithetical to the aims of true religion. To celebrate moderation as an antidote to the dangerous sentiments responsible for the plot was, then, also to challenge the fervent anti-Catholicism that characterized English Puritans calling for more stringent measures against domestic Catholics in the plot's aftermath. Here Andrewes's repetitive emphasis on the minority of disciples asking for violence—"two only, these two only of the twelve"—constructs the position spelled out in his sermon as "moderate," simply by emphasizing its spacious boundaries.

The closing words of Andrewes's sermon confirm this reading of the above passage. In his application of the text to the holiday theme, Andrewes concludes:

This was against Samaritans and by the Apostles, came commended by the movers, they were Apostles; aggravated by the parties against whom, they were of the sect of the Samaritans. We are no Samaritans, I trust, but they no Apostles, I am sure; no Apostles, nor of no Apostolic spirit, which would authorize that which was rebuked in the Apostles themselves. And for Samaritans—which falls to our turn—it may be they count us and call us so.[93]

Andrewes's references to "Samaritans" and "Apostles" are characteristically complex. The jibe against "apostolic spirit" and the pun on *autho*rizing" violence initially identifies the "Apostles" of Andrewes's text as treatise-writing cardinals and other Jesuit opponents of the king; the remark about "sects," however, initially associates "Samaritans" with Puritans. Both remarks imply that the Gunpowder Plot reflected a Catholic misunderstanding of the English Church: that all English Protestants were violently anti-papal Puritans, leaving recusants no hope of conversion to a church so determined to ignore centuries of tradition and for which there was no compromise with even nonpapalist Catholics.[94] Andrewes's insistence that "we are no Samaritans"—"we" in this version meaning "we English"—tells the king and his courtly audience that the mainstream of English Protestant thought is not so immoderately anti-Catholic as to oppose the king's moderate domestic policy. This not only signals a real departure from the kind of Protestantism of the type favored by a majority of clergy with their roots in late Elizabethan religious politics; it redraws the boundaries of moderation to include men of Andrewes's stripe and exclude those moderate Puritans—or bishops like John King—who were critical of James's qualified tolerance of English Catholics.

But Andrewes's complaint goes further, revealing the claustrophobic, internally political nature of the preacher's layered, complex prose. The word *we*, in all its inclusivity, can be more closely focused to refer only to men of Andrewes's stripe. It can mean, therefore, "me, my fellow clerics, and"—in hopeful implication—"Your Majesty." This clubby insinuation, in short, claims a solidarity between James and the kind of clergy labeled "avant-garde" by recent scholars. Andrewes's statement should make us reexamine that label. "They count us and call us so" is a complaint, broadly speaking, about being misunderstood; here Andrewes appears also to be defending his particular brand of churchmanship from a charge of crypto-popery. He takes a swipe at the Puritan polemicists (the "they," in this interpretation) who criticized not only James I's domestic policies regarding Catholics, but also sacramentalists like Andrewes, John Buckeridge, and other ultraconformists at the English court and in the English clergy. More elegantly and effectively than Martin Fotherby, the preacher has aligned himself and his fellow sacramentalist travelers with the king by allying resistance to James with resistance to their particular ecclesiastical vision. This most subtle of Jacobean court preachers has thus implied that James I and Lancelot Andrewes have much in common, not least the threat of potentially murderous forms of "immoderation," Puritanism chief among them.

We have finally uncovered the constituent parts of the image of that peculiarly Jacobean hybrid, the "Puritan-papist." This image represented the equality of the threats posed by each, an idea

that, in the words of a recent historian, "became axiomatic of the
new conformist orthodoxy under James."[95] Traced through a
survey of court propaganda, we can identify this "new orthodoxy" as a product of short-term political needs. The substitution
of anti-Puritan rhetoric for anti-Catholic rhetoric and the pinning
of blame for the plot on Jesuits represent responses to the political mandate of the king's first speech to Parliament after the discovery of the Gunpowder Plot. James's reaction to the plot was
carefully constructed to avoid giving undue offense to either
domestic or foreign Catholics. As a result, in these pivotal years
of governmental response, his preachers concentrated first on
"Puritans," as nonconformists faced the decision to subscribe to
the 1604 canons; and then on "Jesuits," as English Catholics
contemplated the Oath of Allegiance. Andrewes's 1609 sermon
demonstrates how the dovetailing of these two polemics formed
a progressive argument that could pin the official definition of
"Puritanism" to the idea of a foreign threat to the king. This in itself would not be enough to associate moderate Puritanism with
an alienable, dangerous sectarianism, but it did point the way for
one more variation on the themes inspired by Gunpowder Plot.
This strategy contained the potential to indict nonconformity as
something more serious than a disagreement over unessential
matters.

The next, crucial step in the development of Gunpowder Plot–
inspired anti-Puritanism was to combine an already serious critique of Puritanism with an advocacy of the traditional practices
retained in the Church of England. The first printed example of
this strategy can be found in a 1613 Gunpowder Plot sermon
preached at Paul's Cross by John Boys, dean of Canterbury and a
staunch defender of the traditions retained in the Book of Common Prayer. Boys claimed that Gunpowder Day was a religious
holiday equivalent to other saints' days celebrated in the Church
of England, to be celebrated with praise and thanksgiving appropriate both to the solemnity of the day and to the sanctity of a
holy festival.[96] Boys identified as "papist" those who dishonored
the idea of holy days by blasphemously venerating the plotters

and their priests as martyred saints, and then immediately employed what by now had to be the defining characteristic rhetorical strategy for all conformist plot sermons, the paralipsis: "If
I were not (according to the text and the time) forward to prose-
cute the Gunpowder men, as the more dangerous enemies to
God and his Gospell, I might upon this ground take up the
bucklers against idle Novelists, [for] utterly condemning the festivals of holie saints, established in our Church by good order of
law."[97]

Although Boys does not go so far as to claim that Puritans
were "more dangerous" than plotters (something John Howson
felt comfortable preaching to the king two years later),[98] the distinctive (and by now familiar) paralyptical rhetorical flourish
with which he set up his critique makes it impossible to miss his
intention to suggest a provocative parallel. While it could be argued that Boys was merely defending the "lawful" festivals of
the Church, and thereby condemned only sectarianism (which
would have been an unremarkable thing to do), it is nonetheless
significant to find a detailed defense of liturgical practice as the
centerpiece of a Gunpowder Plot sermon. To suggest that ob-
jecting to holidays is akin to gunpowder plotting takes the gen-
eralized complaints against "Puritans" that adorned early Gunpowder Day sermons a step farther toward condemning moderate Puritan activity as dangerously sectarian.[99]

As with all the sermons preached at court on Gunpowder Day
and subsequently published, the juxtaposition of text and context
can provide us with a view into the intent of preachers that their
words alone barely suggest. On the surface, Boys's defense of the
Church is hardly remarkable; as a Gunpowder Day polemic, it
reveals a provocative agenda on the verge of sparking its own
conflagration. In a recent essay, however, John Boys has been described as a cleric of a moderate, "Jacobean Anglican" stamp,
dedicated to "the special character of the Church of England"—
that character being in part defined as an overweening concern
with the forms of polity and liturgy it had established by law.[100]
That Boys was this kind of churchman in print, there can be little

doubt. That his jealous protection of the ceremonies exemplified majority opinion in the Jacobean clergy or the peculiar genius of the Jacobean Church is, on the other hand, highly dubious. Instead, Boys's sermon offers published proof of the direction sacramentally focused conformists took in this period. These were, moreover, conformists with the advantage of a bully pulpit and the king's increasing attention. Focusing in overheated political contexts such as Gunpowder Day on issues of liturgical conformity, these spokesmen created an increasingly alienated characterization of what had been a moderate, assimilable nonconformity. It would take only a transformed image of the English Church and the royal supremacy, and a resacralizing of things once considered adiaphoric, to complete the transmogrification of Puritanism begun from the court pulpit on Accession and Gunpowder Day.

PART II

Two Images of Rule

CHAPTER FOUR

Great Britain's Constantine

Among James I's most engaging personal traits were his extraordinary interest in and talent for religious disputation. While this royal fascination with all things controversial was once considered evidence of a faintly ridiculous, politically insensitive pedantry, it has recently been reassessed in a more sympathetic light, as a sign of James's learned involvement and influence in matters of church and state. Much of this revised opinion comes from historians of James's northern kingdom.[1] The king's early education was conducted in a decidedly monarch-unfriendly laboratory, where the republican theories of his tutor George Buchanan combined with a stringent Knoxian practicum imposed by the Kirk. In the rough and tumble of Scottish ecclesiastical politics, James VI became adept at an art of governing based on theological argumentation and factional manipulation. This was a craft that found its best expression in debate. Upon his accession, James I found it necessary to adapt his hard-won skills to a new, English style of government. Judging from both the style and content of BASILIKON DORON, James saw the English throne, at least in part, as a dais from which he could oversee and influence powerful new disputations.

The king had every reason to believe his working relationship with the English ecclesiastical establishment would be less fraught than had been his experience with an adversarial Kirk. But the relationship between the king and his southern churchmen was actually far more complex. An assumption of doctrinal purity and consensus held the center of English Protestantism, but the doctrine of adiaphora endorsed by churchmen in Elizabeth's reign encouraged her clergy to have subtly divergent opinions on many matters of Protestant practice. England now had a king who, unlike Elizabeth, intended to demonstrate his dedication to the principles of moderation by encouraging rather than suppressing debate. The situation was tailor-made for the public working out of the private issues that divided the English episcopate. As we have seen, they did this not in an obviously oppositional language, but by manipulating a shared rhetoric to voice their solidarity with the king's opinions and their disagreements with each other. The varied way in which preachers interpreted the king's words raises the important question of influence: did the king set the agenda for the court language of government or did his bishops?

To answer this, we must first look at the imagery court preachers used to describe the king's authority, and by implication, their relationship to that authority. In this context, Jacobean court sermons consistently present two typologies of rule: the Solomonic and the Constantinian. These were straightforwardly drawn from the king's reputation (often self-represented) for wisdom and his love of the debating chamber. James acted as overseer of religio-political controversies in a variety of court settings—at post-sermon dinners, where he would expertly question the day's preacher upon arcane points of theology, for example, or at the conferences and formal debates he convened to discuss disputed matters of doctrine and discipline. In addition, the king's writings on religious and political topics traded on his reputation as a theological adept and champion of ecclesiastical debate. When preachers at court with an eye to advancement were assiduous in their praise of James as an astute and careful judge, however, they did more than advance a public image. They also conveyed the idea that James's greatest duty as king was to judge competing claims, not only (or even mainly) between the Church of England and Catholicism or sectarianism, but also between the different styles of legitimate Protestantism that existed amongst the clergy themselves. In fact, in this era devoted to the official maintenance of "moderation" and "consensus," a polemic of veiled extremity characterized Jacobean ecclesiastical infighting: court condemnations of rampant popery and dangerous Puritanism were actually used to influence the king about purportedly "indifferent" religious issues within the Church establishment.[2]

In this atmosphere of polemical subtlety and persuasive subterfuge, Solomonic and Constantinian analogies, while similar, represent disparate and, eventually, competitive metaphors of rule. While both were essential to Jacobean rhetoric, they were by no means interchangeable. In situations like the Hampton Court conference, the king could see himself as a type of Solomon, and his preachers were quick to support this self-representation of wisdom and judgment.[3] The image itself is rooted in the kingship narratives of the Old Testament and carries a particular reference to the story of the Queen of Sheba's first meeting with Solomon (a passage that is referred to time and again in court sermons from this period). Awestruck by Solomon's wisdom, the beauty of his Temple, and the prosperity of his court, the queen heaps lavish praise on her fellow ruler: "It was a true report that I heard in mine own land of thy acts and of thy wisdom; howbeit I believed not the words, until I came, and mine eyes had seen it; and behold, the half was not told me; thy wisdom and thy prosperity exceedeth the fame which I heard."[4] The admission confirms the essentially domestic slant of the Solomonic figure. Like Solomon's, James's wisdom was perhaps best demonstrated—if least appreciated—at home.

The Constantinian model, however, is less studied than the much examined image of Great Britain's Solomon. The king-as-Constantine extended the range of the king's wisdom and influence, invoking the idea of imperial rule to underline James's authority in the wider world of post-Reformation Christendom. This representation, based on the common medieval notion that the mother of the fourth-century emperor Constantine the Great had been British (in fact she was born in what is now Turkey), set the type for James's "peacemaker" image. Constantinian rhetoric originated in the idea of James's representation of the union of England and Scotland, then extended to express the king's dedication to the cause of pan-European confessional peace. The image of the Constantinian James raised kingly attributes in general terms—authority, piety, political acumen—in order to enumerate the benefits those conferred in terms just as universally salutary—peace, orthodoxy, political order. But the ecumenical dimension of James's ambitions, while apparently conciliatory in the international context, also and more immediately served to define and exacerbate the tensions emerging between different factions in the English Church.[5]

A significant test case for this rhetoric was, in addition to Rome or Geneva, Scotland. James's plans for the Kirk demanded a disproportionate amount of space in court sermons published after 1603. This approach gave preachers determined to press an anti-Puritan agenda two remarkably powerful images with which to influence their king: the republican tendencies of Scottish Protestantism, now figuring as an alienable version of "Puritanism," and the need to pursue a simpler, one-size-fits-all doctrinal strategy in continental matters. The king's interest in both Scottish and continental ecclesiastical affairs allowed court preachers selectively to apply "internationalist" or ecumenist language to the domestic religious issues over which they had direct responsibility and in which they had the most interest. In this way, James could be manipulated with his own image, often with his own words. On the other hand, however, that image was also re-manipulated in those royal press releases we know as the political writings of James I. The relationship between the king and his preachers can thus only be seen as symbiotic, the necessary dependence that makes royal courts—which depend on patronage and loyalty—possible. Rather than seeing a single pattern of image management, therefore, we would do best to see the king's image as in process; and in the process lay the impetus for and development of a complex politics.

In order to understand the implications of James's appropriation of the Constantinian image, we have first to return to pre-accession ecclesiastical politics in Scotland. Despite the king's public condemnations of "that firebrand" John Knox, Knox's writings actually provided James's supporters with their most convincing justification for instituting a royal supremacy in Scotland. In *The First Blast . . . Against the Monstrous Regiment of Women* (which has been described by one historian as a "treatise on Anglo-Scottish union"),[6] Knox called for an imperial "godly prince" to lead all Protestants against the popish Antichrist. (The corollary to this position, which advocated the deposition of "ungodly princes," was what led James to denounce Knox.) Religious opinion was split in Scotland, however, over the issue of who exactly was to wield this Christian authority. The presbyterians who represented a majority in the Kirk argued for a separation of the spiritual and political estates, an ideology enshrined in the "Golden Acts" of 1592, which established an independent Kirk. Soon after, James VI asserted his right to order Church and state by instituting the so-called "Black Acts," which imposed a limited episcopal polity that extended the king's jurisdictional reach in both spheres.[7] His show of integrative strength at home, which was given an impressive backup by his accession to the English throne, convinced a number of Scottish clergy (some of whose rapturous works on the union I have already analyzed) that James was indeed the Christian leader to unite an Anglo-Scottish Protestant league against papal power. A rhetoric of Protestant imperialism, therefore, was not only useful to promote the large aims of union; it also supported James VI's unprecedented display of authority in Scotland.[8]

But the political necessities attendant on accession also led James to promote another view, one that expanded the Scottish idea of "Protestant unity" into the larger notion of "the unity of Christendom." Mindful of the persistence of English Catholicism and his need to curry favor with powerful Catholic or crypto-Catholic English nobles, James sent a pre-accession message to Clement VIII, offering the pope a visionary description of universal Christianity.[9] James expressed his concern about confessional polarization in England and his desire for the unity of all his subjects, indeed of all right-minded Christians. The king then proposed a method for establishing a core of central doctrines upon which all professing Christians could agree. Such a consolidation could be accomplished in a "General Council . . . by which all contentions and controversies could be settled and composed" by a process that would cull the "inventions of men" out from the doctrines "agreeable to antiquity, to the first and purer times of the Christian Church."[10] The king's advocacy of decision-making by council found no favor with the pope, who knew full well that conciliarist theory rested on a claim that general councils could not only advise popes but also depose them. Hidden within the velvet gloves of James's appeal to Christian history, then, was a two-fisted attack on papal authority and Catholic traditional doctrine that could hardly have bypassed the notice of His Holiness.

James's letter to the pope was an exercise in polemical management: while sounding promising, it promised nothing. The king's communiqué disclosed another idea, however, one with no real significance for Christendom, but laden with consequences for England. The king mentioned to Clement his desire to see a "divine worship which is common and uniform in all things . . . from which the Church may receive the most joyful fruits of peace and tranquillity."[11] In this proposal, Christian unity would not merely inspire a common style of worship; instead, uniform worship would generate Christian unity. The distinction is important. This advocacy of ceremonial conformity provides early evidence that James's opinions on the issue of adiaphora could be represented in polemic as antithetical to the views expressed by many of England's Calvinist conformists.

After 1603, the Elizabethan justification for ceremonies—that they were merely a matter of order and might some day in some cases be altered—began to break down. The court-sermon rhetoric of the religious "middle way" correspondingly shifted to accommodate a new definition of nonconformist extremism. This transformation can be attributed to the promotion of the king's Constantinian image. James himself was adept with the vocabulary of the golden mean—a lexicon, it must be said, that had had little polemical purchase in his native kingdom. In his first speech to the English Parliament in 1604, the king amalgamated the languages of *via media* and Christian imperialism, calling for a "general Christian union in religion," in order that, "laying willfulness aside on both hands, we might meet in the middest, which is the Center and perfection of all things."[12] The king's penchant for proposing actual international projects transformed the Elizabethan language of the "middle way," reifying it into a broader, universal basis from which to construct a defense of the English Church. In its domestic application, however, this foundation supported an increasingly narrow program. Elaboration by court polemicists turned what had been a flashy but impractical royal appeal to parliamentary opinion into a critique focused on the spectrum of religious opinion in England. As the language of ecumenism dovetailed with that of the "middle way," James's stated desire to counteract religious extremism "on both hands" had its most significant impact on English anti-Puritan polemic.

This Constantinian rhetoric was remarkably generative, producing one of the most persistent and distinctive features in Jacobean court preaching: the promotion of James as the rightful leader of all non-papalist Christians. No matter how sincerely the king believed in and worked toward the creation of a united Christendom, however, James's call for the establishment of Christian unity by means of a General Council and a uniform worship should also be analyzed as a domestic polemical construct.[13] James's model for adjudicating international religious disputes formed a microcosmic paradigm for his national Church. Indeed, it could be argued that the idea functioned much more effectively during the king's lifetime as a domestic rhetorical strategy than it did as an international project.

Unity Revised

The domestic reaction to this ecumenical vision can be charted first in sermons preached in the years immediately after the Hampton Court conference of 1604. Hampton Court was the domestic prototype for the great international assemblies over which James professed himself eager to preside. Court preachers

were quick to note the similarity and incorporate the implications of James's ambitions into their own interpretations of the
events of 1604. While some referred to the king's aim of a general
Christian unity in order to justify the course of events at the conference, other court preachers were wary of James's great notion.
We detect in their words an intriguingly prophetic concern. Despite its great ecumenical intention, James's promotion of the
unity of Christendom, they feared, would narrow the spectrum
of extra-doctrinal beliefs acceptable within the English Church itself.

We should follow their lead and not mistake the rhetoric of
Christian unity for a discourse of toleration in this period. An
analysis of the characteristics of this language, in fact, allows us
to identify strongly opposing points of view within the English
Church. Richard Field, a royal chaplain who later rose to become
dean of Gloucester, preached before James at Whitehall on 16
March 1604 on the third chapter of Jude, "[Y]e should earnestly
contend for the faith which was once delivered unto the saints."
Field is one of the more enigmatic figures of Jacobean religious
history. Faced with the absence of any record of his opinions at
Hampton Court (where he is listed as a participant), recent historians have ascribed to him any number of broadly diverse ecclesiastical personalities. He has been variously described as a Calvinist, a Puritan, or a sacramentalist conformist of the *via media*
camp. (The ascription of all of these opposed characteristics to
one person may indicate how contradictory the language of religion can seem to historians of this period.) However, Field did
preach to the king after the conference. An examination of his
sermon, which was printed the same year, leads us to question
the claim made by Field's son, that his father "did not make use
of his parts for the increase of controversies but rather for the
composing of them."[14]

Field opened his sermon with praise for the authority of the
king and his clergy. Contemporary Church leaders, he claimed,
possessed an unprecedented depth of knowledge. Their erudition was based in part on their familiarity with the work of the

historic councils of the early Church in defining, maintaining, and defending Christian doctrinal orthodoxy. The primitive Church had from time to time entertained "dangerous errors" in matters necessary to salvation. "The contentions of Christians have scandalized many,"[15] Field asserted, but in soteriological matters the early Church had overcome its natural distaste for public contention and subjected such errors to rigorous disputation in council.

Field then compared these disputes over "matters of faith" with contentions over "things mistaken," interconfessional controversies over the nature of grace and the mechanics of predestination. These disagreements reminded the preacher of the Arian controversies of the fourth century. The Council of Nicea had, however, been much too severe:

Constantine [was] resolute to suppress that heresy, and to send into banishment the maintainers of it. The Arians seeing into what straits they were brought, rested not until they had insinuated themselves into Constantine's favour, and perverted Constantius the next succeeding Emperour, a man the Catholics might easily have possessed.[16]

It took the "loving mediation" of Athanasius to establish that the opposing parties, far from being irreconcilable, actually believed "one and the same thing." It was this sort of contention that now divided Protestants, Field asserted, adding that their disputes over such issues as predestination could easily be reconciled in a council such as that over which Constantine had presided.

Of most interest, however, are the logical implications that Field drew from this survey of doctrinal disputes. The negative appeal to a kingly image—the admonition against Constantine's actions—sets up Field's concerns, which are to ensure that this king will not similarly mismanage doctrinal matters in England. Field's warning to James not to define orthodoxy too narrowly challenged the assumption that England had a specifically Calvinist Church. But by reprising the king's own stated desire for establishing a core set of beliefs by general council deliberation, Field struck a blow at nonconformity as well.

Field went on to contrast doctrinal issues with recent events in the Church of England, remarking contemptuously, "in our Church, [disputes are] about round and square, white and black, sitting, standing, and kneeling."[17] He thus dismissed the nonconformist case by belittling it, a polemical task accomplished by this extended exercise in *comparatio*.[18] In this passage, we see one connection between the anti-Calvinist—or less-Calvinist—doctrinal view and the effort to redefine adiaphoric disputes. We can trace the interaction between these issues and the king's own words on the subject of common worship and Christian peace. Appealing to the king's ecumenism to discredit the case for nonconformity, Field also challenges the view, common among conformist Calvinists, that "things indifferent" were by their nature open to reasoned discussion and possible change. In the context of the history of Christian orthodoxy, "things indifferent" become worthy of indifference, issues not important enough to engage the king in lengthy ecclesiastical conference.[19]

Field's opinions contrast sharply with those of a Lincoln clergyman, Henry Hooke, who preached before the king at Whitehall two months later. Like Field's, Hooke's sermon was published the same year, with a title page that featured an apposite citation from Isaiah: "For Sion's sake I will not hold my tongue." And this Hooke certainly did not do, strongly expressing his own doubts about the decisions of religious assemblies in a sermon on the text of Psalm 122:6, "Pray for the peace of Jerusalem."[20] Hooke reminded the king that keeping an already established peace was as virtuous an enterprise as "seeking" a new peace. Assemblies, the preacher claimed, did not always provide the proper setting for the work of true religious reform. Too often they were subject to secular politics and could easily degenerate into showy set pieces with no lasting effect. Thus, "formalist[s] . . . in places of high authority, do for fashion sake shuffle over matters of importance, without any conscionable desire of reformation."[21]

Hooke's reference to "formalists" should catch our attention. Here it appears to refer to the way certain conformists (in this context, Lake's avant-garde or Tyacke's anti-Calvinist clergy) had insinuated themselves into the king's favor and placed their stamp on his ecclesiastical policy. This calls to mind David Calderwood's remarks on the king's pre-accession campaign in England: "the formalists gather matter of hope out of the BASILIKON DORON."[22] This term, the sense of which constructed a dichotomy between "formalist" and "reformer," is rarely used by present-day historians to describe churchmen like Field. Yet, in many ways, it is more accurately descriptive before the 1620's than "anti-Calvinist"; it made an unmistakable polemical impact by its homonymic resonance with words like "conform" and "reform"; and (unlike "avant-garde conformity") it has the advantage of brevity and contemporary usage. But it also has a familiar disadvantage: like the "Puritan," the "formalist" was a shifty character born of polemical contest, useful only when placed in rhetorical perspective.

We have already seen The Formalist featured in a cleverly bitter remark in Anthony Maxey's 1606 Accession Day sermon. There Maxey shared Henry Hooke's lexicon, if not his point, when he complained that the public believed "the reformed though they lose their livings, yet they will keep a good conscience, but the formalists will ever be of the same religion the king is of."[23] Maxey was a Calvinist, not "avant-garde," conformist, and here his sardonic remark, coupled with what we know about his tireless push for preferment, shows evidence of his desire to be as successful with the king as someone like Lancelot Andrewes.[24] These exchanges demonstrate that what was at stake well before the 1620's was as much the definition of "the king's religion" as it was the definition of particular doctrines or practices. "Formalists"—by the accounts of their opponents at court, and those of pushy hopefuls like Maxey—appear in the polemical context already to have gained the advantage.

Hooke's argument reminds us that the vision of moderation supplied by those he called "formalists" was less a religious or political goal than it was a polemical corrective to the dangers they perceived in nonconformity. By this time, "moderation"—

name, not thing—was swiftly emerging as the unassailable vehicle for the advancement of an anti-Calvinist agenda. The king's interest in some minimalist form of ecumenical Christianity provided a rhetorical moment for anti-Calvinists, wherein this strategy and the king's desire to be a new Constantine could appear as mutual interests. Inherent in Hooke's willingness to ascribe nonreligious motives to the sacramentalists was his own corresponding fear that what he regarded as "true religion"—that is, Calvinist, reforming, preaching-focused Protestantism—was being increasingly labeled by clerics close to the king as "immoderate"—namely, radical.

Some Calvinist conformist preachers, therefore, tried to counter the deadly polemical pull to a fictional center by avoiding phrases that advocated formalist-issue *viae mediae*. The week following Hooke's pulpit appearance, Anthony Rudd, bishop of St. David's, preached before James at Whitehall on the text of Psalm 101:2, "I will do wisely in the perfect way till thou comest to me." Rudd recommended this "perfect way" rather than a middle way, remarking that princes had to pursue the same righteous course whether in public decision-making or in private behavior. The wisest rulers, therefore, did not "halt between two opinions," but took the course set out by conscience. Royal wisdom was of necessity politic, but it also transcended politics when true religion was at risk. Referring frequently to Old Testament texts, Rudd claimed that good kings, like David, Solomon, or Hezekiah, would not be swayed by the advice of irresolute, "temporizing States-m[e]n . . . [who] would live safely in all changes of Church and Common-wealth, Court and Country." Here Rudd takes the same line as Hooke, warning his sovereign about "politic practice" at court.[25]

Other preachers would go further, misunderstanding the political subtlety of James's conciliarist paradigm and associating the notion of a British Constantine with Roman Catholicism plain and simple. A year after the Gunpowder Plot, and shortly after a second Hampton Court conference (discussed in the following pages), Richard Stock, a London preacher who had benefited from the notice of James Montague (bishop of Winchester and dean of the Chapel Royal), preached at Paul's Cross. Stock inveighed vigorously against popery from the outdoor pulpit, citing Isaiah 9:14–16, "For the leaders of my people cause them to err; and they that are led by them, are devoured." The text inspired Stock to compare the foundations of Catholicism and Protestantism. Protestant doctrine was based upon inerrant scripture, but Catholics could point only to the questionable authority of tradition to support their beliefs: "[W]e may not doubt of the Scriptures: but of [Councils] it is lawful to doubt, saying, that *Concilia plenaria*, full councils, may err."[26] Here Stock reveals his own doubt about the vision of the Church advanced by traditionalists like Field. For Stock, councils represented the false "excesses" of popery. *Sola Scriptura*, not the deliberations of some general council, would unite Protestant Christendom.[27]

There might have been many views on the nature of the Church broadcast from Jacobean pulpits, even from the Jacobean court pulpit, but in situations wherein the king cast himself as a new Constantine, the most gratifyingly complimentary one would undoubtedly be offered by those Hooke called "formalists." From the other side issued a coded but unmistakable denunciation of the kind of politic considerations that might lead a king to pursue ecumenical goals in the face of papist aggression. The Constantinian image, in other words, was not something to gladden the hearts of the godly minority. In the rhetoric of those more "formally" inclined, therefore, the representation of Constantine was both a gesture to the king's self-image and, as a deliberate polemical strategy, aimed against Puritanism within the Church.

Case Study: The Second Hampton Court Conference, 1606

None of the above is meant to suggest that James was merely the dupe of unscrupulous sacramentalists who twisted his words to implicate the king in conformity programs that he himself would not have countenanced. The longer he ruled in England, the more enamored of the beauties of English holiness James be-

came, and this attraction, as has recently been noted, rather dis-
astrously "gave him an itch to modify Scottish practice."[28] The
first evidence of such desire occurred in 1606, when James de-
cided to discipline a radical presbyterian faction who had held
an unauthorized session of the General Assembly at Aberdeen.
The king reacted swiftly, summoning the eight leading dissident
ministers to London. There they were questioned by the king before the Scottish members of the Privy Council. Significantly, the
king also ordered the Scots ministers to be present at his chapel
services, where English bishops were ordered to preach to them
on the topics of royal authority and the institution of episcopacy.[29] Shortly thereafter, James ordered these sermons to be
published in England. The disciplining of ministers from the
pulpit of the Chapel Royal exemplifies the king's preference for
governing through the medium of sermon polemic, but the print
history of the sermons preached there suggests that the message
the king wanted sent to his dissident Scottish clergy was also
aimed closer to home.[30]

The eight ministers were summoned for the first time to the
Chapel Royal on Sunday, 21 September 1606. According to James
Melville, they were seated separately at a desk "hard by" the
preacher, who on this day was William Barlow, bishop of Rochester. Barlow initiated the homiletic reeducation program with a
sermon on the historical legitimacy of episcopacy based on Acts
20:28, "Take heed to yourselves and to the whole flock, in which
the holy ghost hath placed you Bishops, to feed the Church of
God, which he hath purchased with his own blood."[31] In his preface to the printed version of this sermon, Barlow defended English Church polity against the Scottish charge (as Barlow reported
it) that episcopacy was intolerably popish. He hurled the same
charge back at the Scots: "[E]very opinion or ceremony, which in
the cockpit of elderlings is concluded to be popery, is not so . . .
papists and Puritans would have the king be but an honorable
member, not a chief governor, in the churches of his own dominions." Here Barlow once again shows himself a master of succinct
prefatory invective in defense of the monarchy—and of men like

himself whose ecclesiological attitudes left them open to the charge of crypto-Catholicism. (Adding to the subtle insult was Barlow's sacramentalist address to the ministers of the Kirk: "to my fellow dispensers of God's mysteries.")[32] To refer to "elderlings" is to reduce the authority of Scottish presbyterian leaders to the diminutive; to characterize their meetings as "cockpits" indicted these as low-rent, disorderly ecclesiastical battlefields rather than legitimate religious assemblies.

These representations allowed Barlow to offer in contrast the by now familiar image of the king as an imperial mediator of religious disputes, expressing in periphrastic fashion his "hearty prayer" that James would "be a King of Peace, as in Judah and Israel . . . effecting in us all, both of Kirk and Church, unity in doctrine, unanimity in affection, uniformity in obedience to your Majesty's supremacy, whether in matters either absolutely necessary as enjoined by God, or in themselves indifferent, but authoritatively necessary, as commanded by yourself."[33] This ideal image of the king as the moderator and mediator of the Church would underpin the rhetoric of all his preachers at this second Hampton Court conference. James's court preachers needed to counter the argument of the Scots that presbyterian government was of a more scripturally unadulterated origin than was episcopacy. Accordingly, they proposed a view of the Church that stressed its institutional over its scriptural basis. After all, the apostolic Church was a Church in opposition to the secular powers, they suggested. To ask to return to the days of "pure" Christianity was to make the audacious suggestion that the Church was presently under persecution in both Scotland and, by extension, England.

Preaching the next sermon to the Scots, on 23 September, the royal chaplain John Buckeridge (later bishop of Rochester and then Ely) spelled out the consequences of this alternative Church history:

[A]lthough the church was governed for the first three hundred years before any Emperor or king became a public professed Christian . . . yet the times were different and all things have their time. And therefore as soon as Constantine became a Christian, he assumed this supremacy: he put down idolatry, he established Christian religion, composed differences of bishops, suppressed heresies and schisms, called Councils, and gave his sufferage in them, he heard causes of religion, and judged them in his own person, he made laws, decrees, edicts, and orders for religion. And this saith Eusebius, he did *tanquam communis episcopus a Deo constitutus*, as a common bishop, or overseer ordained of God.[34]

Buckeridge's revised chronicle of the English Church locates this institution within a new, more comfortable setting: the fear of persecution and the rigors of reformation behind them, English Protestants can now reap the benefits of peace and order under the authority of a new Constantine. The king's work, here set out in exhaustive recitative detail, confirms the all-encompassing, "public" nature of a Church governed by royal supremacy. (In addition, making the king a "common bishop" secures his solidarity with the English episcopate.)

But the polemical highlight here is Buckeridge's poetically brusque "yet the times were different and all things have their times." With its biblical cadence and balanced construction emphasizing the *time*, it relegates a defensive, self-protective Protestant reliance on *sola* scripturalism to the past—not the ancient Christian past, but, most emphatically, to the recent sixteenth-century English past.[35] "It seemeth more than reasonable," argued Buckeridge, "that in a reformation, we should conform ourselves *ad regulam antiquorum*, to the rule of the Ancient: Scriptures, Apostles, and Fathers, rather than after the new cut of those who have not above the life of a man on their backs, sixty or seventy years."[36] Here the preacher reappropriates Christian history, privileging the imperial rule of the Church and the episcopacy as the oldest and best form of Church polity and recasting the history of the presbytery as newfangled, innovative and thereby suspect.

Buckeridge's argument was nothing new to the ministers of the Kirk, who must have found such language irritatingly familiar from their experience of earlier public disputations with the king. They would have been reminded, for example, of the experience of Mr. Walter Balcanquall when that Scottish clergyman was called in front of James VI in 1591. Balcanquall had preached once too often against the king's decision to reimpose episcopacy. With his Privy Council as an audience, James harangued the hapless minister, challenging him to cite a historical precedent for such pulpit criticisms of his king. When Balcanquall rather recklessly suggested that the commonwealth of Israel had depended upon godly men to reform their leaders, James offered his own version of religious history, peremptorily proclaiming that "the office of the prophets was ended" and thus ending the argument as well.[37]

We see demonstrated in all these exchanges, not only the centrality of historical argumentation to specific religious issues under dispute, but also the extent to which different versions of history can identify serious differences within a Church settlement. Nowhere is the clash of two versions of Church history more apparent than at this Anglo-Scots conference at Hampton Court in 1606, and in no way is it better exemplified than in disagreements between the Scots ministers and the English bishops over the interpretation of scripture.

Lancelot Andrewes preached the following Sunday, 28 September, explicating the text of Numbers 10:2–3, "Make thee two trumpets of silver . . . And thou shalt have them to assemble the congregation." Andrewes interpreted the verses to illustrate that the trumpets stood for Church and state, and that James had authority over both. But his arcane style failed to impress the Scots, Melville commenting bluntly that the sermon was a subversion of the text.[38] It must be admitted that this time Melville was onto something. This sermon provides us with rare evidence: printed proof that sometimes even Andrewes could be outmatched by his political mandate. Here he discharges his polemical duty within the restrictions imposed by the text's imagery (a task that usually showed Andrewes to be the master of the form) in an awkward, unsubtle style that evokes the efforts of less skilled court preachers like Buckeridge. Despite this, the sermon is the most extensively circulated of the 1606 Hampton

Court sermons. It was reprinted in Latin in 1608 and in English in 1610, contributions to the continuing print controversies over the Oath of Allegiance.

Andrewes contended that the Church had held unauthorized meetings only in times of dangerous necessity, as in the early days of persecution. To tout Church government by presbytery as a return to the purity of the primitive Church was thus an affront to the Christian monarch: "[N]one can seek to have the congregation so called (as before Constantine), but they must secretly and by implication confess they are a persecuted Church as that then was, without a Moses, without a Constantine."[39] Here the preacher opposes two opposed post-Reformation versions of Church history. Andrewes denounces those Protestants who continue to identify with the struggles of the early Christians and invokes the image of Constantine to reassert the centrality of secular power to the survival of an institutional Church. The strategy could hardly have failed to goad the Scots (beyond even their righteous outrage at the sermon's sophistic style of exegesis), whose Reformation had been justified by just such stirring appeals to the Apostolic age.[40]

John King (who would become bishop of London in 1611) expanded upon this aspect of Andrewes's theme when he preached the fourth sermon at Hampton Court the next Tuesday, on the text of Canticles 8:11, "Solomon had a vineyard in Baal-Hamon: he gave the vineyard unto keepers." Like the other preachers at Hampton Court, King based his sermon on the history of Church government by council. He argued that by "keepers," the scripture meant a king and his appointed bishops, not a presbytery independent of the magistrate. King described this arrangement as "part of clergy, part of laity, as of old and new cloth pieced together."[41] But the cloth imagery opens up a line of argumentation that is, in the end, almost despite itself, more conciliatory:

You might as well shape a coat for the moon waxing, waning, changing into so many formes, as set down one manner of discipline for the body of the Church. They call it the Churches livery; which I see not but in the summer of her peace may be of one stuff, of another in the winter of her troubles. . . . If you will call back the uses of those times, make the state of our times equal to them, and put us under a pagan Emperor, and persecution again.[42]

In an attempt to bring the Scots to common ground, King takes the discourse of this second Hampton Court conference back to the issue of "things indifferent." His extended rhetorical image, which in effect enclothes the Church, evokes the sense that these issues in dispute are external and thus mutable. In support of such mutability, King's lunar imagery, summed up in the elegant phrase "waxing, waning, changing," prevents the polemic of royal supremacy from veering onto more dangerous ground, reminding us that, at this time, most preachers at court were still unwilling to claim that polity (or ceremonies) were more than adiaphoric, or that the king's interest in promoting the same was prompted by any motive beyond that of good order and uniform practice.[43]

In fact, King went on to propose the opposite: the episcopate and royal supremacy provided the Church's best protection against a popish-style elevation of adiaphorous issues to doctrinal status. Without the possibility that religious practices could be altered by order of the monarch, the preacher declared, "ceremonies would be taken not to be ceremonies, but matters of substance."[44] This delineation challenges the Scots' conception of both polity and worship, but, significantly, it does not try to counteract their position with a diametrically opposed view of episcopacy that made polity a substantial part of the gospel. King's willingness to stress the secular nature of the king's authority over adiaphora reflects a slightly different attitude than that which underlined the first three sermons at Hampton Court. Its difference, it must be admitted, was so subtle as to miss the notice of the Scots altogether. King's unsubtle deployment of what Melville characterized as "violent invective" against Presbyterianism hardly endeared him to his Scottish auditory; on the other hand, it was calculated to please the king, and anti-presbyterian sentiments united Jacobean bishops no matter what individual views they held on the issue of ceremonies.

By the following summer, the Scots had gone home, sadder perhaps but certainly wiser in the ways of their absentee monarch. All four sermons preached at the Hampton Court conference of 1606 were published in England, however, and so the primarily formalist conformist language of James's authority over the Kirk remained behind to articulate an alternative vision of the English Church and the religion of the king. This vision not only challenged the radical views of the Scots, but also countered the style of much late Elizabethan Calvinist conformism.

Royal Response, 1609–15

This brings us back to the question of who set the agenda for the polemical governance of the English Church. Scholars like Peter Lake and Kenneth Fincham have claimed that the king's own views about the unity of Christendom led him to patronize certain "avant-garde" preachers who could support his immediate political goals. The case of the second Hampton Court conference, however, should make us reexamine the relation between certain ecclesiological viewpoints, a polemic that associated moderate Puritanism with dangerous schismatic positions like that of the Scottish presbyterians, the clerics who were happy to point this correspondence out from the pulpit, and the king who presented them with an image to promote, consistently patronized them and often ordered their opinions into print.

Long before the domestic furor over the Spanish match and the Thirty Years' War led him to hand control over the language of policy to anti-Calvinist formalists like Laud and Buckeridge, James had allowed their style of polemic to flourish in certain other settings at court, thereby creating a storehouse of transformable imagery with which to praise the king's authority and insinuate that moderate Puritanism—far from being unthreatening—was actually dangerous schism biding its time. Even more important, these were the sermons that, because of immediate political expediency, went on in print to public life. The term *avant-garde*, then, seems less useful to the evaluation of how Laud, Buckeridge, or Andrewes functioned within the circle of the court and more useful when comparing their opinions to those of the religious and political worlds outside the court. The king set the agenda; he could not always control the consequences wrought by the lingering half-lives of court sermon polemic. And it may just be that he chose not to, which would mean that those preachers Fincham and Lake call "avant-garde" were actually a distinctive part of a broad and diverse Jacobean mainstream, but not yet dominant enough successfully to eliminate another part of that mainstream, Elizabethan-style Calvinist conformism.

The language and strategies of these court preachers, examined above, made a return appearance in a number of James's own written works, as he defended his kingly authority to a larger world. In his introduction to the most recent edition of James's political writings, J. P. Sommerville remarks that, between 1608 and 1615, "the bulk of James's literary labours consisted of controversial works aimed at Roman Catholics."[45] This is true, yet it is striking to find a remarkable amount of anti-Puritan rhetoric in the king's writings of this period. This must in part be attributed to the fact that the royal works of 1608–15 were heavily ghost-written, often by the same court preachers who developed the original image of James as Constantine.[46]

James's first treatise defending his policies toward English Catholics, *Triplici nodo, triplex cuneus. Or, An Apologie for the Oath of Allegiance* (1608), was the product of a collaboration between the king and the then dean of his Chapel Royal, James Montagu.[47] *Triplici nodo* was so markedly anti-papal, its tone so strident, that it complicated James's European diplomacy. One observer, Sir Thomas Lake, went so far as to complain to Robert Cecil that "the churchmen will draw the king into writing, contrary to his intention."[48] But to what intention, and what sort of churchmen, did Lake refer in 1609? Montagu was an old-style Calvinist conformist, which may account for the vehemency of the anti-Catholic style of *Triplici nodo*. The absence of any specifi-

cally anti-Puritan elements in this tract would seem scarcely
worth comment; it was, after all, an anti-papalist piece of propaganda. The same cannot be said, however, for James's next work,
in which he was assisted, not by Montagu, but by Lancelot Andrewes and William Barlow.[49]

*A Premonition to all most Mighty Monarchs, Kings, Free Princes
and States of Christendom*, published in 1609, was, like *Triplici
nodo*, printed to defend the king's authority against continental
critics of the Oath of Allegiance (and continental critics of *Triplici*). It featured a confession of royal religious faith, in which
James attempted to explain the relation of his personal beliefs to
his secular governance in the wake of the Gunpowder Plot, in the
midst of the controversy over the Oath of Allegiance, and, quite
possibly, in the face of the kind of criticism he was getting from
preachers like Stock or Hooke. In the *Premonition*, James pursued
the Constantinian tack of the sermons of 1604–6, dissociating
himself from radical Protestantism as well as papal Catholicism
and establishing instead the definition of what he would consider true Christian "Catholicity."[50]

The centerpiece of the *Premonition* was James's personal "confession of faith." It begins with an account of his baptism, which
was into his mother's Catholic faith, but not, he stressed, into a
"superstitious" Catholicism: "At my Baptism (although I was
baptized by a Popish Archbishop) she sent him word to forbear
to use the spittle in my Baptism; which was obeyed, being indeed a filthy and an apish trick, rather in scorn than imitation of
Christ. And her own very words were, 'that she would not have
a pocky priest to spit in her childs mouth.'"[51]

James's purpose in presenting his mother as a reformed
Catholic was twofold. It allowed him to distance himself from
his religious bloodline so that he could criticize certain superstitious aspects of Catholicism while stressing his personal experience of the common doctrine and history shared by Catholics
and Protestants. This could appear as an enlargement or variation of union rhetoric, in which James represents, in his own person, the amalgamation of both confessions.[52]

More likely, however, is that the passage reflects the line of argumentation Lancelot Andrewes employed in his other works against Bellarmine, wherein he challenged the cardinal's assertion that true Catholics believed in such things as transubstantiation, the intercession of saints, and the secular claims of the papacy. The content of James's personal Catholicism was very precisely defined.[53] James described himself in the *Premonition* as a "Catholic Christian, as believeth the three creeds, that of the Apostles, that of the Council of Nicea, and that of Athanasius." He declared himself bound by the decisions made by the first four general councils of the Church, as well as all the writings of the Church Fathers, insofar as they agreed with Scripture. The application of this principle allowed James to attack idolatry in the Roman Church—the intercession of saints, private masses, belief in transubstantiation and purgatory, and worship of images and relics. These idolatries were "novel," said James, abhorrent to the plain sense of Scripture, certainly, but not central to the Catholic faith.[54] They were instead evidence of corrupt leadership of the Church.

With the stage set for a stinging denunciation of the pope, James skillfully sidestepped, borrowing a strategy from Gunpowder Plot rhetoric and producing instead an argument for government by bishops. The king defended episcopacy as necessary to the maintenance of order and decency, thereby introducing a recital of royal objections to "Puritans." These the king chose to identify by their objections to the apostolic origins of episcopacy:

That Bishops ought to be in the Church, I ever maintained it, as an Apostolic institution, and so the ordinance of God; contrary to the Puritans, and likewise to Bellarmine; who denies that Bishops have their jurisdiction directly from God. But it is no wonder that he take the Puritan's part, since Jesuits are nothing but Puritan-papists. And as I ever maintained the state of Bishops, and the Ecclesiastical Hierarchy for order sake, so was I ever an enemy to the confused Anarchy or parity of the Puritans, as well appeareth in my *Basilikon Doron*.[55]

With this reference to confusion and "anarchy," James ends the

Premonition, calling for the reinstitution of an ecumenical general council under the enlightened jurisdiction of Christian monarchs. All members would have to profess the ancient Christian faith, broadly interpreted; excluded from the proceedings would be "all the incendiaries and Novelist fire-brands on either side, as well Jesuits as Puritans." The passage signals a domestic context for this internationally pitched print debate, and reminds us of a style of polemic familiar to readers of many court sermons between 1604–8. Considering that the audience for James's political writings would have been an educated one, it seems obvious that one sure audience of *A Premonition* would be the king's own highly placed clergy. An internationalist or ecumenist rhetoric justified by a condemnation of English Puritanism could scarcely have failed to make its point about who the king considered his domestic enemies: those who did not share his vision of catholicity.[56]

After 1610, developments on the Continent cast a different light on James's calls for a unified and enlightened Christendom. The Arminian controversy in the Low Countries, which began as a theological dispute in the University of Leyden, soon became a pretext for Spanish aggression in the region. James put his ecumenic theories to another test. In 1612, he wrote *A Declaration Concerning the Proceedings with the States General, of the United Provinces of the Low Countries in the Cause of D. Conradus Vorstius.*[57] In the *Declaration*, James claimed that "charity" had prompted his solicitude for his Protestant neighbors, citing the geographical proximity of the Low Countries as posing a particular danger to his own kingdom: "[England] had to fear the like infection within our own dominions." The danger James spoke of, however, was not only the malignant doctrines of Arminius, but the danger of religious disunity and republicanism, which made "a fearful rent not only in [the] Ecclesiastical, but also in [the] Political state."[58]

England had more to fear from its Protestant neighbor than simply the influence of heretical doctrine on young English students at Leyden or the destabilization of a religious ally during a period of growing Spanish aggression. James also viewed the Vorstian heresy as something that reached past foreign diplomatic interests to have some serious implications for the home front. Where Protestants embraced Arminianism, recusants could take advantage of what they saw as a declination in the State's vigilance for uniformity: "In this confusion, and liberty of prophesying, [they] would thrust in for a part; conceiving it more reasonable, that their doctrine should be tolerated by those of our Religion, then the doctrine of Vorstius."[59]

James's primary concerns center on Arminianism in the Low Countries and its effect on "the good amity and correspondence which is between us and the United Provinces."[60] His reference to "prophesying," however, is significant, and shows the subtle work involved in the choice of a word to describe a phenomenon. In this passage, it takes on synecdochic weight to establish a secondary domestic context. *Prophesying* was one Puritan term for preaching, and for those English clergy who remembered the trials of Archbishop Grindal, it would also have called up the reminder that, in a fight between individual conscience and royal supremacy, the monarch always won. It would seem that once again James had chosen to characterize his international opponents by their resemblance to his domestic opponents. Indeed, the followers of Conradus Vorstius had more in common with Jacobean nonconformists than they would have with the Arminian ceremonialists of Laudian England. Dutch Arminians had no prayer book, nor had they any overweening desire for Church hierarchy or the "beauty of holiness." James feared Dutch Arminianism, therefore, for much the same reason he feared English Puritanism. For this reason, it is not all that surprising to see the defense of Calvinism so prominent at the Synod of Dort collapse on the home front by the 1620's. As we shall see in Chapter 5, much of that defense would be nullified by the attachment of sacramentalist concerns to English Arminianism.[61]

The prevailing image in James's writings of this period was that of a Constantinian king, presiding over the affairs of the

Church in a general council. This was a representation first developed in disputes with Puritans and Scots at home. The image of Constantine proclaimed the king's authority to lecture foreign monarchs on matters of religion, but it also refined the picture of his own Church to exclude even moderate Puritans. James's condemnations of precisianism and intolerance challenged the radical origins of English Protestantism, thus making the image of Constantine a central feature of the polemics of anti-Puritanism in Jacobean England. The scope of the king's anti-papal writings reflects the domestic agenda of preachers like Andrewes or Barlow, and demonstrates that the interdependence of royal and "formalist" arguments for order and authority predated the uproar over foreign policy in 1617–18.

James's Constantinian rhetoric led him to assert his written authority in a wider European context, but it is also necessary to analyze Jacobean internationalist language in the context of domestic politics, where it may have had a more significant and long-lasting effect. It has been recently noted that the diversity of opinions that characterized James's government in matters of religion "produced much factional and personal rivalry at court," especially between bishops advocating leniency for either moderate Puritans or loyal Catholics.[62] Nowhere is the powerfully internecine quality of this situation better exemplified than in the discourses carried on between the lines of the sermons analyzed above. Richard Field praised moderation and unity in matters of doctrine, hardly incendiary goals on first glance; Henry Hooke advised his king to rule wisely and religiously, not exactly a matter for the Tower. Even Richard Stock, who did not preach at court, but who appears to have been patronized by one of the court's old-style Calvinist power brokers, expressed only anti-Catholic views, nothing unusual at Paul's Cross after the discovery of the Gunpowder Plot; he focused upon Scripture as the inerrant basis for religion, something upon which it would seem all Protestants could agree. Yet these clerics actually offered James diametrically opposed "visions of the English church," as has recently been noted.[63] The opposition of their viewpoints emerged in acts of professional rivalry, but it was also encoded in the languages of the court pulpit.

A close examination of the defense of episcopacy and the king at the second Hampton Court conference reveals no dangerous claims for the divine origin of the episcopate or even of the royal supremacy, yet hidden under the unassailable discourses of royal supremacy, we begin to detect a picture of the Church that would later prove controversial in the extreme, and not only to radical Scots. This casts the "evenhanded" rhetoric of some court conformists in a slightly different light. The rhetoric of broad Christian unity, paradoxically and more than a little ironically, exposed the disunity at the heart of the Jacobean ecclesiastical establishment, yet it also identifies a faction within this establishment to which James would turn at moments when his authority needed the most support. Their polemic was powerful enough in this period, but much of its power would wait in reserve for the domestic political crises of the final decade of James's reign.

The Jacobean consequences of James's vision, however, can be seen in the rationale it provided for the formalist liturgical initiatives of the last years of his reign. A description of the English Church as an institution wherein tradition and the king's mandate had an authority rivaling *sola scriptura* could underpin a new view of sacramental worship as more than simply adiaphoric. The notion of a united Christendom would inspire the actions of ultra-ceremonialist clerics, justifying their vigorous defense of the centrality of the sacraments and their equally vigorous rejection of Calvinism. The Caroline formalist Peter Heylyn's suggestion that James himself intended to unify the reformed churches in a common liturgy suggests that Laudian clergy were happy to look back and claim not only Lancelot Andrewes but also James I as their inspiration. And so it is to the impact of Jacobean sacramentalist language on the rhetoric of the king, the politics of the court, and the fortunes of "formalist" churchmanship that we finally turn.

CHAPTER FIVE

Kneeling and the Body Politic

If we examine theological debates from 1603 to 1625, we find that James I ruled over a better reformed Church than did either his predecessor or successor. If we examine the records of ecclesiastical enforcement, we find James ruled over a better conformed Church. In fact, many scholars have all but eliminated every possible point of contention that might have divided the Jacobean Church, and yet now we know that James's was not an entirely reformed, quiet, or contented religious settlement. When we analyze the rhetoric of religion, we recognize that James I ruled over a powder keg.

As we have seen in the preceding chapters, both the evidence for and the source of this problem can be found in the polemical style of government that characterized the early Stuart Church. Without question, James I managed a religious settlement that was remarkable in its age for theological consensus and nonconfrontational policy. But it is also true that he did so while always tolerating and often promoting an official rhetoric of scorn and contumely against subjects identified as "papist" and "Puritan" who placed themselves outside the bounds of that settlement.[1] In the case of Puritanism, this proved particularly destabilizing. If Puritanism truly was contained for the most part within the English religious settlement,[2] then the alienating language of the king's Church would have been provocatively set against Puritan experience.

It may be true that the ecclesiastical policy of James I was designed to distinguish moderate Puritans from radical. But in the controversial rhetoric commissioned for that very purpose, these carefully drawn political distinctions broke down under the constant rough handling of biased religious polemicists bent on dominating the ecclesiastical tenor of the Jacobean court. In this chapter, I analyze the most significant rhetorical development of this pulpit tradition: the creation of a strand of mainstream anti-Puritan polemic that would transform the acceptable categories of "things indifferent," sacralizing formalist behavior. Making such a daring claim for the doctrinal import of liturgical practice allowed James's public spokesmen not only to insist that "moderate Puritans" were in actuality schismatics determined to break the unity of the Church given the chance; it finally provided the necessary leap in logic to support the anti-Calvinist campaign of the 1620's.[3]

Throughout James's reign, the sermons issuing in print from the court and Paul's Cross at times of domestic crisis lumped the many acceptable, but subtly different, approaches to conformity to be found in the Church of England into two very broadly drawn but distinct categories: "praying" and "preaching" Protestants. These oppositionally poised stereotypes lent themselves to a particularly crude type of verbal imaging: humility juxtaposed to pride, embodied in the *praxis* of worship. Such images played a significant role in the rhetoric of the Hampton Court conference of 1604; they formed one basis for the political critique of Puritanism throughout the reign; and, finally, they underwent a curious transformation. In the last years of James's reign, political pressures transformed what had been a secular polemic and bequeathed a fully developed language of sacramentalism to the subsequent disastrous ecclesiastical policies of Charles I and his archbishop of Canterbury, William Laud.

The purpose of this chapter is to trace the long trajectory of rhetorical pre-Laudianism in the Jacobean Church, in order to refute in part the claims for that Church's quiescence and unity. The first section considers a piece of anecdotal evidence, featuring A King, A Bishop, A Puritan, and a scene-stealing gesture. The second section recasts a familiar ecclesiastical debate into cultural and political terms. And, last, the third section examines the effect of political anxiety on religious rhetoric and tracks its subsequent transformation into controversial doctrine. This approach, while diverse, focuses upon one subject, the debate over the meaning of the act of kneeling: a gesture symbolic of both religious and secular obedience, and thus exemplary of the power, interdependence, and ultimate vulnerability of political and religious discourse in the age of James I.

Scene: The Hampton Court Conference

On Monday, 16 January 1604, the second day of the Hampton Court Conference, the Puritan spokesman John Reynolds expressed his hopes to James I that "good Pastors might be planted in all Churches to preach" the "pure" doctrine of the Church of England. The request was voiced in terms calculated to please a king who had publicly voiced his approval of both Calvinist doctrine and educated clergy. Taking up this point in debate, James expressed his own concerns over the maintenance of learned men in Church livings when Richard Bancroft, the bishop of London, suddenly fell to his knees with the following entreaty:

Because I see this is a time of moving petitions, may I humbly present two or three to your Majesty: First, that there be amongst us a *praying* ministry; it being now come to pass, that men think it the only duty of ministers to spend their time in the pulpit. I confess, in a church newly to be planted, preaching is most necessary, not so in one so long established, that prayer should be neglected.[4]

On the surface, these words seem unremarkable, and certainly more temperate than most of what the bishop had to say about the Puritan platform presented at Hampton Court. But they are fighting words nonetheless. Bancroft made a distinction between "praying" and "preaching" ministries in an attempt to win the king over to his view that there were two opposed parties in the Church of England.[5]

In his call for a ministry that was "learned," Reynolds had employed a buzzword, familiar to everyone in the chamber, that signified "godly reforming preachers." Dr. Reynolds's reluctance in debate to identify these evangelizing worthies (or himself, for that matter) as "Puritan" displayed a politic delicacy matched only by recent historians. These days the Jacobean Puritan is an endangered species, the victim of overenthusiastic revisionism. The historiography of the Church of England under James I has produced a picture of a Church marked by theological consensus and moderated by a king well versed and adept in religious controversy, not overzealous to enforce ecclesiastical canons, and determined to disarm extremists. This picture is misleading in its very accuracy. The problem of those pesky Puritans remains, and its persistence begs a question: what exactly did their opponents find so offensive about them? If the singular crime of Puritanism in this period was that of deviant ecclesiology,[6] what danger could it possibly represent in the mild and moderate reign of "Great Britain's Solomon"?[7]

The problem is one of methodology—both ours and theirs. To begin, historians of the early Stuart Church would do well to temper their preoccupation with theologians more or less enthusiastic about predestination. Recent analyses have focused almost exclusively on the doctrinal beliefs of Calvinists and anti-Calvinists, thereby limiting the focus of their debate to the definition of systems of salvation. This is not to suggest that the debate was, or is, marginal. To reduce the Church to a soteriological think tank, however, narrows its interests and leaves us with a picture of an institution isolated from the political and cultural issues of its day.[8]

A concentration on the taut logic of theology leaves no room for consideration of the politic flexibility of post-Reformation religious language. It must be remembered that the very impression of doctrinal solidarity that most Jacobean polemicists worked tirelessly to convey was itself a political and cultural construct. These writers did little to prepare us for the ecclesiastical crises of the 1630's; indeed, much of their discursive repertoire consisted of rhetorical strategies designed to defuse the notion of societal conflict.[9] In this polemic, words like "praying" and "preaching" were more than innocent descriptions of Christian worship: they were concealed weapons. To understand the meaning behind the Bancroft-Reynolds exchange at Hampton Court, modern historians must learn new ways to decipher the subtle declarations of war encoded in the deceptively moderate and consentient language of early Stuart religious controversialists.[10]

In moving away from a naïve consideration of a complex rhetoric, however, care must be taken also to preserve the broad-brush-stroked concept of Puritanism for this period. To reduce it to an assimilated and tolerable nonconformity, or to break it up into increasingly precise, individualized descriptions along the radical-conformist continuum, leaves us without a satisfying characterization of a persistent, crude, and vivid cultural phenomenon. Jacobean churchmen, like Jacobean theater audiences, knew a Puritan when they saw one. The word itself had a resonance that present-day scholars find almost impossible to describe.[11] Puritans were not simply people who refused to wear surplices, make the sign of the cross, or call their communion tables "altars." The visibility of that refusal projected matters of private conscience into the public realm; it "symbolized negative opinions," according to one seventeenth-century writer, and so exemplified societal as well as confessional disunity.[12]

What follows is an analysis of one aspect of the prayer-preaching controversy in the Church of England: the debate over kneeling in worship. The issue of kneeling was neither minor nor strictly ecclesiastical: it occupied that volatile space where religious, political, and cultural matters contend. This is because the physical act itself supported the weight of many meanings. Kneeling conveyed the idea of obeisance to God; it conveyed the idea of obeisance to the monarch. In an Erastian Church, it conveyed these ideas simultaneously. Herein lay the heart of the problem—just where in matters of religion did secular loyalty end and religious conviction begin? What was the spiritual duty of the subject confronted with the arbitrary rule of a royal supremacy? And, come to think of it, just how arbitrary was that rule—or that conscience?

These questions cut across theological lines, penetrating the religious and political culture of Jacobean England in a way that debates over predestination could not. Gestures, unlike beliefs, were visible. The former could be discerned, indeed enforced, while the latter posed an entirely different problem. In addition, it is arguable that, soft on its enforcement as he was, the king was more preoccupied by the kneeling issue than any of the other conformity issues of his reign.[13] For these reasons—as well as the fact that the language of gesture can be opened up to demonstrate the kind of broad, rhetorically effective stereotypes that challenge the careful particularity of much recent historiographical descriptions of Puritanism—the debate provides a new and valuable perspective on what was at stake in the struggle to define the Church of England in the reign of James I.

To return to the mise-en-scène described above: in rhetorical terms, Bancroft's juxtaposition of "praying" with "preaching" ministries was studied and succinct. He bypassed the theological consensus that may well have existed between two parties—after all, Calvin's theology has no exclusive relation either to prayer or to preaching—and pointed instead to what he really found offensive about Reynolds's program. The bishop of London ingeniously transformed the idea of an educated preaching clergy, one of the cornerstones of Protestant reform, into a threat to the royal supremacy.[14]

Conflating the intent of Puritan petitioning with the aims of Protestant preaching, Bancroft implied that evangelicalism was little more than a respectable-sounding excuse for popular agitation. His allusion to newly planted churches intensifies the force of this contention. If preaching ministries supplied the inspiration for an immature Church to initiate and complete the work of religious reformation (as it had throughout the history of Christianity and most memorably in the preceding half-century), then to endorse such a ministry was to criticize the present state of religion under the rule of the new Constantine. By suggesting that, in calling for better preaching, Reynolds had actually voiced a more general dissatisfaction with James I's religious settlement,

Bancroft repackaged the Protestant desire for reform as evidence of disloyalty.

Credit for brilliant politicking must be given to Bancroft, both for his unerring strike to the heart of what the king would have found dangerous about Puritanism and for his rhetorical devaluation of a powerful and influential evangelical agenda for the established Church. But what is as important if less noticed about the scene is how the bishop wrested control of the agenda from Reynolds by the simple expedient of falling to his knees. In doing so, the bishop quite literally "fleshed out" his moderate words with an action guaranteed to make his underlying intent uncompromisingly clear. Bancroft's argument became well-nigh irresistible: not only did he perform the devout behavior he wished to promote, but in the same elegant gesture, he also displayed his own submission to the king.[15]

Speaking on his knees, Bancroft turned a "praying ministry" into an obedient ministry, and identified it with the posture of humility and obeisance. An alternative image of "preaching" could then be silently suggested: the godly auditory sitting in their pews, hats on heads, stubbornly stiff-necked. This view of the "proud Puritan" lent itself easily to conformist propaganda. Bancroft's action served to illustrate to James I that the conscientious refusal of Puritans to kneel at worship could look very similar to a refusal to kneel before the king himself. In the same way that the loyal bishop turned himself into a living representation of the concept of conformity, the language of religious consensus was transformed into a medium of political conflict in the debates at Hampton Court.

Context: Kneeling and the Sixteenth-Century Reformation

While Church historians generally treat the debate over kneeling as an ecclesiastical dispute, its long association with the rhetoric of politics and court culture is less noted. The narrative of this association begins with a sermon by the Scottish reformer John Knox to Edward VI and his court in 1552, one so fiery that it inspired a hasty addition to Edward's second Book of Common

Prayer.[16] The authors added a new set of instructions on communion kneeling that declared that obeisance implied no adoration of Christ's body on the altar, but was instead an expression of thanksgiving, undertaken to "avoid profanation and disorder." This "Black Rubric" was thus oddly but aptly named. Kneeling continued to be prescribed as ritual in the prayer book, but was left stripped of its religious coloration.[17]

This reinterpretation of ritual action relegated kneeling at the communion rail, if only by implication, to the status of the merely ceremonial gestures of prayer described in the 1549 prayer book—such things as "kneeling, crossing, holding up of hands, knocking upon the breast," actions that could be "used or left" to the worshiper's discretion.[18] These "things indifferent" were practices neither prescribed nor proscribed in Scripture. Consequently, they required a process of decoding subject to more controversial forms of authority. The prayer book stated that ceremonies could be "altered and changed, and therefore [were] not to be esteemed equal with God's law," a statement that, when combined with an act of supremacy, could greatly strengthen the claims of the royal prerogative over things adiaphoric. To describe communion kneeling as expressive solely of humility and good order made possible, therefore, not only its description as mere ceremonial, but also its analogy to secular obedience.

The radical nature of Edwardian reform, in matters of both doctrine and practice, is exemplified in the language of the 1552 prayer book. But its influence was cut short by Edward's death soon thereafter and the accession of Mary I, who repealed it. As a consequence, the newest version of the prayer book had never been in widespread general use by English congregations. Its significance instead lay in its preservation and use by English exiles on the continent, and in its power (and theirs) to shape attitudes toward a later Book of Common Prayer. After a brief Catholic reign punctuated by the execution of heretics who denied the doctrine of transubstantiation, Protestantism was reinstated under Elizabeth. This was, however, no return to the heady days of Edwardian reform, a fact demonstrated in the construction of the Elizabethan prayer book and Act of Uniformity.[19]

Elizabeth I preferred a more conservative formulation of communion; in the matter of the Eucharist, therefore, the 1552 prayer book exerted a partially negative influence on its 1559 successor. The Black Rubric, with its explicit denial of a materially real presence of Christ in the elements, was not included, leaving communion kneeling open to a number of diverse interpretations, including those of a Catholic nature.[20] The queen's moderation disappointed many of her reform-minded subjects who had expected finally to strip the English Church of all its popish ceremonies, the remnants and reminders of a disconcertingly recent Catholic past. Conflicts over conformity and obedience were fierce in this period, as evidenced in the vestiarian controversy, the "Admonition to the Parliament" of 1572, and the correspondence of Elizabeth's bishops with their continental brethren.[21] Royal apologists responded to resistance by citing Elizabeth's authority to retain as well as to alter things adiaphoric, thereby taking Knox's old argument to another logical, if disheartening, conclusion.

With doctrinal attitudes toward the Sacrament so unsettled at this time, kneeling at communion presented an interpretive minefield for Protestants to cross. Unlike the wearing of a surplice, it was an action commanded of an entire congregation. Thus a refusal to do so took on the appearance of a popular insurrection rather than that of a ministerial indiscretion or eccentricity. Despite this, the injunction to kneel could be and often was overlooked in many parishes. The appearance of obedience was often sacrificed to a greater principle by a minister on behalf of his parishioners. An order to kneel imperiled Puritan consciences, which after years of wrestling with the doctrine of the Real Presence were acutely and characteristically sensitive to the popish appearance of the English communion service.[22]

By 1603 and the accession of James VI to the throne of England, however, the idea that ceremonies like kneeling were in

themselves adiaphoric actually began to work to the benefit of
the King's Puritan subjects. This is in part owing to the relative
broadmindedness of the Jacobean episcopate, who in their visi-
tation examinations frequently found room to maneuver around
tricky situations. Where the need for men of good preaching and
pastoral ability was particularly acute, Jacobean bishops were
willing to compromise with nonconformists.[23] This would not
have been possible if ceremonial practices had been considered
essential in this period to the orthodox interpretation of sacramental theology. In a sense, therefore, the ideology of the Black
Rubric was expressed de facto if not de jure in the religious culture of Jacobean England.

In some court-sermon rhetoric, the argument that obedience
itself was divinely ordained could be attached to a defense of the
ceremonies. Early on, this argument centered upon the divine
commandment to show visible obeisance to the monarch. Thomas Bilson's 1603 Coronation Day sermon (preached on Romans
13:1, "[T]he powers that be, are ordained of God") explored the
synecdochal relationship between religious gesture and respect
for the king's authority in this light: "When S. Peter saith,
'honour the King,' we must not thence exclude bodily honour,
which is sensible to others, and restrain it to the honour of the
mind, which neither we can shew, nor they can see, but by external signs. The commandments of God bind the whole man: no
part is exempted where submission is required."[24]

Bilson's call for an obedience confirmed by kneeling before
the king could be extended into an advocacy of kneeling in worship in submission to monarchical authority in adiaphoric matters. Refusing to kneel in church at the king's command, Bilson
implied, looked like refusing to kneel before the king himself;
judged by appearances, such refusals could be equally treasonous. This particular line of argument was a favorite of court
preachers defending the king's right to demand conformity and
subscription.[25]

James's accession was the catalyst for an initial period of intense print activity focusing on the topic of ceremonies. James's

1599 book *BASILIKON DORON*, with its conciliatory but ambiguous remarks about Puritanism, had raised hopes, long suppressed in Elizabeth's reign, of further liturgical reformation. The "Millenary Petition" of 1603 that outlined Puritan scruples in this matter prompted the Hampton Court Conference (and Bancroft's snide remark about "moving petitions" described above).[26] While some concessions were made to Reynolds and his brethren at the conference, however, they were allowed no leeway on adiaphoric issues.

The post-conference conformity campaign of 1604–5 was hardly the wholesale "harrying" with which James had threatened his recalcitrant clergy at Hampton Court. Few Puritans were actually deprived for refusing to perform certain liturgical practices. After all, Jacobean bishops were not the only ones to practice the politic art of compromise. Convinced of the concept of spiritual "indifferency"—or, perhaps convinced that no further discussion was possible—, most ministers eventually found it possible to accommodate themselves to the ceremonies. The fact that James preferred to subdue his Puritan clergy by requiring subscription to, rather than actual observance of, the canons of 1604 also made it possible for the godly but pragmatic to avoid total compliance.[27]

Nonetheless, some stiff-necked ministers refused even the piecrust promise of conformity. Notable were the clergy of the diocese of Lincoln, who in 1605 sent a treatise to the king justifying their refusal to subscribe.[28] This was only one of a multitude of treatises and sermons printed in this period that explored the reasons for and against conformity.[29] A decline in these publications after 1607 parallels a relative decline in episcopal enforcement. For some scholars, official inactivity signals the end of Puritan resistance (and for a few, this effectively means the end of "Puritanism") until the Laudian campaigns for conformity in the 1630's.[30]

But the battle over ceremonies was always more extensively and exactingly conducted on the page than in the Church courts during the reign of James I. In this forum, Puritanism continued to be, at the very least, the ongoing creation of negative polemics. Circa 1617, the print campaign in England shifted once more into high gear, driven by a campaign for ecclesiastical conformity in Scotland.[31] It is not the purpose of this chapter once again to examine the mechanisms, rhetorical or otherwise, of the king's authority in his native Kirk. But it is important to note some aspects of the Scottish situation that had a significant effect on the second great English debate on ceremonial conformity conducted in the final decade of James's reign.

The fifth of the Five Articles of Perth enjoined kneeling at communion, which was the only specific ceremonial performance to be thus commanded.[32] This distinguishes the campaign from that of 1604–5 in England, which involved a broader and more general subscription to conformity. In addition, the earlier conflict had proceeded upon the assumption that communion kneeling could be thought of in the same way as all other "indifferent" worship gestures. Now the debate was refocused; not only did kneeling become the central issue and image in the ensuing controversy, but the stage was set for a much narrower and less forgiving dispute, one that pitted the interpretation of the Eucharist against the meaning of obedience to the monarch.

The angry sense that the rules of engagement had shifted flashes from a contemporary account of an assembly held to discuss the Articles prior to their official passage.[33] David Calderwood, one of the Scottish ministers present, provides a characteristically harsh assessment of the king's move to reimpose a small measure of ceremonial uniformity on what had been a vastly more reformed church than its English counterpart. In his partisan report, recalcitrant clergy are portrayed as maneuvering unsuccessfully between the Scylla of religious conviction and the Charybdis of royal prerogative. Throughout, Calderwood portrays the debate on one article as symbolic of the entire enterprise: "Kneeling," according to the minister, "was chiefly agitate."[34] His outraged testimony paints a vivid picture of a hateful submission to monarchical authority in matters of religion.

Calderwood's fears centered around the reimposition of

kneeling as part of a royal campaign to reestablish "popish rites and superstitions" in Scotland, and they were only intensified by the progress James made to Scotland that same year. James had had the Chapel Royal at Holyrood redecorated in ornate fashion, which occasioned much concern on the part of the Scots as to whether this display of the beauty of English holiness was a harbinger of things to come in their own churches.[35] But the Five Articles of Perth would prove to be as imperfectly enforced as the English canons of 1604, a fact that should be filed separately from the evidence of the numerous tracts and sermons supporting the practice of kneeling that date from this period. In 1617, as in 1604, the rhetoric stimulated by a conformity campaign had a longer shelf life, a longer reach, and a more extensive effect than did the campaign itself.

The very real differences between the Scottish and English debates over ceremonial only serve to make their similarities more intriguing. It is at this point that the effect of the king's liturgical policy in Scotland must be considered in another context.[36] Its timing coincides with and should be related to a developing crisis of obedience catalyzed by James's plans to marry his son to a Catholic princess. In England as in Scotland, policy ran perilously counter to public sentiment; fears of court-based popery were aired in pamphlets and from pulpits.[37] The debate over kneeling stimulated by the king's Scottish policy was easily absorbed into the rhetorical atmosphere surrounding the so-called "Spanish Match," not simply because both provoked violent anti-Catholic sentiment, but, more interestingly, because the defenders of the king in both situations employed the same forms of synechdochic imagery.[38] The brilliant figures and memorable tropes used to advocate kneeling to the Scots proved so attractive that they became the height of rhetorical fashion, guaranteed to clothe any conformist polemical attack in the latest style.

Here it is oddly apt to introduce one last element, the polemical preoccupation of a number of conformist Jacobean court preachers: the promotion of the "beauty of holiness." In one sense, this concept can be traced from the Knoxian contention that worship should be conducted with order and decency, the guarantor of that style being the royal supremacy. But, as we shall see, these relatively uncontroversial notions could exist in the Jacobean clergy alongside more dangerous interpretations. The appearance and prominence of language extolling the beauty of holiness in court polemic can be directly related to the defense of the king's authority in the increasingly tense political and rhetorical atmosphere of the second half of his reign. The defense of kneeling should be examined in the context of this more general polemic; indeed, it provides the final, necessary connection between the polemical texts and their historical context.

Connections: Religion, Rhetoric, and Transformation

The Jacobean notion of the beauty of holiness was rooted in a metaphor of the monarch as builder and overseer of the Church, and preachers at James's court deployed strikingly architectonic imagery in the service of this concept. On Easter 1611, Lancelot Andrewes preached on Psalm 118, "The stone, which the builders refused . . . is become the Head of the Corner." Andrewes drew from this text the lesson that every Christian was required to "make God an house": "If we be but ourselves . . . build God an oratory . . . if we have a household . . . build him a chapel . . . if a country or kingdom, then a Basilica or Metropolitan Church, which is properly the Prince's Building."[39] The logic of this passage, with its hierarchical, metaphoric progression from prayer to Basilica, eventually locates the prayerfully devout believer within the structures of the king's religion. The analogy to the royal supremacy is clear and uncomplicated.

Precisely because of its clarity, this image could be manipulated in a variety of ways. Andrewesian language graces a 1612 sermon preached before the king at the deteriorated abbey church of St. Alban's. William Westerman, a chaplain to Archbishop Abbot, cited his text, "And there was Jacob's well" (John 4:6), in a contemporary application to James's (in the Latin *Jacobus*) own stop on progress at a holy place.[40] The preacher's purpose was to secure funds for the rebuilding of the abbey, and he used a familiar image to persuade James that such patronage was appropriate: "Kings . . . in the profession of our religion . . . erected Basilicas, Kinglike Palaces."[41] We see, therefore, the influence of Andrewes's rhetorical strategies, now placed in the service of a straightforward campaign implicating the king in the actual beautification of the church.

At Hampton Court in 1621, Christopher Swale made use of these same themes in a sermon on Jacob's vow (Genesis 28:22): "This Stone, which I have set up as a pillar, shall be God's house." Swale applied the text to the contemporary situation of the Church and called upon the king to use his authority to ensure its physical maintenance. The literal thrust of his contemporary application makes it possible, therefore, to interpret his assertion, "no good thing will [God] with-hold from them, that worship him in the beauty of holiness," in the material as well as in the spiritual sense. Swale then pressed this aesthetic vision of the Church into service as a criticism of nonconformity: "Private Conventicles are not to be compared with the public Assemblies of the Church."[42] What distinguishes this style of anti-Puritan rhetoric is not only its physical aesthetics, but also its logic in associating the idea of the "beauty of holiness" with the visible, established Church.

This aspect of Swale's sermon—the dichotomy presented between Church and conventicle—demonstrates how the increasingly materialistic rhetoric of the "beauty of holiness" could provide a useful language to support and shape what Ken Fincham and Peter Lake have identified as characteristic Jacobean ecclesiastical policy.[43] (The drawbacks of the approach are discussed below.) The distinction between public and private could be used to divide radical from moderate Puritans by implying that any objection to this aesthetic of worship could only come from outside the Church. Such rhetoric could work in tandem with a doctrine of adiaphora, since, by concentrating on the external, it could leave the workings of the individual conscience alone. Moderate Puritans could, therefore, interpret ceremonial action in light of their inclusion in the visible Church, while their personal beliefs, like their membership in the Church invisible, remained matters not subject to ecclesiastical law.

In fact, the attention paid to appearances can be seen as evidence of the broad theological consensus that characterized James's reign. Since orthodoxy was not the issue at stake in the Jacobean debate over kneeling, some of the king's polemicists concentrated instead on the visible impression made by kneeling or not kneeling. Bishop Thomas Morton offered an analysis that owes its ideology to the Black Rubric:

Although there be not a proportion of equality, between a Civil and Religious reverence, yet is there a proportion of Similitude, and the one doth singularly illustrate the other, in this case. For as a civil gift ought to be taken with a civil reverence, from the hand of an earthly Sovereign, so must a spiritual gift; and the Instruments thereof, be received with a Spiritual and Religious Reverence . . . our religious receiving of Holy Rites, doth magnify the Author, but no way deify the gift.[44]

Morton's carefully drawn distinction between "proportion of equality" and "proportion of similitude" is a brilliant, complex statement about the inadequacy of any worship gesture to demonstrate sincerity or orthodoxy of belief. His defense of kneeling is rooted in the idea that the reverent gesture is itself an indifferent matter, as the reassurance about "religious receiving" not "deifying the gift" of communion indicates. The reference to obeisance to the king as "singularly" illustrative of communion kneeling makes the adiaphorous nature of the act even more explicit: the proper, uniform conduct of the communion thus becomes the "gift" of the sovereign to an obedient and grateful people.

James himself contributed to the debate over kneeling in 1619, with his treatise *A Meditation upon the Lord's Prayer Written by the King's Majesty for the Benefit of All His Subjects Especially of Such as Follow the Court.* Prefaced by a lengthy anti-Puritan diatribe, in which James presented his meditation as a defense of liturgical prayer, the royal argument is drawn from a familiar polemical dichotomy. The king claimed that his meditation was designed to counteract a recent trend: Puritans had rewritten the apostolic injunction "pray continually" to read "preach continually."[45] In his view, such spiritual arrogance was visibly demonstrated in a refusal to kneel at the Sacrament. James condemned those who sat "Jack-fellowlike with Christ at the Lord's Table." The tableau illustrates the constituent characteristics of Puritanism: pride, insolence, and irreverence.[46]

The king viewed this manifestation of what he called "the private spirit of Reformation" as a first step down the slippery slope of sectarianism. The airing of Puritan scruples about ceremonies encouraged others who were more radically minded to leave the established Church altogether. The king employed his own architectonic metaphor to explain this assertion more fully: "because that all our goodly material churches were built in time of popery . . . therefore to the woods and caves must they go like outlaws, to their sermons . . . thus have I sufficiently proved, I hope, that our Puritans are the founders and fathers of the Brownists, the latter only boldly putting into practice what the former do teach, but dare not perform." The denunciation carries real polemical force; it was a warning to those who saw themselves as conscientious objectors in the adiaphoric tradition that the king deemed their attitudes irreconcilable to the established Church. This focus differs from Morton's, whose language is designed to convince Puritan brethren that uniformity of worship was a thing spiritually indifferent. *A Meditation upon the Lord's Prayer* demonstrates that the concept of adiaphora had become an inadequate political and rhetorical strategy for maintaining the unity of the Jacobean Church.

It might seem that the king was the prime mover, then, in this controversial campaign to sacralize acts of unity and uniformity, but we must consider the possibility that the very nature of this long-developing and complex print debate meant that here polemical content followed rhetorical form. By the time he wrote *A Meditation*, James could draw upon a set of rhetorical conventions to condemn Puritanism. These conventions could be reduced to a single, succinct image. The amalgamation of the language of the Perth campaign and the defense of the king's foreign policy meant nonconformity was frequently in danger of being exclusively defined as non-kneelery. The image was central to a polemic that paid increasing attention to the problem of irreverence altogether. By the second half of James's reign, court sermons invariably featured a detailed description of the misbehavior of people in the pews, in lively language that must have been intentionally entertaining. Anthony Maxey, a perennially preferment-seeking conformist Calvinist, complained in a sermon to the king that most worshipers were "like Elephants . . . they have no joints in their knees, they talk, whisper, and gaze about, without any kind of bodily reverence, and as it may be thought, without any inward devotion at all." Maxey then went on to add that "the inward mind is expressed by the outward gesture,"[47] a remark that is worth noting in more detail.

Neither Maxey's zoological metaphor nor his reference to kneeling as the external symbol of an internal sanctification is original; they echo the rhetoric of other sermons, most notably a 1614 Easter sermon at court preached by Lancelot Andrewes.[48] The entertainment value of picturing elephants in England's pews most certainly ensured the metaphor's elevation into a sermonic buzzword. What is more significant here, however, is the way in which this very memorable and effective description is combined with and complicated by the claim, not only that the quality of worship in England had somehow deteriorated in the past decades (a claim, it must be said, that is difficult to sustain with fact) but also, and more controversially, that the quality of devotion was inevitably expressed in gesture (or the lack of it). By contrast, performance of secular obedience required no reference to the "inward mind"; in part, this was what detached adiaphoric observance from the necessity of a particular doctrinal interpretation. To speak of true religious devotion as necessarily expressed in external behavior opened up the conduct of the liturgy to assertions of its theological meaning.

Not that this was what Maxey had in mind. Maxey and Morton (whose treatise represents the ironic counterpoint to a remarkably unsuccessful record against persistent nonconformity in his diocese)[49] fit into a familiar category of Jacobean church-manship. These clerics supported conformity as an adiaphoric concept useful for the support of the royal supremacy. This lan-guage of support, of course, could be usefully employed to com-bat the king's political opponents. But their condemnations of Puritanism, frequent as they were, were undertaken on the as-sumption that the king's opponents in ceremonial matters were also his theological allies. For the Maxeys and Mortons of this age, the beauty of holiness had little if any substantial doctrinal import.

Maxey and Morton simply commandeered a cultural com-plaint against the behavior of the laity at worship that could also support a more pointed rhetoric against the physical and spiri-tual decay of the Church. This common complaint rhetoric would be drawn upon by persons with different theological be-liefs in a time when Puritanism was implicated in political pro-tests that went beyond matters of ceremonial nonconformity, which brings us finally to the drawbacks of Jacobean ecclesiasti-cal policy and some increasingly audacious statements on behalf of the beauty of holiness. Considered in political context, a care-ful reading of the texts illuminates how the debate over kneeling could lead to serious questions in the 1620's about the king's the-ological commitments, not only to reformed Protestantism, but also to the English Calvinist consensus.

It was one thing to claim that uniformity was aesthetically pleasing, but quite another to locate aesthetic values in the Sac-rament itself. In fact, the excess of attention paid to the Eucharist by some court preachers might have made the connection be-tween court religion and potentially popish sacramentalism all too apparent. In the final decade of James's reign, the rhetoric of obedience became vulnerable to a less adiaphoric interpretation, one going beyond the king's requirements. The theme of the beauty of holiness, while present in many court sermons, had been the persistent preoccupation of Lancelot Andrewes. His eloquence made him James's favorite preacher, but his own anti-

Calvinism made his defense of conformity problematic.[50] Despite the fact that Andrewes's personal theological opinions were controversial enough to be suppressed by royal fiat,[51] they continued to shape his rhetoric on issues of conformity and obedience.

In a sense, then, Andrewes provides an interesting confirmation of Maxey's Theorem: in the outward effect of his sermon style, his inward mind was invariably expressed. The success at court and prominence in print of Andrewes's sermons ensured flattering imitations, even by men whose actual churchmanship had a very different character.[52] As the rhetoric of the kneeling campaign in Scotland was applied to the political situation in England, Andrewesian language extolling the beauty of holiness became the discourse of the hour. The imagery of kneeling acquired an unprecedented significance. A new, shriller style of anti-Puritan rhetoric called into open question the very existence of a broad consensus in the English Church.

Andrewes's Easter sermon of 1614 is evidence that his attention to the topic of kneeling predated the Scottish campaign. In expounding his text, "at the name of Jesus every knee will bow" (Philippians 2:10), Andrewes warned the king that irreverence was more to be avoided than popery: "heed would be taken, that by taking heed we prove not superstitious we slip not into the other extreme before we be aware: Which, of the two extremes, Religion worse endureth; as more opposite to it."[53] Andrewes's concentration on outward performance rather than inward conviction was controversial enough to earn a moderate reproof from one court preacher a scant week later. Norwich Spackman, a chaplain to the bishop of Bath and Wells, preached at court on Matthew 9:13, "I will have mercy and not sacrifice," in which he interpreted "sacrifice" to mean "the whole outward service of God." Countering Andrewesian language with good old-fashioned adiaphoric rhetoric, the chaplain insisted that ceremonies took second place to "inward worship"; they were "indifferent," "simply necessary" for believers, but certainly not "absolutely necessary for God." Spackman had no quarrel—at least not in this setting—with ceremonial conformity overall; it is obvious, however, that he felt that Andrewes had overstepped the polemical boundaries of the debate on kneeling.[54]

Andrewes did not get called out very often. He was as politic as he was anti-Calvinist, and his careful avoidance of open religious controversy lent his polemic a multivalent quality often absent in that of other controversialists. Other preachers were far less subtle. Given the opportunity to defend James's campaign in Scotland, John Buckeridge, bishop of Rochester, turned on its head the old conformist view that kneeling was orderly and obedient, but not necessary to salvation. In 1617, he preached a controversial sermon before James that explored the nature of the relationship between secular and sacred obedience. Referring to both Scottish and English nonconformity, Buckeridge made the following statement, which represents a departure from conformist rhetoric like Morton's:

All [James's] Kingdoms must be obedient to his *venite*, and join together, not only in *unitate*, in the unity and substance of Religion, and worship of God, but also in *uniformitate*, in uniformity of outward order and ceremony of Gods service, if possibly it may be; especially in . . . Adoration, and Prostration and Kneeling, which are not ceremonies (Rom.13.4) but parts of divine service; and for disobedience must be subjected to his coercion, who bears not the sword in vain.[55]

Here Buckeridge asserts that the act of kneeling was subject to the king's will, not because it was indifferent, but indeed because it was essential. The rationale for James's authority becomes the duty to have the act itself performed—not the duty to display obedience to the royal supremacy. In short, the focus has moved from an idea of service to the king to one of service to God.

Where Buckeridge deviates from other conformist rhetoric is not simply in his discussion of obedience, but in the connection of arguments for obedience with those promoting a non-adiaphoric view of the Sacrament. The bishop wrote a longer treatise on kneeling the following year. In its preface, he implied that his ideas had proven so thought-provoking he had been asked to apply them more specifically, to the "particulars of the Sacrament." In doing this, Buckeridge revisited the politics of the debate over the Edwardian Prayer Book, effectively reversing the intent of that discourse. In 1552 the language of the Black Rubric presented the gestures of the Lord's Supper in the less highly charged language of adiaphoric prayer gestures. With the kneeling issue refocused upon the Eucharist, Buckeridge placed ecclesiastical law back in the service of God and undermined the notion of the political nature of the royal supremacy.

The effect of Buckeridge's rhetoric was to assert an obligation greater than secular obedience, one that bound monarch and subject alike:

So the Church of England, reforming by the rule of the Primitive Church, hath learned, and practiced by her example, to prostrate and kneel at the receipt of those great and sacred Mysteries. In which I dispute not, whether it be duty of necessity, or a Ceremony of Indifferency; I conceive upon reason, in mine own judgment, that it is a Duty, or part of Gods worship, not to be omitted in public and solemn Adoration, but in case of evident necessity.[56]

While there is enough theological ambiguity in the above passage to protect Buckeridge from a charge of heterodoxy, it is obvious that here the language of moderation has been stretched to its breaking point. The resort to his "own judgment" boasts of a liberty of conscience equal to that deplored in James's Puritan opponents. The king, in searching for a polemic to counter religious opposition based on private dictates, ended up promoting the same dangerous claims from the other side. More significant, when Buckeridge claimed the personal freedom to interpret certain ceremonies as essential rather than indifferent, this interpretation could be applied to practices that were enforceable under the ecclesiastical canons of 1604.

Like Andrewes, Buckeridge had always been given a mandate to air his ultraconformist views when it was most needed—at those times when the king was beset by bothersome Puritans or Scottish presbyterians. His sermons reestablished a kind of equilibrium of extreme rhetoric; therein lay their value.[57] But this was less problematic when the extremity served the theme of obedience than when it delved into eucharistic theory. That the king finally allowed such an obviously provocative discussion of the Lord's Supper to issue from the court pulpit and to be displayed in published works is a measure of how badly he needed a rhetorical counterweight to the opposition to his foreign diplomacy. Andrewes's 1614 and 1621 Easter sermons and Buckeridge's 1617 sermon and 1618 treatise are astounding, given the ambiguous nature of most statements of court religion. They answer objections to the practice of kneeling by implying the very thing that objectors feared most—that Puritanism was worse than superstition, and that ceremonies were not to be thought of as adiaphoric. This exemplifies the dangerous shift in direction conformist views could take when traveling in tandem with a less-reformed sacramental theology.

In the overheated polemics of James's later reign, the employment of the concept of the beauty of holiness as a rhetorical device to discredit Puritanism finally led to a significant shift in the way the Sacrament of communion was discussed at court. This passage from Lancelot Andrewes's sermon of Easter 1621 indicts irreverence as potentially treasonous by deliberately calling to mind Andrewes's own 1610 Gowry sermon and its treatment of the theme of "touch not the lord's anointed":

Take this with you: Christ can say *noli*, then. For I know not how, our carriage, a many of us, is so loose; covered we sit, sitting we pray; standing, or walking, or as it takes us in the head, we receive; as if Christ were so gentle a person, we might touch Him, do to him what we list, He would take all well, He hath not the power to say *noli* to anything.[58]

Andrewes's use of *noli me tangere*, with its evocation of *nemo me impune lacessit*, also appears designed to remind the king of the insult done to his authority in Scotland; preached at Whitehall, it serves as a warning about similar Puritan attitudes about the king's policies in England. "The matters likewise, princes' affairs . . . [are] points too high, too wonderful for us to deal with," explained the preacher, "to these also, belongs this 'touch not.'" Here Andrewes associates the *arcana imperii* with the mysteries of Christ's presence in the Eucharist. Making James's political experience into a material type of the passion, however, invariably shifts the focus to the stronger image. The implication is that nonconformity defiles the literally "tangible" person of Christ in the same way it could the king. Andrewes's language admits a close-to-materialist interpretation of eucharistic doctrine, opening up new ground for the theological explorations of Laudian sacramentalists. More significant, it assigns the defense of this subtly transformed view of the Sacrament to James I, by implying that his own experience gives him a peculiar sympathy with the passion narrative.[59]

Royal apologists wrote not only to persuade the king's target audiences, but also to influence the king himself. One way to do this, as we have seen time and again, was to use the king's own words. As the king and his preachers ventriloquized each other, their writings eventually generated a polemical heir: a focused cultural critique with consequences both rhetorical and religious. The debate over kneeling provides an example of just how far James could implicate himself in programs that reflected desires once antithetical to his own. This can best be seen in his own contribution to the debate, his last published treatise, the 1619 *A Meditation upon the 27th, 28th, and 29th Verses of the 27th Chapter of Saint Matthew, or, A Pattern for a King's Inauguration.*

The biblical image upon which *A Pattern* focuses is the passage wherein Roman soldiers strip and crown Jesus with thorns, kneel, and then mock him. From this grim narrative, James constructed a similitude with his own situation: unwilling to acknowledge the divinity of Christ, the soldiers perform "a civil homage, done to a temporal king." This abuse functions as a type of worship, contends James; God must "wring his glory out of corruptions." The observation has novel implications for nonconformity: "These therefore, that will refuse in any place or at any time to worship Christ as well in body as in soul, are in that point inferior to those profane soldiers: which I wish were well observed by our foolish superstitious Puritans, that refuse to kneel at the receiving of the blessed Sacrament."[60]

The king's purpose here is to shame and thus correct nonconformity by means of a hyperbolic comparison: knees bent in mockery are superior to necks stiffened in religious opposition. To transform hypocrisy into a model of worship seems audacious and, on the surface, inappropriate. An analysis of how James fashioned a new argument from a wealth of current rhetorical strategies, however, provides a clue to his purpose. We see in this passage echoes of Morton's conformist polemic, but it is a rhetoric altered by the notion of *noli me tangere*.

Morton had linked the figures of Christ and king with a similitude—the "civil gift" of religion received by a compliant and grateful people in the secular reflection of religious devotion. *A Pattern* offers a strikingly different linking image, the bent knees of mocking and abusive obeisance, civil scorn. The title of this work makes it clear that James has tied himself to the figure of a discredited Christ and to a Sacrament for which he cannot enforce proper reverence. To borrow a phrase from Andrewes, neither Christ nor king have the power to say *noli* to anything. It is an oddly haunting final image, one with such representative resonance that Andrewes was clever enough to feature it in his Easter sermon of 1621. Here we see the king rewriting his autobiography in conjunction with his polemicists, transforming Great Britain's Solomon, the new Constantine, into a king defiled. James I had indeed lost control: not of policy, but of the language of policy.

The sermons and tracts examined above point out the significance of a simple gesture. Following the Black Rubric of 1552, criticism of nonconformity had centered upon the appearance—not the mentality—of kneeling, and thus the act itself remained open to a variety of religious interpretations. Once the interpretation fixed upon the Sacrament, the description of religious obeisance shifted away from the adiaphoric. These works demonstrate how a once familiar language of conformity could be transformed by the supercharged politics of anti-Puritanism of the late reign of James I. That the transformation was accomplished without the strong arm of royal enforcement makes it no less significant or real. The actual enforcement or nonenforcement of kneeling at communion in the Jacobean Church bears little relation to the utilization of the idea of kneeling as a rhetorical device in the polemic of the period.

A final important point to make requires our return to Andrewes's 1621 Easter sermon, and his insistence, through powerful and evocative physical imagery, that the presumptions of nonconformity were analogous to taking a impious swipe at the king. Andrewes continued this line of thought as we have seen above, developing a concept of unworthy touch that connected Jesus's warning to Mary Magdalen, the king's warning to tract-writing Puritans upset over ceremonies, and Andrewes's own warning to highly placed court ecclesiastics not to presume to contradict the king on matters of state like the Spanish match. And then, in what must have been one of his finest and most daring homiletic moments, Andrewes stepped over the line:

And if of the king's secrets this may truly be said, may it not as truly of God, of his secret decree? May not they, for their height and depth, claim to this *noli* too? Yes, sure; and I pray God, he be well pleased with this licentious touching, nay tossing his decrees of late; this sounding the depths of his judgements with our line and lead, too much presumed upon by some in these days of ours. *Judicia eius abyssus multa* (saith the psalmist): His judgements are the great deep. St. Paul, looking down into it, ran back and cried, O the depth! the profound depth! not to be searched, past our fathoming or finding out. Yet are there in the world that make but a shallow of this great deep, they have sounded it to the bottom. God's secret decrees they have them at their fingers' ends, can tell you the number and order of them just, with 1.2.3.4.5 . . . Mary Magdalen's touch was nothing to these.[61]

This is a passage that begs us to picture the great preacher: undoubtedly, at this point in the sermon, Andrewes dramatically raised his hands and counted. The five points he ticked off on his own fingers' ends certainly must have referred to the five Calvinist articles recently ratified at the Synod of Dort: finally, Lancelot Andrewes was ready to declare there was an essential con-

nection between the doctrine of predestination and a nonconformity he had long been willing to label as politically radical
and worse than popery. The effect must have been electrifying.
Here the language of gesture and the gesture itself merge, as
rhetoric calls forth—as it was designed to do—action.

Words, however, are not actors here; people manipulating
words are. If we examine the debate over kneeling against the
backdrop of political developments in the later reign of James I,
we find a language initiated by Calvinist conformists and re-
shaped by anti-Calvinist conformists. The latter would seize the
polemical initiative in the next reign, at which time they could
claim the considerable advantage of a tradition to support their
once-suppressed doctrinal assertions. The rhetorical re-sacraliz-
ing of the act of kneeling was to be the first warning of more
trouble to come. The development of a new polemic emphasizing the beauty of holiness in terms of eucharistic practice set the
tone for the disastrous ecclesiastical policies of the 1630's.

CHAPTER SIX

The Politics of Memory

If the cultural origins of the English Civil War can be traced, at least in part, to Laudian ecclesiastical policy, then the discursive origins of that policy can be found, at least in part, in the sermons of the Jacobean court. In this book I have traced the development of an anti-Puritan conformist polemic that had both the capacity and the opportunity to transform the notions of Puritanism that had governed the Church of England since the later Elizabethan period. We have seen the "Jacobethan" religious settlement, under which Calvinist orthodoxy was assumed and ceremonial practice was adiaphoric, transformed into a settlement under which Calvinism was contested and ceremony took on an unprecedented soteriological significance.

This change, it seems safe to say, was startling and fundamentally destabilizing, but it also gives both the Laudian and the Puritan (to use two very general and problematic, if contemporary, adjectives) arguments of the 1630's an uncannily familiar ring. While petitioners complained that ecumenism and sacramentalism were Caroline innovations tending to Rome and demanded a return to the certainties of the Elizabethan and Jacobean religious settlement, William Laud claimed that he was only defending the faith outlined in the 1604 canons and the definition of English Protestantism saved for posterity in the works of clerics like Lancelot Andrewes. Both sides deployed entirely defensible and supportable arguments, which gives us some insight into the complexity of James's polemical mode of government.

James's preachers were not, on the whole, anti-Calvinist or ultra-sacramentalist. Records of preaching appointments and the work of the Jacobean episcopate provide evidence that the Church of England under James consisted in the main of Calvinist conformists who were often sympathetic to the Puritan desire to rid the English Church of its unreformed ceremonies and polity. The record left to us in printed sermons, however, suggests that published court sermons most often featured an indiscriminate anti-Puritanism that could be deployed against even conformable Puritans within the Jacobean religious settlement. Published sermons issuing from the court thus challenge our picture of the religious settlement defended by the Jacobean episcopate and (especially in the early years of his reign) the king himself.

Some general comments are in order. Much of the disparity between the print culture of court religious polemics and the actual operations of James VI and I's ecclesiastical establishment can be attributed to the method of governing preferred by the king. The chronology of publication for court sermons and Paul's Cross sermons by court preachers shows an upswing in certain years: 1603–4, the period spanning the accession and Hampton Court Conference; 1606, the year after the Gunpowder Plot when the Scottish ministers were censured by sermon at Hampton Court, and 1617–18, the years of the conformity campaign in Scotland and the worsening crisis in England over the Spanish match. This suggests that the king's favorite method of dealing with threats to his authority took a remarkably logocentric turn, featuring the triple threat of the publication of court sermons (in addition to James's own religious works), publication of the 1604 canons, and the requirement of written subscription to those canons rather than the actual performance of conformity.

Also important to our understanding of government by polemic is the extent to which the publication of court sermons frequently and primarily addressed James's problems as king of Scotland. This is particularly apparent in the printed sermons of 1606 (the sermons censuring the Scots at Hampton Court account for more than a third of all court sermons published that year— this despite the polemical imperatives of the discovery of the

Gunpowder Plot) and 1617–18, when James traveled to Scotland to impose the Articles of Perth upon an unwilling Kirk.

We have also seen how frequently the Scots figured (or were figured, in the rhetorical sense), for good or ill, in sermons inspired by James's accession and the 1604 Hampton Court conference. This does not mean that the English government in this period was dominated by a "British problem"; rather, it suggests strongly that the "government by pen" that James as an absentee king required in Scotland presented a rare opportunity for preachers to construct sermons with a dual Scottish and English anti-Puritan thrust. In so doing, they were able to incorporate by analogy their own interpretations of England's religious situation into their defense of James's ecclesiastical authority. The king's desire for what John Morrill has called "congruity" of his national churches led him to encourage and authorize the publication of a large number of such sermons.[1] These could easily be assimilated to the anti-Puritan agenda of ceremonialists at the Jacobean court, thereby making published court sermons from this period overwhelmingly anti-Puritan in their orientation. This evidence alone might persuade us to reconsider the claim that James I "balanced" the threats of Puritan and papist by hewing to a broad "middle way." This may well have been the king's general intent, but his specific and localized polemical requirements allowed many of his preachers to construct a very different governmental message.

The significance of these findings must be tempered by our realization that printed court sermons constituted a relatively small percentage of what was available from court and other pulpits of Jacobean England, and an infinitesimal proportion of all religious polemic published in this period. Despite the fact that there was more preaching at the Jacobean court than ever before, owing to James's overweening enthusiasm for the religion of the ear, only a fraction of the sermons preached at his court were printed during his reign. In my sample, the voice of Lancelot Andrewes stands out, with eleven sermons preached before the king also printed between 1603 and 1625, by far the largest number from a single court preacher in this period. (Next in line is the ambitious Calvinist conformist Anthony Maxey, with five, but his sermons were not published by the king's own printer, as those of Andrewes were.) This alone, however, should prompt us to reexamine the claim that Andrewes did not represent the mainstream of Jacobean religion, but rather an avant-garde challenge to its ceremonial and doctrinal consensus.

Although Andrewes's ecclesiastical style may have seemed only mildly important during James's reign (as proof that Andrewesian Protestantism was not central to James's religious outlook, historians are fond of pointing out that James passed him over for the post of archbishop of Canterbury), it became the hallmark of an ecclesiastical industry after his death. With the publication by William Laud and John Buckeridge of Andrewes's *Ninety-Six Sermons* in 1629, four years after the death of James I, the number of Jacobean court sermons in print almost doubled. After 1629, therefore, works by Andrewes constitute about half of all the printed sermons available to readers looking for clues as to the nature of the Jacobean religious settlement.[2]

Andrewes has long been considered the premier example of Anglicanism—the proudest jewel in the crown of English pulpit oratory. But this is a mistake that confuses a later history with an earlier. It is largely owing to the thorough work of Laud and Buckeridge, although also because of the tireless efforts of ecclesiastical and literary historians to keep the flame of Anglo-Catholicism burning, that Andrewes has enjoyed such a lengthy and undisputed posthumous reign over the rhetoric of the early Stuart Church. The Anglican enthusiasms of (among many others) Cardinal John Henry Newman and T. S. Eliot, who promoted a sacramental and meditative religion of the *via media*, have kept the myth of "the church of Andrewes" alive.[3] Subsequently, tireless Church of England historians, determined to promote the status quo ante, have read the history of the nineteenth-century Church back into that of the early seventeenth-century Church.[4]

In the context of the Jacobean court, Lancelot Andrewes more accurately functions as the representative voice of a small group of preachers whose styles of divinity challenged the predominant understanding of mainstream Church of England clergy at the turn of the seventeenth century. Andrewes differed from most of his court-preaching colleagues in two respects: his theology was anti-Calvinist, and his personal piety was "formalist," or sacramentalist. The first, for James and other court preachers, may well have seemed negligible until the 1620's: doctrine was seldom explicated at length in the court pulpit, or on national holidays. The second aspect of Andrewes's thought is more significant, leading us to consider its relation to what Maxey would have called "the religion the king is of." Andrewes was allowed to expound upon his sacramentalist leanings (as were other likeminded preachers) at times when James was under attack for not reforming the Church sufficiently or for attempting to bring the Kirk into conformity. This Andrewesian polemic, which was more boldly (if crudely) explicated by men like John Buckeridge, was especially distinct at the end of James's reign and laid the groundwork for the Laudian campaign against Calvinist "Puritanism."[5]

Puritans did not enjoy the regard and admiration of any of James's preachers; as we have seen, they were the object of pulpit scorn and contumely on any occasion that called for official preaching. But "Puritan" meant different things to different people. The term functioned as a handy catch-all pejorative label, one that until late in James's reign moved through a series of very subtle but significant transformations. James's concept of Puritanism was derived from his Scottish experience, but it was vulnerable to the biases of his English episcopate. Very few ministers were actually deprived for nonconformity under James; many were allowed some scruples as long as they protested their allegiance to James and promised a reasonable degree of conformity. Good intentions counted in the Jacobean Church. "[Use] justice upon the obstinate, [show] grace to the penitent, and [enlarge] them that seem a little schooled by the rod of affliction," James wrote to Robert Cecil after the Hampton Court conference, in the tones of an aggrieved but indulgent father.[6]

For most of the reign, James's preachers pursued their monarch's dreams of moderation, transforming them through the intriguingly polarized language of inter-Protestant factional rivalry. This was not a clash of "Anglican" and "Puritan," but of two different types of court conformists; the very internality of this debate lent it a quality of claustrophobic tension. Thus we have the ironic experience of reading sermons by court preachers that denounce Scotland on the day a Scottish king came to rule England; that denounce Puritans on a day that celebrated the discovery of a Catholic Plot; that preach international ecumenism while denouncing Protestant brethren at home; and that offer up the image of a crucified monarch in order to highlight the king's authority in the face of political opposition.

James appeared personally to prefer "preaching" Protestantism to "praying" Protestantism, especially in the first half of his reign: he was notorious for abruptly ending the liturgy upon his entrance into the Chapel Royal and ordering the sermon to begin immediately. In any case, James's establishment of an extra day of sermons at court every week in honor of his delivery from the Gowries and the Gunpowder Plotters would have been sufficient demonstration of his enthusiasm for the preaching ministry.[7] This made gaining his ear easier, perhaps, but even more, it made it crucial. And thus we have the ultimate irony: that a group of formalist, anti-Puritan ecclesiastics were forced to do their special pleading from the persistent vantage point of a pulpit. Their many sermons warning against a religion based on preaching not only stocked the Caroline anti-Calvinist magazine but also bequeathed to an admiring posterity the glorious imageries of the "golden age of pulpit oratory." Avant-garde, indeed!

Court preachers wielded a serious, intentional, and public language; their typology of Puritanism produced an unforgettable and influential cultural portrait. The maintenance of an assumed but ambiguously articulated common orthodoxy could not last long in a world where words possessed such substantiality. Like all such politically intentioned rhetoric, Jacobean court sermons may have had temporary aims, but their essence remained to be exploited during the next reign. William Laud could point proudly to the work of a preacher whose words had pleased James for reasons of state and personal vanity and just as pointedly ignore the Calvinist, reforming legacy of the Jacobean court pulpit, rapidly fading in the bright sun of Andrewes's posthumous reputation.[8]

By remembering the Calvinist consensus of which many Jacobean court preachers were a part, however, we can best understand the real dilemma of the official pulpit and move beyond the question of court Calvinism. What we learn from court sermons is how political necessity allowed James's preachers precipitously to alter the very definition of Calvinism by associating its doctrinal content with the cultural and political offenses of Puritanism, which almost all court preachers had denigrated steadily throughout the reign. Herein we observe the peculiar function of court-sermon rhetoric in this period. While James used it as a tool for instruction and a kind of correction, we have seen (for example, in the case of nonconformity) that it often bore no tangible relation to the execution of his actual policies. In this sense, court sermons were ephemeral: offering points and counterpoints, they constantly redrew the artificial boundaries of a construct called "moderation" in response to events and demands. But in another sense, these same ephemera had the power to create a discourse of exclusion that redefined the meaning and significance of nonconformity. The result was the most dangerous and far-reaching schism in the history of the post-Reformation Church of England. The need to erase this divisive legacy led first to the myth of an Anglican *via media*, as defined by Andrewes, and then, much later, to the myth of the "moderate" Church, defined by revisionist scholars.

To read published Jacobean court sermons and many Paul's Cross sermons is to trace the failure of the Calvinist consensus. And it should lead us to question the use of the term *avant-garde* to describe preachers such as Andrewes and Buckeridge, who were so publicly identified with the opinions of the king. In one sense, of course, that of artistic influence, Andrewes was a model of the avant-garde: his style of preaching—and, ultimately, his ecclesiology of the "beauty of holiness"—had a catalytic effect, not only on the Laudians, but even on the king and on Calvinist conformists at court. (And, like modern avant-garde artists, in fact, he and his cohort also spent much time seeking preferment by ambitious self-promotion.) But the prominence in print polemic of Andrewes and his imitators reminds us that the rhetorics of conformity that supported James I were their creation and responsibility from 1603 to 1625. It is more accurate to describe this style of polemic, ecclesiology, and, ultimately, doctrine as consistently dominant in the claustrophobic but powerful world of the court—a force that, given a few shifts in the political climate, was capable of relegating moderate Puritans and the bishops who indulged them to roles as dangerous schismatics.

A final look at some later Laudian polemic will demonstrate the progress of the Jacobean campaign to establish the "moderate" mainstream of English Protestant thought in Andrewesian formalism rather than in mere adiaphoric conformity. In 1638, the anti-Puritan controversialist Christopher Dow pointed to the reluctant conformists of the Jacobean period as the ideological forebears of Caroline "doctrinal Puritanism."[9] While stubborn nonconformists had been deprived of their livings after the Hampton Court conference of 1604, Dow claimed, other like-minded clergy had "yield[ed] a kind of conformity" in public while privately continuing to express their "dis-affection" for the enjoined ceremonies. Unwilling to risk losing their ministry, yet as unwilling to be visible examples of conformity, these men employed a stratagem:

[T]hey did wisely avoid all occasions that might draw them to the public profession of conformity by using the ceremonies, and betook themselves to the work of preaching, placing themselves . . . in Lectures and . . . getting conformable Curates under them to bear the burden of the ceremonies. Thus saving themselves, and maintaining their reputation with the people, they gained the opportunity to instill into them their principles, not only of dislike of the Church-government and rites, but also of the doctrine established.[10]

Dow locates the source of 1630's theological conflict in Jacobean moderate Puritanism, the very same phenomenon that has inspired recent historians to cite the Jacobean religious settlement as a model of consensus. Most significant, therefore, is Dow's contention that moderate Puritan clergy had been overrepresented as preachers in the previous reign, and that their unimpeded access to the pulpit allowed them to promote a heterodox Calvinism that resulted from, rather than inspired, their disdain for ceremonial conformity.[11]

Dow's tract is a Laudian propagandist's portrayal of Puritanism[12] that confirms the peculiar substantiality of rhetoric. He defines "real" (and by this he means more dangerous) separatism as a domestic, discursive phenomenon. But the lexicon of Puritanism, if Dow is to be our witness, appears to have been as moderate on its surface as was the behavior of the Jacobean "Puritan" clergy he condemns:

[They] made, though not a local (as some more zealous among them have, by removing to Amsterdam and New-England) yet a real separation, accounting themselves the "wheat among the tares," and monopolizing the names of "Christians," "God's Children," "Professors," and the like: styling their doctrine, "The Gospel," "The Word," and their Preachers, "The Ministers," "The Good Ministers," "Powerful Preachers," and by such other distinctive names.[13]

To us, perhaps, the "names" in which Dow saw such dangerous intent are not all that distinctive: there is nothing overtly presumptuous or potentially radical, surely, about Protestants calling their doctrine "The Gospel" or their preachers "The Good Ministers." The people speaking these words, however, were distinctive; Dow's audience would have recognized this language as characteristic Puritan expression. This is the process by which ordinary words, and the concepts they describe, become controversial. It is also the reason why scholars, reading resolutely across the surface of seemingly unremarkable discourse, can be fooled by a deceptive, elaborately coded ordinariness. What Dow is actually proclaiming in 1638 is the capture of the rhetorical mainstream by the forces of Laudianism. Any monopoly on words went by rights to the victors.

Dow's tract thus demonstrates the peculiar triumph of anti-Puritan rhetoric in the reign of Charles I, but his words would have been unsupportable without the foundations provided by the anti-Puritan rhetoric of James and his preachers. The alienation of what had been a conformable, assimilable Puritanism was fully accomplished when Jacobean rhetoric was backed up by new and provocative Caroline action. This is not to say that Jacobean government by polemic was by contrast less effective. The power granted to words in this logocentric age eloquently testifies to its substantiality.

Reference Matter

Notes

The following abbreviations are used throughout the notes:

CSPD	*Calendar of State Papers, Domestic Series, for the Reign of James I* (4 vols., for 1603–25; London, 1857)
CSP (Ven.)	*Calendar of State Papers (Venetian), 1603–7* (London, 1900)
CTJI	Thomas Birch, *The Court and Times of James I* (2 vols.; London, 1848)
DNB	*Dictionary of National Biography* (London and New York, 1885–1993)
JBS	*Journal of British Studies*
OED	*Oxford English Dictionary*
Venn	John Venn and J. A. Venn, *Alumni cantabrigienses: A Biographical List of All Known Students, Graduates and Holders of Office at the University of Cambridge, from the Earliest Times to 1900* (10 vols.; Cambridge, Eng., 1922–54)
Wood	Anthony Wood, *Alumni oxonienses: The Members of the University of Oxford, 1600–1714; Their Parentage, Birthplace, and Year of Birth, with a Record of Their Degrees. Being the Matriculation Register of the University, Alphabetically Arranged, Revised and Annotated,* ed. Joseph Foster (4 vols.; Oxford and London, 1891–92)

Chapter 1

1. Notable exceptions appear almost exclusively in the Donne literary camp: to cite a few examples, R. Strier, "Donne and the Politics of Devotion," in *Religion, Literature and Politics in Post-Reformation England, 1540–1688,* ed. D. Hamilton and R. Strier (Cambridge, Eng., 1995), 93–114, and the scholars in the special double issue "Donne as Preacher," *John Donne Journal* 11, nos. 1–2 (1992).

2. These historians and their works include P. Collinson, *The Religion of Protestants* (Oxford, 1992); N. R. N. Tyacke, *Anti-Calvinists: The Rise of English Arminianism c. 1590–1640* (Oxford and New York, 1987); K. Fincham and P. Lake, "The Ecclesiastical Policy of James I," *JBS* 24,

no. 2 (April 1985): 173–92; id., "The Ecclesiastical Policies of James I and Charles I," in *The Early Stuart Church*, ed. K. Fincham (Stanford, 1993), 23–50; and K. Fincham, *Prelate as Pastor: The Episcopate of James I* (Oxford and New York, 1990).

3. M. Todd, "Introduction," in *Reformation to Revolution: Politics and Religion in Early Modern England* (London, 1995), 5.

4. For a succinct account of Whig historiography, see D. Underdown, *A Freeborn People: Politics and the Nation in Seventeenth-Century England* (Oxford, 1996), 1–3.

5. See Kevin Sharpe's survey of the historiographical landscape, "Religion, Rhetoric, and Revolution in Seventeenth-Century England," *Huntington Library Quarterly* 58, no. 3 (July 1995): 255–58.

6. J. Morrill, "The Religious Context of the British Civil War," *Transactions of the Royal Historical Society*, 5th ser., 34 (1984): 155–78, recently reprinted in J. Morrill, *The Nature of the English Revolution: Essays by John Morrill* (London, 1993), 45–68.

7. Todd, "Introduction," 3. Underdown calls this recourse to religious conflict the "big bang theory of civil war" (*Freeborn People*, 6).

8. N. R. N. Tyacke, "Puritanism, Arminianism, and Counter-Revolution," in *The Origins of the English Civil War*, ed. C. Russell (London, 1973), 119–43, and id., *Anti-Calvinists*.

9. Fincham and Lake, "Ecclesiastical Policy of King James I," 173–92, later expanded and updated as "Ecclesiastical Policies of James I and Charles I." See also Fincham, *Prelate as Pastor*, passim.

10. Collinson, *Religion of Protestants*; id., "Protestant Culture and the Cultural Revolution," in *The Birthpangs of Protestant England: Religious and Cultural Change in the Sixteenth and Seventeenth Centuries* (New York, 1988), 94–126; and id., *Godly People* (London, 1983).

11. In point of fact, these historians are often identified (when such identification is called for) as "counter-revisionists," since their analyses invariably demonstrate that religion was a point of contention in this period. See Todd, "Introduction," 8.

12. The description of this anti-reformist view, which was associated with a number of preaching clerics at the Jacobean court, as avant-garde, comes from Peter Lake, "Lancelot Andrewes, John Buckeridge, and *Avant-garde* Conformity at the Jacobean Court," in *The Mental World of the Jacobean Court*, ed. L. Peck (Cambridge, Eng., 1991), 113–33.

13. Sharpe, "Religion, Rhetoric, and Revolution," 257.

14. Chief among these are K. Sharpe, *The Personal Rule of Charles I* (New Haven, Conn., 1993), and P. White, *Predestination, Policy and Polemic: Conflict and Consensus in the English Church from the Reformation to the Civil War* (Cambridge, Eng., 1992).

15. M. Lee, Jr., *Government by Pen: Scotland Under James VI and I* (Urbana, Ill., 1980).

16. These roots are discussed by C. Haigh, *English Reformations: Religion, Politics, and Society Under the Tudors* (Oxford, 1993), in a thesis that challenges A. G. Dickens's *The English Reformation* (1964; 2d ed., London, 1989). Dickens's was for years the undisputed narrative of sixteenth-century English Protestantism; various scholarly challenges to Dickens's view of a successful and devoutly wished-for Reformation have been summarized by Haigh, "The Recent Historiography of the English Reformation," *Historical Journal* 25 (1982): 995–1007.

17. The old view begins with Anthony Weldon's scurrilous *Court and Character of King James: Written and Taken by Sir A. W.* (London, 1650), often underlines Gardiner's account of the reign, and appears to have infected all modern biographies of James until M. Lee, Jr., *Great Britain's Solomon* (Chicago, 1990). For a more balanced view, see M. Schwartz, "James I and the Historians: Toward a Reconsideration," *JBS* 13 (1974): 114–34; J. Wormald, "James VI and I: Two Kings or One?" *History* 68 (1983): 187–209; and the prevailing temper of the essays in *Mental World of the Jacobean Court*, ed. Peck.

18. By *ecclesiology*, I mean churchmanship as defined in attitudes to the outward face of worship, rather than the study of church buildings.

19. The phrase "Calvinist consensus" is modern; see P. Lake, *Moderate Puritans and the Elizabethan Church* (Cambridge, Eng., 1982), 227, cited in G. Bernard, "The Church of England, c. 1529–c. 1642," *History* 75, no. 244 (June 1990): 192n.

20. The authorial side of James has recently been given some welcome attention by Kevin Sharpe, "The King's Writ: Royal Authors and Royal Authority in Early Modern England," in *Problems in Focus: Culture and Politics in Early Stuart England*, ed. K. Sharpe and P. Lake (London: 1994), 117–38, and "Private Conscience and Public Duty in the Writings of King James VI and I," in *Public Duty and Private Conscience in Seventeenth Century England*, ed. J. Morrill, P. Slack, and D. Wolfe (Oxford, 1993), 77–100; the introductions to both twentieth-century collections of James's writings have also been helpful: see *The Political Works of James I*, ed. C. H. McIlwain (1918; rpt., New York, 1965), and *King James VI and I: Political Writings*, ed. J. P. Sommerville (Cambridge, Eng., and New York, 1994). Sommerville has astutely opened up the range of James's "political works" by including treatises on religion that McIlwain thought apolitical; McIlwain's approach would have been anathema to the king's first editor, the dean of his Chapel Royal, James Montague, whose introduction to James's works in 1616 remains the best evidence of the impact these works had in their

own time: see *The Workes of that most High and Mightie Prince James . . . Published by James Bp. of Winton. and Deane of his Majesties Chappell Royall* (London, 1616).

21. M. MacLure, *The Paul's Cross Sermons, 1534–1642* (Toronto, 1958), is the most recent work on Paul's Cross sermons. Forthcoming from Cambridge University Press is Peter McCullough's *The Sermon at the Court of Elizabeth and James*. I thank Dr. McCullough, who is a scholar of English literature, for allowing me to read the Jacobean portion of his manuscript in full prior to publication. The books of both MacLure and McCullough feature extensive calendars of sermons: MacLure's, while badly needing an update, has been—as McCullough's will be—indispensable to the study of the sermons of this period.

22. J. Shami, "Introduction: Reading Donne's Sermons," *John Donne Journal* 11 (1992): 2.

23. For example, see W. Fraser Mitchell, *English Pulpit Oratory from Andrewes to Tillotson* (London, 1932), 335; or the description of John Preston in J. Chandos, *In God's Name: Examples of Preaching in England from the Act of Supremacy to the Act of Uniformity, 1534–1662* (Indianapolis, 1971), 287. Certainly, the introductions to the many volumes of the magisterial collection of Donne's sermons edited by G. R. Potter and E. M. Simpson tend to turn these works into background material for the poetry. This last issue is addressed by Jeanne Shami in her excellent preface to *John Donne Journal* 11 (1992): 2–3, 7.

24. I discuss the significance of this legacy and its peculiar print history briefly in the conclusion to this book.

25. L. A. Ferrell, "Donne and His Master's Voice, 1615–1625," *John Donne Journal* 11, nos. 1–2 (1992): 68.

26. L. A. Ferrell, "Kneeling and the Body Politic," in *Religion, Literature and Politics,* ed. Hamilton and Strier, 70–92.

27. Fincham, "Introduction," 6–10; N. R. N. Tyacke, "The Fortunes of English Puritanism 1603–1640" (London, 1989), 121.

28. P. Collinson, *The Elizabethan Puritan Movement* (Oxford, 1990), 461.

29. James I, *Apology for the Oath of Allegiance,* in *Political Works of James I,* ed. McIlwain.

30. Quoted in J. Nichols, *The Progresses . . . of James I* (London, 1828), 2: 286–87.

31. B. Galloway, *The Union of England and Scotland* (Edinburgh, 1986), 173.

32. D. G. Mullan, *Episcopacy in Scotland: The History of an Idea* (Edinburgh, 1986), 98–102.

33. An earlier version of Chapter 5 was previously published, under the same title, in *Post-Reformation England,* ed. Hamilton and Strier.

Chapter 2

1. R. Wakeman, *Salomons Exaltation: A Sermon Preached Before the King at Nonesuch, April 30 1605* (1605), 13.

2. J. Wormald, "The Union of 1603," in *Scots and Britons: Scottish Political Thought and the Union of 1603*, ed. R. Mason (Cambridge, Eng., 1994), 18–19.

3. Parliamentary speech of 19 March 1603/4, first printed as *The Kings Majestys Speech as it was delivered by him in the Upper House of the Parliament, to the Lords Spiritual and Temporal, and to the Knights, Citizens and Burgesses there assembled* (London: 1604), sigs.B.*v–r*; reprinted in *The Political Writings of James VI and I*, ed. J. P. Sommerville (Cambridge, Eng., and New York, 1994), 135.

4. The problem of multiple kingdoms has been brought to our attention by Conrad Russell, *The Causes of the English Civil War* (Oxford, 1990), and id., *The Fall of the British Monarchies, 1637–1642: The Ford Lectures Delivered in the University of Oxford, 1987–8* (Oxford, 1991).

5. Relatively few pages of either Nicholas Tyacke's *Anti-Calvinists: The Rise of English Arminianism, c. 1590–1640* (Oxford, 1987) or, more recently, Anthony Milton's *Catholic and Reformed: The Roman and Protestant Churches in English Protestant Thought, 1600–1640* (Cambridge, Eng., 1995) discuss the problems posed by Scotland or the influence of its example in English religious debate prior to the late 1630's.

6. K. Fincham and P. Lake, "The Ecclesiastical Policies of James I and Charles I," in *The Early Stuart Church*, ed. K. Fincham (Stanford, 1993), 23, 29. See also J. Morrill, "A British Patriarchy? Ecclesiastical Imperialism Under the Early Stuarts," in *Religion, Culture and Society in Early Modern Britain: Essays in Honour of Patrick Collinson*, ed. A. Fletcher and P. Roberts (Cambridge, Eng., 1994), 209–37.

7. Some of John Gordon's writings are analyzed later in this chapter.

8. B. Levack, *The Formation of the British State: England, Scotland, and the Union, 1603–1707* (Oxford, 1987), 114–15.

9. W. Ferguson, *Scotland's Relations with England to 1707* (Edinburgh, 1977), 78–80; D. G. Mullan, *Episcopacy in Scotland: The History of an Idea* (Edinburgh, 1986), ch. 2, passim.

10. J. Wormald, "James VI and I: Two Kings or One?" *History* 68 (1983): 194–96.

11. Mullan, *Episcopacy in Scotland*, ch. 3, passim; J. Kirk, "The Polities of the Best Reformed Kirks: Scottish Achievements and English Aspirations in Church Government After the Reformation," *Scottish Historical Review* 59 (1980): 42–43; Morrill, "British Patriarchy," 210–12.

12. Peter McCullough has demonstrated that there was a concerted behind-the-scenes effort by Archbishop Whitgift and the bishop of

London, Richard Bancroft, to pack the court-preaching *rota* with chaplains who could be counted upon to hold a stern line against what they feared would be an influx of Scots presbyterian preachers coming south with the king after his accession. Their fears were unjustified, but they also resulted in what McCullough terms "one of the more significant changes from an Elizabethan to a Jacobean court religious life": the appointment of a dean of the chapel to oversee the religious services of the court. See McCullough, *The Sermon at the Court of Elizabeth I and James I* (Cambridge, Eng., forthcoming, 1998).

13. Cf. Morrill, "British Patriarchy," who challenges Conrad Russell's claim that the early Stuarts "sought to anglicize (or in ecclesiastical terms anglicanize) all three of their kingdoms"; it worked the other way around, at least in the English court. For James's view, see Wormald, "Union of 1603," 33–34.

14. Levack, *Formation*, 103.

15. Not so Conrad Russell, who calls James's claim to the 1604 Parliament that his kingdoms were "already united in religion" a "bluffing assertion . . . sustained by a largely cosmetic series of adjustments to both churches" (Russell, *Causes*, 45).

16. For examples, see *The Jacobean Union: Six Tracts of 1604*, ed. B. Galloway and B. Levack (Edinburgh, 1985). While Levack does examine some aspects of ecclesiastical union, he devotes most of his energies to the 1630's, 1660's, and 1707, and he is primarily interested in the problems posed by union in ecclesiastical government. In *The Causes of the English Civil War*, Conrad Russell devotes the lion's share of one Ford lecture to Anglo-Scottish religious differences in James's reign, and, like Levack, he appears interested in the main by problems of Church government. This may explain why Russell claims that James's main problem with his two churches was economic rather than ecclesiastical. Generally speaking, historians of Scotland have done rather better with this topic, in part because James's reimposition of episcopacy on Scotland during this period was a major development in the history of the Kirk, and in part because contemporary Scottish writers often seem more concerned about the state of the Church of England than English writers were about the state of the Kirk.

17. Robert Pont, *De Unione Britanniae Seu De Regnorum Angliae et Scotiae* (Edinburgh, 1604): "Calumnia hec est. In doctrina enim optimum conveniunt. Quod autem quaedam est in disciplina diversitas religioni non adeo obest, quin bona consistat inter regna harmonia et Ecclesiarum unitas."

18. Robert Pont, "Of the Union of Britayne" (translation of *De Unione Britanniae*), in *Jacobean Union*, ed. Galloway and Levack, 7–8.

19. Pont's tract also demonstrates a hopeful optimism about religious unity (if doomed to failure) that is notably missing from Scottish writers who did not look to the king's patronage. These writers, all representatives of the Kirk, warned against the pollution of the Kirk by the example of a ceremonially unreformed, episcopal Church of England (Morrill, "British Patriarchy?" 212).

20. Francis Bacon, *A Breif Discourse of the Happy Union of the Kingdoms of England and Scotland, with Certain Articles concerning the same* (rpt., London, 1700), 16–17.

21. Levack, *Formation*, 114.

22. But cf. Conrad Russell, "The Anglo-Scottish Union, 1603–1643: A Success?" in *Religion, Culture and Society in Early Modern Britain: Essays in Honour of Patrick Collinson*, ed. A. Fletcher and P. Roberts (Cambridge, Eng., 1994), 243. Russell calls Anglo-Scottish relations in this period a "cooperation across the border with co-religionists," rather than cooperation with fellow Britons.

23. But see P. Lake, *Anglicans and Puritans? Presbyterianism and English Conformist Thought from Whitgift to Hooker* (London and Boston, 1988), 164–69, for Richard Hooker's view, later taken up by some Church of England clergy, that retention of ceremonies was positive theology.

24. The mixed reactions of English Puritans to this rhetoric remind us that their attitudes to conformity were as diverse as the ways in which they interpreted the bounds of the adiaphoric. See J. S. Coolidge, *The Pauline Renaissance in England: Puritanism and the Bible* (Oxford, 1970), 56–58.

25. 1559 Book of Common Prayer, "Of Ceremonies." I owe this brief discussion of *adiaphora*, always a tricky term to define both well and succinctly, to the *Oxford Dictionary of the Christian Church* and the discussion provided by Lake, *Anglicans and Puritans?* 16–17.

26. See Fincham and Lake, "Ecclesiastical Policies of James I and Charles I," 25, for the authors' contention that this was a "key statement of royal intent," aimed at making a clear distinction between radical and moderate opinion.

27. *BASILIKON DORON, or His Majesties Instructions to his Dearest Sonne, Henry the Prince* (1599; rpt., London, 1603), sig. A7v.; also reprinted in *King James VI and I: Political Writings*, ed. Sommerville, 6–7.

28. Morrill contends that James did not intend there to be an "institutional union" of his Scottish and English churches, but does not question how the king's polemic and that of his propagandists might have left readers and listeners with that idea ("British Patriarchy," 214–21).

29. See Chapter 4.

30. *The Kings Majesties Speech as it was Delivered by Him*, sig. B2r., reprinted in *The Political Works of James VI and I*, ed. C. H. McIlwain (1918; rpt., New York, 1965), 272. See also M. J. Enright, "King James and His Island: An Archaic Kingship Belief?" *Scottish History Review* 55, nos. 159–60 (1975): 29–32, in which James's language is called "almost a commonplace," with antecedents as diverse as puritan and Celtic traditions; and D. Daitches, *Scotland and the Union* (London, 1977), 17, on "Quae Deux coniunxit nemo Separit."

31. J. G. A. Pocock, "Two Kingdoms and Three Histories?" in *Scots and Britons: Scottish Political Thought and the Union of 1603*, ed. R. Mason (Cambridge, Eng., 1994), 303.

32. *CSPD 1603–10*, 230, 321, 334, 348, 364, 408; *CSP (Ven.)*, 456; and *Dictionary of National Biography* entry for James Hay for an account of the negotiations, the father of the bride's reluctance to see his daughter marry a Scot, and the economic inducements offered by the king.

33. This sermon has attracted virtually no notice, but the sumptuous masque performed at the wedding festivities, which demonstrates the same themes in a theatrical genre, has been analyzed by David Lindley, *Thomas Campion* (Leiden, 1986), 176–90, and id., "Campion's Lord Hay's Masque and Anglo-Scottish Union," *Huntington Library Quarterly* 43, no. 1 (1979): 1–11. The masque may have been paid for by Robert Cecil, despite his dislike of the union scheme. See D. Lindley, "Who Paid for Campion's Lord Hay's Masque?" *Notes and Queries* 26, no. 2 (1979): 144–45.

34. R. Wilkinson, *The Merchant Royall. A Sermon Preached at Whitehall before the Kings Majestie* (London, 1607), sig. C3v–r.

35. Ibid., sigs. F1r–F2v.

36. This is not to say the more ambitious campaign was a total failure: trade had been regularized between the two kingdoms and a significant legal victory was achieved in the case of the *post-nati*: see B. Galloway, *The Union of England and Scotland, 1603–1608* (Edinburgh, 1986), 151–57.

37. Wilkinson, *Merchant Royall*, sig.B4v.

38. It was this act that unleashed the largest flood of union-related tracts between 1603 and 1605. See *Jacobean Union*, ed. Galloway and Levack, xxx.

39. Some tracts interpreted the proclamation as anti-parliamentary rather than as a limited and legitimate display of the king's authority. See Galloway, *Union of England and Scotland*, 20–21, 28–29.

40. T. Bilson, *A Sermon Preached at Westminster before the King and Queenes Majesties at their Coronation* [1603], sigs. A6v–A7r: "The likeness

that princes have with the kingdom of God and of Christ consisteth in the society of their names. . . . As Christ giveth Princes his name by calling them Gods and Sons of the most High: so he taketh their Names and Signs to show the unity and sovereignty of his kingdom, and to sever itself from all other kinds of government." For this claim on behalf of the royal supremacy, see also sig. C5v–C7r.

41. Russell, *Causes*, 47–48.

42. Wormald, "Union of 1603," 27–28. The English were not the only ones concerned about what this would mean; the anti-episcopal faction of the Kirk also feared the anglocentric consequences of religious union. See M. Lee, Jr., *Government by Pen: Scotland Under James VI and I* (Urbana, Ill., 1980), 31–32.

43. At least according to the author, John Gordon, *Henotikon: Or a Sermon of the Union of Great Britain in Antiquity of Language, name, religion, kingdom: preached by John Gordon Dean of Salisbury, the 28 day of October 1604, in presence of the King Majesty at Whitehall* (London, 1604), 17.

44. Ibid., 22–23.

45. Ibid., 24.

46. Ibid., 50.

47. One issue not investigated here is the economic aspect of union: Gordon appears to be focused, not merely on unity as a religious mandate, but on how such a unity demanded parity between the English and the Scots in matters of "dignities, honours and preferments" (13, 16, 18–19). This sermon certainly supports Levack's contention that the main problem between English and Scottish Protestants was the English fear of losing benefices (Levack, *Formation*, 118–19).

48. For the internationalist dimension to Scottish apocalyptic thought, and its comparison to the English variety, which was nationalist in scope, see A. Williamson, *Scottish National Consciousness in the Age of James VI* (Edinburgh, 1979), 21.

49. The less dutiful were delighted, of course, with the opportunity opened up with the accession; see, e.g., Miles Mosse, *Scotlands Welcome: A Sermon Preached at Needham* (London, 1603). My thanks to Patrick Collinson for pointing out this treatise.

50. For earlier hopeful attempts along these lines, see G. Donaldson, "The Attitude of Bancroft and Whitgift to the Scottish Church," *Transactions of the Royal Historical Society* (1942): 95–115.

51. J. Hopkins, *A Sermon Preached before the King's Majesty* (London, 1604), sigs. C3v–4v. In 1604, Hopkins received an M.A. from Cambridge; he eventually became vicar of Great Wenham, Suffolk: Venn, 2:405.

52. Hopkins refers to Ezek. 37:17–22, wherein God instructs the

prophet to write the name of Israel on one stick, the name of Judah on the other, and hold them together. God promises that the stick "will become one" in the prophet's hand, thereby miraculously showing the people that "one king shall be king of them all, and they shall be no more two nations, neither shall they be divided into two kingdoms any more at all" (sigs. C3r–4v). The passage also confirms the preacher's own rhetorical strategy, in which vivid imagery provides the evident proof of the rightness of an idea.

53. Hopkins, *Sermon*, sig. B2r. The rhetorical figure Hopkins uses here is *acclamatio*, a succinct summing-up of the points of an argument, which is enhanced by his employment of *dissolutio*, a figure wherein connecting particles are absent in parallel clauses. See B. Vickers, *In Defence of Rhetoric* (Oxford, 1988), 493, 494.

54. Hopkins, *Sermon*, sigs. C8r–D4r.

55. Ibid., sigs. D4r–5v. Also see the conclusion to the quotation cited in the preceding paragraph, wherein Hopkins describes the alliance formed by England and Scotland as also including Ireland: "[W]e are that threefold gable which being well twisted, will not easily be broken" (sig. C4r). Morrill picks up on this familial language when discussing the Irish Church in "British Patriarchy," 212–14.

56. On the petitions, "millenary" and otherwise, see *SP 14/3/83*, letter of Bancroft and Whitgift to Cecil, dated 24 September 1603; B. W. Quintrell, "The Royal Hunt and the Puritans, 1604–1605," *Journal of Ecclesiastical History* 31 (1980): 43–59, and S. B. Babbage, *Puritanism and Richard Bancroft* (London, 1962), 43–73. Naturally, John Chamberlain observed and commented upon this outpouring of petitions; see T. Birch, *The Court and Times of James I* (London, 1848), 1: 7.

57. Sermons preached before the king in this period that particularly focused on the Solomonic virtues of justice, judgment, and wisdom include those by Rudd (1604, 1605); Hopkins (1604), already cited; and R. Smith, *The Black-smith* (1604).

58. R. Field, *A Learned Sermon Preached Before the King at Whitehall on Friday the 16 of March 1604* (London, 1604), sig. A7r.

59. Wakeman, *Salomons Exaltation*, 45–60, esp. 58–60.

60. Ibid., 25.

61. For differing views on the Hampton Court conference's impact on the puritan cause in England, see M. Curtis, "The Hampton Court Conference and Its Aftermath," *History* (1961): 1–16; F. Shriver, "Hampton Court Revisited: James I and the Puritans," *Journal of Ecclesiastical History* no. 32 (1982): 48–71; and Babbage, *Puritanism and Richard Bancroft*, 59–73. For the moderation of the Puritan representatives to the Conference, see P. Collinson, *The Elizabethan Puritan Movement* (London,

1967), 455, and P. Lake, *Moderate Puritans and the Elizabethan Church* (Cambridge, Eng., 1982), 247–48.

62. One of James's Scottish chaplains, Patrick Galloway, had encouraged the English nonconformists, implying that the king would look favorably upon their cause (Collinson, *Elizabethan Puritan Movement*, 451; Tyacke, *Anti-Calvinists*, 9).

63. L. A. Ferrell, "Kneeling and the Body Politic," in *Religion, Literature and Politics in Post-Reformation England, 1540–1688*, ed. D. Hamilton and R. Strier (Cambridge, Eng., 1995), 71–74.

64. R. Bancroft, *A Sermon Preached at Pauls Cross the 9 of February, being the first Sunday in the Parliament, Anno. 1588. by Richard Bancroft D. of Divinity and Chaplain to the Right Honorable Sir Christopher Hatton Knight and Lord Chancellor of England* (London, 1588), sig. E3v. The quotation is from Mic. 7:5–6,"Trust ye not in a friend . . . a man's enemies are the men of his own house." Significantly, this sermon was reprinted in 1636. Also important for the Elizabethan context is Bancroft's infamous *Dangerous Positions and Proceedings, published and Practiced within this Island of Britain, under pretense of Reformation and for the Presbyterial Discipline* (London, 1593), especially sigs. Ar–A2r, the "Contents of the Second Book," which demonstrates the bishop's preoccupation with the "railing" of Scottish-influenced English clergy against the established Church.

65. Bancroft was influenced by Archbishop Adamson's 1585 defense of the so-called "Black Acts," which established James's authority over the Kirk and his right to appoint bishops to oversee it; see R. Mason, "George Buchanan, James VI and the Presbyterians," in *Scots and Britons*, ed. Mason, 131–33.

66. The bishop of Durham's account of the Hampton Court Conference is in E. Cardwell, *A History of Conferences and Other Proceedings Connected With the Revision of the Book of Common Prayer from the Year 1558 to the Year 1690* (Oxford, 1840), 161–66; this is included with other accounts of the conference in Cardwell, 151–217. For William Barlow's more partisan anti-puritan account, *The Summe and Substance of the Conference* (London, 1604), see Cardwell, 167–212.

67. 1 Kings 3:7–10.

68. A. Rudd, *A Sermon Preached at the Court at Whitehall before the Kings Majesty upon Sunday being the 13. of May 1604* (London, 1604), 6–8. Rudd was appointed to the see of St. David's in 1594, where he remained until his death in 1615 (Venn, 3: 495; *DNB*).

69. Tyacke, *Anti-Calvinists*, 17; K. Fincham, "Episcopal Government, 1603–1640," in *Early Stuart Church*, ed. id., 75–76; and Milton, *Catholic and Reformed*, 21.

70. For another aspect of this confusion, seen through the lens provided by scurrilous underground prose, see A. Bellany, "A Poem for the Archbishop's Hearse," *JBS* 34 (April 1995): 137–64.

71. *CSP (Ven.)* 1603–7, 280: "The question of the Union will, I am assured, be dropped; for his Majesty is now well aware that nothing can be effected, both sides displaying such obstinacy that an accomodation is impossible; and so his Majesty is resolved to abandon the question for the present, in the hope that time may consume the ill-humours"; also quoted in Galloway, *Union of England and Scotland*, 80. The French ambassador had said much the same thing in 1604 (Lindley, *Campion*, 177, n.6). For the abandonment of the union issue in Parliament, see *CTJI*, I: 52, letter of the earl of Shrewsbury to Sir Thomas Edmondes, 12 February 1605/6. See also C. V. Wedgwood, "Anglo-Scottish Relations, 1603–1640," *Transactions of the Royal Historical Society* 32 (1950): 32. Wedgwood describes the period from the failure of the scheme in 1608 to the end of the reign as "quiescent," with the exception of James's "steady reorganization" of the Kirk.

72. J. Wormald, "Gunpowder, Treason and Scots," *JBS* 24 (April 1985): 157–68, esp. 161–64; Galloway, *Union of England and Scotland*, 79–81.

73. Pocock, "Two Kingdoms," 309–10.

74. Russell, *Fall*, 34.

75. This was after he had been summoned to a second Hampton Court conference with fellow presbyterians to be subjected to harangues on James's authority over the Church. The four sermons, preached by William Barlow, Lancelot Andrewes, John Buckeridge, and John King, were published in London and Oxford that same year. For a detailed analysis of this "second Hampton Court Conference," see pp. 125–32 above.

76. A. Maxey, "The Third Sermon. The Churches Sleepe," in *The Golden Chaine of Mans Salvation* (3d ed., London, 1607), sigs. L4r–M4r. Maxey, who has been described as a "simonist of the first water," was rector of several churches between 1591 and 1618. He eventually became dean of Windsor and Wolverhampton in 1612, although he campaigned tirelessly, sparing no expense, for the vacant see of Norwich in 1618, the year he died. The *DNB* contends that James was attracted to Maxey as much for his hatred of tobacco as for his "florid pulpit eloquence" (Venn, 3: 165; *CSPD* 1611–18, 532).

77. Maxey, "Third Sermon," sigs. I4r–5v. This sermon was first published in *The Churches Sleepe, expressed in a sermon preached at the court* (London, 1606).

78. The phrase "natural child" was in definitional flux in the early

seventeenth century; in public use it could connote either consanguinity, to distinguish these children from those adopted; or it could connote bastardy (*OED*).

79. On the 1604 canons, see Babbage, *Puritanism and Richard Bancroft*,
74–102. On the effects of the canons, see ibid., 375–78, and K. Fincham
and P. Lake, "The Ecclesiastical Policy of King James I," in *JBS* 24, no. 2
(April 1985): 174–79.

80. Maxey, "Third Sermon," sig. I4r.

81. On the conflicting attitudes in England to the example of the Genevan Church, see Milton, *Catholic and Reformed*, 400–401, 427–28, 450.

82. For the actions that landed the Scots in prison in 1606, see
Chapter 4. Maxey also concludes this section with a ringing denunciation of religious wars and ecclesiastical dissention. Among such notable
examples as the "massacres in France" and the "wearisome broils of
Flanders," he includes the Scottish conspiracy of the Gowries against
James VI: "If we set before our eyes the high indignities offered hereto-
fore in Scotland [here a marginal reference to the Gowrie conspiracy] to
our most worthy and religious King James; the sodaine and sundrie
mutinies, and uprores ever and anon rising from their Presbyteriall discipline ... then we must needes confesse, happy are we in our settled
peace" (Maxey, "Third Sermon," sigs. L2v–r). In his denunciation of
Knox and Buchanan, Maxey was repeating James's condemnation of
their works as "infamous invectives" in BASILIKON DORON, sigs. K7r–8v
(R. Mason, "George Buchanan, James VI and the Presbyterians," in
Scots and Britons, ed. Mason, 125).

83. Lake, *Moderate Puritans*, 58, 113; Patrick Collinson, *Archbishop
Grindal: The Struggle for a Reformed Church* (Berkeley, Calif., 1979), passim; id., Elizabethan *Puritan Movement*, 61, 159–60.

84. On English presbyterianism, see Lake, *Anglicans and Puritans?*
and Fincham and Lake, "Ecclesiastical Policy of King James I," 180–81;
they cite N. R. N. Tyacke, "Puritanism, Arminianism, and Counter-
Revolution," in *The Origins of the Civil War*, ed. C. Russell (London,
1973), 125. For the Scottish response to the Hampton Court conference,
see Morrill, "British Patriarchy?" 218–19.

85. Lancelot Andrewes, *XCVI Sermons by the Right Honorable and
Reverend Father in God, Lancelot Andrewes, late Bishop of Winchester*
(London, 1629), 124.

86. Ibid., 123–24.

87. Another reading is possible here, one that allies the "images" of
popery to the "imaginations" that erect them out of heterodox beliefs.

88. Andrewes, *XCVI Sermons*, 127.

89. This was a double celebration, secular and religious: Accession

Day and Easter Sunday fell on the same day in 1611. Unlike the previously cited Andrewes sermon, this sermon was published in the year it was preached. The vast majority of sermons by Andrewes were published posthumously in the 1629 edition of *XCVI Sermons*; see P. McCullough, "Making Dead Men Speak: Laudianism, Print, and the Works of Lancelot Andrewes, 1626–1642," *Historical Journal*, forthcoming; and see also pp. 169–71 above.

90. L. Andrewes, *A Sermon Preached Before His Majesty at Whitehall, on the 24. of March last, being Easter day, and being also the day of the beginning of his Majestys Most Gracious Reign* (London, 1611), 18–26.

91. Andrewes, *Sermon Preached . . . on the 24. of March last*, 26.

92. See Chapter 4 above.

93. R. Mason, "George Buchanan, James VI and the presbyterians," in *Scots and Britons*, ed. Mason, 121. The quotation is from BASILIKON DORON, sigs. E4v–r.

94. J. S. Morrill, *The Scottish National Covenant in Its British Context* (Edinburgh, 1991), 8–11; "British Patriarchy?" 216, 220–21.

95. Wormald, "Two Kings?" 203.

96. Tyacke's observation (in "Puritanism, Arminianism, and Counter-Revolution," 125) that there were no treatises against presbyterianism licensed for publication between 1611 and 1618 says more about the decline of this method of attacking nonconformity than it does about the actual threat of presbyterianism in England between 1603 and 1611; see Fincham and Lake, "Ecclesiastical Policy of James I," 181n.

Chapter 3

1. And we would not be the only skeptics: speculation that the plot was micromanaged from above was voiced as early as the following week by the Venetian ambassador to the court. *See CSP (Ven.) 1603–7*, 291–92; and J. Hurstfield, *Freedom, Corruption and Government in Elizabethan England* (London, 1973), 334–36.

2. M. Nicholls, *Investigating the Gunpowder Plot* (Manchester, 1991), 220. According to Nicholls, the image and celebration of Gunpowder Plot was thus preserved for the intolerant anti-Catholic politics of later periods.

3. This in contradistinction to Professor Hurstfield's famous saying, that determining the authenticity of Gunpowder Plot had become "a pleasant way to spend a rainy afternoon, like dating Shakespeare's sonnets, but hardly an occupation for adults" (J. Hurstfield "Gunpowder Plot and the Politics of Dissent," in *Early Stuart Studies*, ed. H. Reinmuth [Minneapolis, 1976], 110).

4. There is hardly reason to look any further than Gardiner's nine-

teenth-century account, although Nicholls puts the facts in a more modern and useful order and has many valuable things to say about the
mechanics of Gunpowder Plot investigation. The trend has shifted to
discussion of the plot's place in the construction of anti-popery. See
C. Z. Weiner, "The Beleagured Isle: A Study of Elizabethan and Early
Jacobean Anti-Catholicism," *Past and Present* 51 (1971); R. Clifton, "Fear
of Popery," in *The Origins of the English Civil War*, ed. C. Russell (London, 1973), 144–67; and P. Lake, "Anti-Popery: The Structure of a Prejudice," in *Conflict in Early Stuart England: Studies in Politics and Religion,
1603–1642*, ed. A. Cust and R. Hughes (New York, 1989), 72–106. On the
celebration of 5 November as a national holiday, see D. Cressy, *Bonfires
and Bells: National Memory and the Protestant Calendar in Elizabethan and
Stuart England* (Berkeley, Calif., 1989).

5. Nicholls, *Investigating the Gunpowder Plot*, 47–49.

6. M. Maclure, *The Paul's Cross Sermons, 1534–1642* (Toronto, 1958),
11–14.

7. For example, Lancelot Andrewes, who, according to the biogra-
pher of John Hacket, had to fall to his knees before his king and beg
James to confirm that he had told the truth about the Gowry conspiracy;
see Hacket, *A Century of Sermons Upon Several Remarkable Subjects:
Preached by the Right Reverend Father in God, John Hacket, Late Lord Bishop
of Lichfield and Coventry* (London, 1675), viii. This probably apocryphal
story, which appears to have originated in later seventeenth-century re-
vulsion at the Jacobean court, is repeated in N. Lossky, *Lancelot Andrewes the Preacher, 1555–1626* (Oxford, 1991), 289–35; and P. Welsby,
Lancelot Andrewes, 1555–1626 (London, 1958), 141–42.

8. The majority of Andrewes's sermons were printed in the reign of
Charles I for a related but substantially transformed polemic purpose.
This assertion forms the basis for the conclusion to this book.

9. K. Fincham and P. Lake, "The Ecclesiastical Policies of James I
and Charles I," in *The Early Stuart Church*, ed. K. Fincham (Stanford,
1993), 32.

10. Andrewes's Gunpowder Plot and Gowry sermons have been examined in a strict theological context by Lossky, *Lancelot Andrewes*, who
finds them demonstrative "not so much [of] a political theory . . . as [of]
the embryo of a Christian anthropology," maturing into the "elements
of a theology of man" (324–25).

11. Hurstfield, *Freedom, Corruption and Government*, 330.

12. See William Barlow's assertion that James feared gunpowder be-
cause of his womb-memory of Bothwell's murder by explosives of
James's father, Lord Darnley (Barlow, *The Sermon Preached at Paules
Crosse the tenth day of November, being the next Sunday after the discoverie of*

this late Horrible Treason [London, 1606], sigs. Ev–r). James himself had stated this in his parliamentary speech (*The Workes of that most High and Mightie Prince James, by the Grace of God King of Great Britain, France and Ireland, Defender of the Faith, &c. Published by James Bp. of Winton. and Deane of His Majesties Chappell Royall* [London, 1616], 500).

13. The Gunpowder Plot was actually better known by the sobriquet "Gunpowder Treason" in the early seventeenth century (Hurstfield, *Freedom, Corruption, and Government*, 327).

14. Nicholls, *Investigating the Gunpowder Plot*, 149–50.

15. S. Adams, "Spain or the Netherlands? The Dilemma of Early Stuart Diplomacy," in *Before the Civil War*, ed. H. Tomlinson (London, 1983), 139–72.

16. A point David Lindley makes his introduction to his translation *Thomas Campion: De Puluerea Coniuratione* [On the Gunpowder Plot] (Leeds, Eng., 1987), viii–x.

17. A. Milton, *Catholic and Reformed: The Roman and Protestant Churches in English Protestant Thought, 1600–1640* (Cambridge, Eng., 1995), 55–58.

18. For more on this interesting group, as well as some sharply observant thought on their significance in view of early Stuart ecclesiastical policy, see A. Walsham, *Church Papists* (London, 1994).

19. The king wanted to send Parliament back to its constituencies in order to patrol for any disaffected papists on the run after the plot and to prevent further disorder (speech of 9 November 1605 to Parliament in *Workes*, 504).

20. James I, *Workes*, 504; also in *The Political Works of James I*, ed. C. H. McIlwain (1918; rpt., New York, 1965), 285. The speech was attended by representatives of the Spanish king and of the infanta (letter of Sir Edward Hoby to Sir Thomas Edmonds, November 1605, quoted in T. Birch, *The Court and Times of James I* [London, 1848], 1: 39–40). For the sensitivities of the ambassadors, see *SP* 14/19/27, letter of Robert Cecil to the earl of Mar, 9 March 1606.

21. For the view that James did not, generally speaking, persecute Catholics with noticeably increased vigor after the discovery of the plot, see Nicholls, *Investigating the Gunpowder Plot*, 47–49; also J. Bossy, *The English Catholic Community, 1570–1850* (London, 1975), 280; E. Norman, *Roman Catholicism in England* (Oxford, 1985), 33–34; and E. E. Reynolds, *The Roman Catholic Church in England and Wales: A Short History.* (Wheathampstead, Eng., 1973), 261–74. But cf. *The Condition of Catholics Under James I: Father Gerard's Narration of the Gunpowder Plot*, ed. J. Morris (London, 1871), 16.

22. This process has been briefly described by Fincham and Lake: "Ecclesiastical Policies," 25.

23. Milton, *Catholic and Reformed*, 15–16. The expression "paper tiger" is from P. Collinson, *The Elizabethan Puritan Movement* (1967; rpt., Oxford, 1990), 448–67.

24. *DNB*, entry for Ruthven.

25. James I, *Workes*, 500.

26. Ibid., 505–7, for the king's irritated acknowledgment of the same: James's assertion throws light on Jenny Wormald's contention that the Gunpowder Plotters were, if not entirely motivated by anti-unionist feelings, entirely happy to justify their treason on the basis of their hatred of the Scots: see Wormald, "Gunpowder, Treason, and Scots," *JBS* 24 (April 1985): 141–68. If James planned to be present in Parliament on 5 November only to oversee the articles, we can give an even higher priority to the union as a cause of the plot. If he only used that idea to demonstrate how entirely fortuitous it was that gunpowder was discovered on that day, it is still telling that he chose to claim that he only planned to attend Parliament because of union matters.

27. James I, *Workes*, 505.

28. See Chapter 2.

29. *His Majesties speech in this last session of Parliament concerning the Gunpowder Plot; as near his very words as could be gathered at the Instant. Together with a Discourse of the Manner of the Discovery of this late intended Treason, joined with the Examination of some of the Prisoners* (London, 1605), 92 quarto pages; reprinted in entirety in *Harleian Miscellany* (London, 1745), 4: 234–55.

30. James I, *Workes*, 503.

31. *Summe and Substance* was published in London in 1604.

32. Barlow, *Sermon . . . at Paules Crosse*, sigs. A3r–A4r.

33. Ibid., sig. A3r.

34. Literary-critical scholarship on the concept of theatricality is vast and forbidding. For a succinct survey of the issues involved, see Thomas Whitaker, "Some Reflections on 'Text' and 'Performance,'" *Yale Journal of Criticism* 3, no. 1 (1989) 143–62; and, with specific reference to Elizabethan sermon style, see B. Crockett, *The Play of Paradox: Stage and Sermon in Renaissance England* (Philadelphia, 1996).

35. Pathopoeia, the rhetorical art of stimulating fearful emotions, is described in B. Vickers, *The Defence of Rhetoric* (Oxford, 1988), 331.

36. Barlow, *Sermon . . . at Paules Crosse*, sig. Cr–C2v. For another account of this sermon that emphasizes the awkwardly sycophantic aspects of Barlow's efforts, see Maclure, *Paul's Cross Sermons*, 88–89.

37. Lindley, "Introduction," in Campion, *De Puluerea Coniuratione*, xviii. This discussion of the rendering of Gunpowder Plot into epical panegyric by the process of "dematerialization" contains points applicable to the rhetoric of post-plot Jacobean sermons as well as to other imaginative literature.

38. English antipathy, both contemporary and recent historiographical, to the Scots and James has been well documented by J. Wormald: "James VI and I: Two Kings or One?" *History* 68 (1983): 187–209.

39. For a description of the rhetorical form *aversio* (also known as *apostrophe*), see Vickers, *Defence of Rhetoric*, 298, 492. Vickers ranks *aversio* "gale force nine" in transmitting emotional intensity. In fact, Barlow uses all the rhetorical figures associated with the emotive "grand style" (on which see Vickers, 316) in this particular sermon.

40. Barlow, *Sermon . . . at Paules Crosse*, sigs. E3r–E4r, the exhortatory conclusion to the sermon.

41. Ibid., sig. E4r.

42. Although it is possible that Barlow also had to observe the principle of haste in the publication of the sermon as well. His pointed reference to not having enough time would have made a similarly arresting break in the pulpit. On time in the Paul's Cross pulpit, which usually extended to two turns of the hourglass, see MacClure, *Paul's Cross Sermons*, 8–9. On *paralipsis* (also known as *occupatio*), the rhetorical form used to such interesting effect by Barlow and others in this chapter, see Vickers, *Defence of Rhetoric*, 306, 496.

43. It is probably more accurate to describe the demands as "less-conformist," since truly radical opinion only made its apprearance at Hampton Court in the mouths of James's bishops, who used it to discredit their moderate puritan opponents there: see L. A. Ferrell, "Kneeling and the Body Politic," in *Politics, Religion, and Literature in Post-Reformation England, 1540–1688*, ed. D. Hamilton and R. Strier (Cambridge, Eng., 1996), 73–74.

44. Of course, James would also have singled out Knox and Buchanan as particular enemies and did so in BASILIKON DORON but here Barlow takes the time to expand on James's brief anti-puritan rant and reconnect it to the anti-Scottish polemics of the Hampton Court conference. See Chapter 5 for a further analysis of the language of conformity at Hampton Court.

45. On Barlow's ecclesiology, see Milton, *Catholic and Reformed*, 296, 472, 532–33, and K. Fincham, "Episcopal Government, 1603–1640," in *Early Stuart Church*, ed. id., 77–78; for his doctrinal positions, see N. R. N. Tyacke, *Anti-Calvinists: The Rise of English Arminianism, c. 1590–1640* (Oxford and New York, 1987; rpt., 1991), 20, 28.

46. For another analysis of Andrewes's sermon, see Cressy, *Bonfires and Bells*, 141–56.

47. William Barlow, *A Brand. Titio Erepta* (London, 1607), sig. E4r.

48. Ibid., sig. Fv.

49. Ibid., sigs. Dv.

50. Ibid., sigs. Dv–Dr. The emphases are reproduced from the printed text.

51. P. Collinson, "The Theatre Constructs Puritanism," in *The Theatrical City: Culture, Theatre, and Politics in England, 1576–1649*, ed. D. Smith, R. Strier, and D. Bevington (Cambridge, Eng., 1995), 164–67.

52. A second conference at Hampton Court, in 1606, at which James subjected his presbyterian Scottish clergy to sermons preached by Barlow, Lancelot Andrewes, John Buckeridge, and John King on episcopacy and the royal supremacy, certainly informed the episcopal apologetic in Barlow's sermon as well, and links his anti-presbyterian language to the earlier campaign for English conformity. On this second Hampton Court conference, see Chapter 4.

53. Martin Fotherby, *Four Sermons, Lately Preached, whereunto is added, an answer by him concerning the use of the cross in baptism: written in 1604, and now commanded to be published by authority* (London, 1608), 75–76. At this time, Fotherby was the archdeacon of Canterbury. He later rose to become bishop of Salisbury in 1618 (Venn, 1: 165).

54. Fotherby, *Four Sermons*, 76–77.

55. Ibid., 84–85.

56. Ibid., 84.

57. Maclure, *Paul's Cross Sermons*, 14.

58. Ibid., 91. The preachers at Paul's Cross were not all court servants; but almost all Paul's Cross sermons were characterized by Calvinist sentiments during James's reign (Tyacke, *Anti-Calvinists*, 27–28, 253–60).

59. *The Works of Lancelot Andrewes*, ed. J. P. Wilson and J. Bliss (Oxford, 1841–44), 4: 234.

60. Andrewes's other Gowry sermons were printed in the *XCVI Sermons* of 1629; one other sermon, preached by John Hacket at the end of the reign (perhaps when Andrewes was not well enough to preach) was not printed until 1675 (Hacket, *Century of Sermons*, 731–41).

61. T. Playfere, *Caesaris superscriptio. Sive conciuncula, coram duobos Potentissimis Regibus, in superiori atrio splendidae illius domus, Honoratissimi Comitis Sarisburiensis, quae vocatur Theobaldus* (London, 1606). A sermon that was preached by Henry Parry, bishop of Gloucester and Worcester, on 10 August, may also have been printed: *De Regno Dei et Victoria Christiana, Conciones Duae Auctore D. Henrico Parraeos Theologiae*

Doctore et Decano Cestrensi (London, 1606). See J. Nichols, *The Progresses of James I* (1828), 2: 91: "On Sunday the Kings, Queen, and Prince, lying the night before in the Bishop's palace at Rochester, had a Latin sermon in the Cathedral Church preached by Dr. Parry, who delivered so good matter with so good a grace as their Majesties were very well pleased to hear him. His text was *Fac judicium et videbus faciem Domini*." Andrewes's Latin Gowry sermon was not translated into English until the 1641 edition of *Ninety-Six Sermons*.

62. "A Triple Wedge for a Triple Knot": James's "wedge" is aimed to destroy the knot, which in turn represents the two papal breves and a letter from Cardinal Bellarmine to the English arch-priest Blackwell, forbidding English Catholics to take the Oath of Allegiance. See *King James VI and I: Political Writings*, ed. J. P. Sommerville (Cambridge, Eng., and New York, 1994), xxi, 283, 497n. A third Gowry Sermon, which was preached at Paul's Cross in 1607, was printed in 1610: John Milward, *Jacob's Great Day of Trouble, and Deliverance. A Sermon Preached at Pauls Cross, the fifth of August 1607 upon His Majesties deliverance from the Earl Gowries treason and conspiracie* (London, 1610). See MacLure, *Paul's Cross Sermons*, 227.

63. James I, *Political Writings*, ed. Sommerville, xxi.

64. Fincham and Lake, "Ecclesiastical Policies," 29.

65. For other pageantry during the visit of the king of Denmark, see Nichols, *Progresses*, 2: 54–95.

66. Hoby's concerns quoted in *Court and Times*, 1: 45–46. For fears about Catholic loyalty, see Maclure, *Paul's Cross Sermons*, 90–91. But cf. Tyacke, *Anti-Calvinists*, who sees in the Oath of Allegiance an attempt to "distract attention from the dangers of Puritanism," 27.

67. For example, in *CSPD 1603–1610*, 317 (SP 14/21/26), examination of John Tucker, shipmaster, relative to the speeches uttered by the recusant Robert Moore during passage to England; and 270 (SP 14/17/32), examination of Thomas Strange and "Points to be noted in the booke of equivocation" (SP 14/17/33).

68. L. Andrewes, *XCVI Sermons by the Right Honorable and Reverend Father in God, Lancelot Andrewes, late Bishop of Winchester* (London, 1629 [1641]), 1011. The rhetorical pattern of the passage is characterized by *reduplicatio*, also known as *anadiplosis*, where the last word of a phrase is repeated as the first word of the next phrase. This was considered a very "forceful figure," which could impart a "passionate tone" to rhetoric (Vickers, *Defence of Rhetoric*, 305, 491).

69. Andrewes, *XCVI Sermons* (1641), 1012–13.

70. Ibid., 1013.

71. R. Tynely, *Two Learned Sermons* (1609), sig. A3r.

72. Ibid., 5. The comical poet is Plautus.

73. Ibid., 6.

74. Ibid., 6–7.

75. Milton, *Catholic and Reformed*, 43.

76. J. King, *A Sermon Preached at Whitehall the 5. Day of November. ann. 1608* (Oxford, 1608), 26–27. This sermon was printed by royal command.

77. J. Chamberlain, *Letters of Chamberlain*, ed. N. E. Maclure (Philadelphia, 1939), 1: 269.

78. The book, *Responsio ad Librum inscriptum Triplici Nodo Triplex Cuneus* was written by Cardinal Bellarmine (a well-known secret) and was answered by Lancelot Andrewes: *Tortura Torti: sive, ad Matthaei Torti librum responsio* (London, 1609).

79. King, *Sermon Preached at Whitehall*, 37.

80. Ibid., 37–39. The emphasis here is mine.

81. For correspondence related to the 1608 "Balmerino" affair, see *Letters of James VI and I*, ed. G. P. V. Akrigg (Berkeley, Calif., 1984), 301–10. On James's early contact with the pope, see W. B. Patterson, "King James I's Call for an Ecumenical Council," in *Councils and Assemblies: Papers Read at the Eighth Summer Meeting and the Ninth Winter Meeting of the Ecclesiastical History Society*, ed. G. J. Cuming and D. Baker, Studies in Church History, No. 7 (Cambridge, Eng., 1971), 267–77.

82. On King's Calvinism, puritan sympathies, and anti-Catholicism, see K. Fincham, *Prelate as Pastor: The Episcopate of James I* (Oxford and New York, 1990), 253–65; N. R. N. Tyacke, *Anti-Calvinists* (London, 1987), 63; and R. Babbage, *Puritanism and Richard Bancroft* (London, 1962), 63n. On Franco-Spanish relations, see T. Cogswell, *The Blessed Revolution* (Cambridge, Eng., 1989), 12–15.

83. King, *Sermon Preached at Whitehall*, 34–35.

84. Ibid.

85. One important issue that will not be discussed here is the relation of the Burges case to factional realignment at the early Jacobean court. Recent work on the Burges cause célèbre includes A. Bellany, "A Poem for the Archbishop's Hearse," *JBS* 30, no. 2 (1995), 161; and L. Levy Peck, "John Marston's *The Fawn*: Ambivalence and Jacobean Courts," in *Theatrical City*, ed. Smith, Strier, and Bevington, 117–36.

86. Fincham and Lake, "Ecclesiastical Policies," 32; Fincham, "Episcopal Government," 74.

87. It also demonstrates the depth of James's personal Protestantism, which was built upon the necessity for discipline and admonition from the pulpit.

88. R. Cust and A. Hughes, "Introduction: After Revisionism," in *Conflict*, ed. Cust and Hughes, 17; Lake, "Anti-Popery," 73.

89. *Works of Lancelot Andrewes*, ed. Wilson and Bliss, 4: 61.

90. See p. 162–63 above; for Andrewes's treatment of "Noli me tangere" (John 20:17) in his 1621 sermon before the king: "A Sermon Preached Before the Kings Majesty at Whitehall on the first of April 1621, being Easter Day," in *XVCI Sermons*, 548–49.

91. *Works of Lancelot Andrewes*, ed. Wilson and Bliss, 4: 243. Andrewes had preached upon this text before Queen Elizabeth in much the same vein: see ibid., 5: 318, cited in W. F. Mitchell, *English Pulpit Oratory from Andrewes to Tillotson* (London, 1932), 150.

92. *Works of Lancelot Andrewes*, ed. Wilson and Bliss, 4: 245.

93. Ibid., 257.

94. This was to become an increasingly popular theme with those clergy (like Andrewes, John Buckeridge, and Andrew Harsnet) inclined to anti-Calvinist doctrine (to use Tyacke's formulation) and avant-garde ceremonialism (to use Lake's formulation): that even moderate puritanism, if tolerated in the Church of England, would hinder the conversion of English Catholics to Protestantism. See Milton, *Catholic and Reformed*, 64–65.

95. Milton, *Catholic and Reformed*, 46–47.

96. J. Boys, *An Exposition of the Last Psalme, Delivered in a Sermon Preached at Paules Crosse the 5th of November 1613 which I have joined to the festivals as a short apologie for our holy daies in the Church of England* (London, 1615).

97. Ibid., 12.

98. J. Howson, *Certain Sermons Made in Oxford. anno. Dom. 1616* (London, 1622), 159, 162–63; cited in Milton, *Catholic and Reformed*, 47. This was not a plot sermon. Howson claimed that, because it was far more widely dispersed in England, puritanism was a much more serious problem than popery.

99. For another account of this sermon, see Maclure, *Paul's Cross Sermons*, 235.

100. P. White, "The *Via Media* in the Early Stuart Church," in *The Early Stuart Church, 1603–1642*, ed. K. Fincham (Stanford, 1993), 215–16. The other part of this "special character," according to White, was the rejection of stringent Calvinist doctrine.

Chapter 4

1. It is part of these historians' generally more favorable attitude toward James altogether: see M. Lee, Jr., *Great Britain's Solomon* (Chicago, 1990), 1–63; J. Wormald, "James VI and I: Two Kings or One?" *History* 68 (1983): 141–68; M. Schwartz, "James I and the Historians: Towards a Reconsideration," *JBS* 13 (1974): 114–34.

2. K. Fincham and P. Lake, "The Ecclesiastical Policies of James I and Charles I," in *The Early Stuart Church, 1603–1642*, ed. K. Fincham (Stanford, 1993), 32.

3. The proof of the ubiquity of this characterization, in fact, can be found in its inspiration for less positive presentations as well. The scurrilous Anthony Weldon, for example, obviously employed a deliberate parody of this well-publicized image when he called James the "wisest fool in Christendom" (*The Court and Character of King James. Written and Taken by Sir A. W.* [London, 1650], 186–87).

4. 1 Kings 10:6–7.

5. But cf. Fincham and Lake, who point out that James's "belief in Christian unity, based upon a very limited number of crucial Catholic doctrines," could unify his disparate clergy in such projects as the defense of the Oath of Allegiance ("Ecclesiastical Policies," in *Early Stuart Church*, ed. Fincham, 31). This chapter suggests how the king's ecumenism could provoke an altogether different response.

6. A. Williamson, *Scottish National Consciousness in the Age of James VI* (Edinburgh, 1979), 11.

7. "Golden" and "Black" are, of course, informal names for these legislative acts; both epithets originate in presbyterian polemic (John Morrill, "A British Patriarchy? Ecclesiastical Imperialism Under the Early Stuarts," in *Religion, Culture and Society in Early Modern Britain: Essays in Honour of Patrick Collinson*, ed. A. Fletcher and P. Roberts [Cambridge, Eng., 1994], 214–15). Episcopal authority in Scotland under the "Black Acts" was, presbyterian protests to the contrary, limited (D. G. Mullan, *Episcopacy in Scotland: The History of an Idea* [Edinburgh, 1986], 106–11).

8. Williamson, *Scottish National Consciousness*, 1–43 passim.

9. W. B. Patterson, "James I's Call for an Ecumenical Council," in *Councils and Assemblies: Papers Read at the Eighth Summer Meeting and the Ninth Winter Meeting of the Ecclesiastical History Society*, ed. G. J. Cuming and D. Baker, Studies in Church History, No. 7 (Cambridge, Eng., 1971), 270–75; Lee, *Great Britain's Solomon*, 112–13.

10. Patterson, " James I's Call for an Ecumenical Council," 270–71. James had communicated with Clement VIII earlier, in 1599, thanking His Holiness for not interfering with the accession process: see J. Rushworth, *Historical collections of private passages of state, weighty matters in law, remarkable proceedings in five Parliaments, beginning the sixteenth year of King James, anno 1618, and ending . . .* [with the death of King Charles I, 1648] (London, 1659–1701), 1: 166, cited in *Letters of King James VI and I*, ed. G. P. V. Akrigg (Berkeley, Calif., 1984), 488. James's queen, Anne of Denmark, had recently converted to Catholicism and had written the

pope as well, promising His Holiness that James would be lenient to English Catholics should he become king there.

11. Anthony Milton, *Catholic and Reformed: The Roman and Protestant Churches in English Protestant Thought* (Cambridge, Eng., 1995), 496.

12. *The Political Works of James I*, ed. C. H. McIlwain (Cambridge, Eng., 1918), 275–76.

13. The topic of James's foreign policy, and its relation to his notion of a united Christendom and ecumenism, has been the subject of many important essays by W. B. Patterson (cited throughout this chapter), and will be the subject of a forthcoming book by him. This chapter has a narrower scope: to show how foreign policy rhetoric has an influence on domestic policy rhetoric.

14. Of Field's categorization in Jacobean ecclesiastical circles, the reports are widely varied. Patrick Collinson remarks, "[He] was one of several members of the conference who cannot be placed easily in either camp." Despite being described by the Puritans as a cohort, he apparently confined his participation at Hampton Court to one speech only, and that of an anti-puritan nature (Collinson, *The Elizabethan Puritan Movement* [London, 1967], 503n). Nicholas Tyacke admits the doctrinal classification of Field is "problematic," pointing out that his works cannot place him in the camp of anti-Calvinists, but that his opinion on predestination was "strikingly" moderate, i.e., lukewarm. More recently, two other historians have analyzed Field's views with a view to placing him in a recognizable niche in the Jacobean spectrum. Anthony Milton, whose work is based upon an extensive analysis of Field's magisterial work *On the Church*, is most convincing on the subject of the elusive cleric, whom he describes as a worthy protégé of Hooker, whose written works created a separable view of the Church that distinguished the "true" from the "visible" Church (Milton, "The Church of England, Rome, and the True Church: The Demise of a Jacobean Consensus," in *The Early Stuart Church, 1603–1642*, ed. K. Fincham [Stanford, 1993], 206–7). In the same volume, however, Peter White disputes Tyacke's assessment of Field, presenting him (on the basis of a hagiographical biography of Field by his son and a disputed report by Peter Heylyn) as the kind of "moderate" "Anglican" that characterized the Jacobean Church (White, "The *Via Media* in the Early Stuart Church," in ibid., 217). The filial encomium is quoted by White.

15. R. Field, *A Learned Sermon Preached Before the King at Whitehall, on Friday the 16th of March, by M. Dr. Field: Chaplaine to His Majestie* (London, 1604), sig. B4r.

16. Ibid., sig. B8v.

17. Ibid., sig. B6v.

18. B. Vickers, *The Defence of Rhetoric* (Oxford, 1988), 111, 492. Another term for *comparatio* is *antithesis*, about which figure Vickers remarks: "The real function of *antithesis* . . . is less neutral classification than polemical discrimination."

19. Field, *Learned Sermon*, sigs. B5r–6v.

20. Henry Hooke was a rector at Nettleton in Lincoln until 1617, when he became archdeacon in the West Riding of Yorkshire: Wood, 1:740.

21. H. Hooke, *A Sermon Preached before the King at White-hall, the eight of May. 1604* (London, 1604), sig. Bviiir.

22. D. Calderwood, *The History of the Kirk of Scotland* (Edinburgh, 1842–49), 6: 220.

23. See p. 56 above.

24. It is worth noting that the term *formalist* is distinguished from the word *conformity* by its lack of a prefix. *Conform* can convey the notion that something or someone has been shaped, possibly in obedience. What is left in *formalist* may connote a kind of positive value to the "form," or its visual aspects, in itself.

25. A. Rudd, *A Sermon Preached at the Court at White Hall before the Kings Majesty, upon Sunday being the 13. of May 1604* (London, 1604), 6–7.

26. R. Stock, *A Sermon Preached at Pauls Crosse, the second of November, 1606* (London, 1607), 54–55. Stock was at St. John's College, Cambridge, and eventually became rector at All Hallow's, Bread Street, in London. He was well known as a public preacher: Wood, 2: 1425; *DNB*.

27. Stock's sermon can "hesitatingly" be called "Puritan" and "potentially schismatic," observes M. MacLure, *The Paul's Cross Sermons 1534–1642* (Toronto, 1958), 95. Certainly, Stock himself was a great friend to a good many people one could unhesitatingly call "puritan," including Thomas Gataker and Richard Brooke. Stock was also accused of allowing a suspended nonconformist access to his (Stock's) London pulpit. I thank Paul Seaver for pointing this out.

28. Morrill, "British Patriarchy?" 218.

29. The implied insult to James in this process was the Kirk's contention that in times of grave risk to the Church, a council could be called by the ministers instead of the king—the risk being, of course, James's own episcopal policies. On the Aberdeen assembly, see Mullan, *Episcopacy in Scotland*, 107.

30. The conference was also held at Hampton Court, which has led some historians of Scotland to draw comparisons with the 1604 sessions. See Mullan's index in *Episcopacy in Scotland*, which contains two listings for "Hampton Court Conference," one for 1604 and one for 1606. On the 1606 Conference, see ibid., 98–102, and Calderwood, *History of the Kirk of Scotland*, 6: 477–81, 568–83.

31. W. Barlow, *One of the Foure Sermons Preached Before the Kings Maiestie, at Hampton Court in September Last. This Concerning the Antiquitie and Superioritie of Bishops. Sept. 21, 1606* (London, 1606), sigs. A4v–r. On James's reimposition of episcopacy in the ministers' absence, see Calderwood, *History of the Kirk of Scotland*, 6: 481–539.

32. Barlow, *One of the Foure Sermons*, sig. A3v.

33. Ibid., sig. A2r.

34. J. Buckeridge, *A Sermon Preached at Hampton Court before the Kings Majestie, on Tuesday the 23. of September, ANNO 1606* (London, 1606), sigs. D4r–Ev.

35. The rhetorical figure here used is *epanalepsis*, in which the same word begins and ends a phrase. Vickers cites the sixteenth-century rhetorician Henry Peachum's *The Garden of Eloquence* on the proper use of *epanalepsis*: "a word of importance [placed] in the beginning of a sentence to be considered, and in the end to be remembered" (Vickers, *Defence of Rhetoric*, 326).

36. Buckeridge, *Sermon*, sigs. F2r–F3v.

37. Calderwood, *History of the Kirk of Scotland*, 5: 161–62.

38. L. Andrewes, *A Sermon Preached Before the Kings Majesty at Hampton Court, concerning the Right and Power of Calling Assemblies, on Sunday the 28 of Sept. ANNO 1606. By the Bishop of Chichester* (London, 1606). See also Mullan, *Episcopacy in Scotland*, 100–101, who echoes Melville in pointing out that in Num. 10:3–4, the two trumpets actually represent the leaders and the people, thus rendering Andrewes's sermon a "blatant exegetical impropriet[y]."

39. Andrewes, *Sermon*, sig. G4r.

40. On the radical counterclaim to Protestant history, see P. Christianson, *Reformers and Babylon: English Apocalyptic Visions from the Reformation to the Eve of the Civil War* (Toronto, 1978), 13–47; J. Facey, "John Foxe and the Definition of the English Church," in *Protestantism and the National Church*, ed. P. Lake and M. Dowling (London, 1987), 162–92.

41. J. King, *The Fourth Sermon Preached at Hampton Court on Tuesday the last of September 1606* (Oxford, 1606), 14–15. King was dean of Christ Church in Oxford at this time. For his reputation as a preacher and his favor with James, see K. Fincham, *Prelate as Pastor: The Episcopate of James I* (Oxford and New York, 1990), 87, 264–65.

42. King, *Fourth Sermon*, 29.

43. The phrase is highlighted by the rhetorical figure *homoioteleuton*, wherein words are connected by both the similarity of their meanings and the similarity of their endings (Vickers, *Defence of Rhetoric*, 495).

44. King, *Fourth Sermon*, 29.

45. *King James VI and I: Political Writings*, ed. J. P. Sommerville (Cambridge, Eng., and New York, 1994), xx.

46. D. H. Willson, "James I and His Literary Assistants," *Huntington Library Quarterly*, 8 (1944–45): 35–57.

47. Ibid., 41–42.

48. *CSPD*, 570, letter of Lake to Salisbury, 11 December 1609; also quoted in Willson, "James I and His Literary Assistants," 42.

49. Willson, "James I and His Literary Assistants," 44–46.

50. Anthony Milton has convincingly argued that "'catholic' as an adjective was usually understood as referring to purity and apostolicity of doctrine," and therefore the use of the term was common to all styles of divinity in the Jacobean Church. "Catholic Church," however, according to Milton, "was bedevilled by the same sort of semantic confusion that accompanied all Protestant discussions of the church during this period" (*Catholic and Reformed*, 150, 150–57).

51. *The Workes of that most High and Mightie Prince James, by the Grace of God King of Great Britain, France and Ireland, Defender of the Faith, &c. Published by James Bp. of Winton* (London, 1616), 301.

52. On the religion of Mary Queen of Scots, see G. Donaldson, *All the Queen's Men* (London, 1983), 54, 70. That Mary was not interested in James's confessional loyalties is also apparent from Mary and James's correspondence, in which it appears that Mary's maternal concerns were entirely centered around whether James would consent to share the Scottish throne with her (*Letters of King James VI and I*, ed. Akrigg, 44–48, 55–57).

53. Milton, *Catholic and Reformed*, 216.

54. James I, *Workes*, 301–7.

55. Ibid., 305.

56. *Political Works of James I*, ed. McIlwain, 156, 319–29.

57. F. Shriver, "Orthodoxy and Diplomacy: The Vorstius Affair," *English Historical Review* 85 (1970): 449–50, 453–55. The Jesuits accused James of sharing the "Vorstian heresy," and Shriver argues that the *Declaration* protected James from the "vagaries of Dutch theology" (ibid., 474). See also, C. Grayson, "James I and the Religious Crisis in the United Provinces, 1613–19," in *Reform and Reformation: England and the Continent c. 1500–c. 1750*, ed. D. Baker, Studies in Church History, Subsidia 2 (Oxford, 1979), 195–219.

58. James I, *Workes*, 365–56. James's letter to Dudley Carleton, ambassador to the Low Countries, is reprinted in the *Declaration* (*Workes*, 350–51).

59. James, *Workes*, 351–66, 379.

60. Ibid., 379.

61. Shriver, "Vorstius Affair," 474; K. Fincham and P. Lake, "The Ecclesiastical Policy of King James I." *JBS* 24, no. 2 (April 1985): 189–91.

62. Fincham and Lake, "The Ecclesiastical Policies of James I and Charles I," in *The Early Stuart Church, 1603–1642*, ed. K. Fincham (Stanford, 1993), 32.

63. Ibid., 32.

Chapter 5

1. K. Fincham and P. Lake, "The Ecclesiastical Policy of King James I," *JBS* 24, no.2 (April 1985): 173–92.

2. Puritans formed a "separation within the Church," says P. Collinson, "The Cohabitation of the Faithful with the Unfaithful," in *From Persecution to Toleration: The Glorious Revolution and Religion in England*, ed. O. Grell, J. Israel, and N. R. N. Tyacke (Oxford, 1991), 62.

3. This is, of course, the phenomenon described by Nicholas Tyacke in his justly influential essay on anti-Calvinism, "Puritanism, Arminianism and Counter-Revolution," in *The Origins of the English Civil War*, ed. C. Russell (London, 1973), later expanded in his book *Anti-Calvinists: The Rise of English Arminianism, c. 1590–1640* (Oxford and New York, 1987; rpt., 1991). The doctrinal development he describes is entirely convincing; the purpose of my book is to show what issues of practice predated the all-out, open Arminian campaign against Calvinism in and out of court that Tyacke dates from the 1620's.

4. T. Fuller, *The Church History of Britain*, ed. J. S. Brewer (rpt., Oxford, 1865), 288; W.Barlow, *The Summe and Substance of the conference . . . at Hampton Court* (London, 1604), 53–54.

5. For the attitudes of the Jacobean episcopate on the significance of prayer and preaching, see K. Fincham, *Prelate as Pastor: The Episcopate of James I* (Oxford and New York, 1990), 231–40, and P. Lake, "Lancelot Andrewes, John Buckeridge, and *Avant-Garde* Conformity at the Court of James I," in *The Mental World of the Jacobean Court*, ed. L. Levy Peck (Cambridge, Eng., 1991), 115–19, 124–30.

6. For the purposes of this book, my use of the term *ecclesiology* (which is defined in the *Shorter Oxford Dictionary* as the "science of church buildings and decorations") is enlarged generally to mean the perceptible or apparent practices of the Church as opposed to its theology.

7. This picture is finally undergoing a much needed revision. "Puritanism," both name and thing, can be found in most of the essays on the Jacobean Church in *The Early Stuart Church, 1603–1642*, ed. K. Fincham (Stanford, 1993). In this volume, Fincham and Peter Lake have

updated their 1985 *JBS* article to include a discussion of the relation of Jacobean policy to its Caroline successor ("The Ecclesiastical Policies of James I and Charles I," 23–50).

8. Peter Lake has recently voiced the same complaint in an essay on the Church in the 1630's ("The Laudian Style," in *Early Stuart Church*, ed. Fincham, 162).

9. K. Sharpe, *Politics and Ideas in Early Stuart England* (London, 1989), 9–20.

10. I refer here to such works as Tyacke, *Anti-Calvinists*, and P. White, *Predestination, Policy and Polemic: Conflict and Consensus in the English Church from the Reformation to the Civil War* (Cambridge, Eng., 1992), as well as the *Past and Present* debate involving these two authors, "The Rise of Arminianism Reconsidered," *Past and Present* 115 (May 1987): 201–29. Peter Lake added his mediating opinion in "Calvinism and the English Church, 1560–1640," *Past and Present* 114 (Feb. 1987): 32–76. Patrick Collinson's work also figures in this view of the Church of England. The work of Collinson, Lake, and Kenneth Fincham is a welcome move away from strict considerations of theology.

11. Collinson, "Cohabitation of the Faithful," 53–55.

12. T. Morton, *A Defense of the innocency of the Three Ceremonies of the Church of England* (London, 1618), prefatory epistle.

13. Fincham, *Prelate*, 239; D. Calderwood, *Perth Assembly* (Leiden, 1619), 4–10.

14. Bancroft was a Calvinist, although he had misgivings about what he called "puritanical" interpretations of the doctrine of predestination. His dislike of puritanism stemmed from his hatred of presbyterianism: see S. Babbage, *Puritanism and Richard Bancroft* (London, 1962), 33–36; Fincham, *Prelate*, 291–92; Tyacke, *Anti-Calvinists*, 16–17.

15. This is not to suggest that this incident was the only one in which Reynolds was interrupted by importunate and suppliant bishops at Hampton Court, or even that Reynolds himself failed to show proper obeisance to James (Barlow, *Summe*, 26, 41).

16. A. G. Dickens, *The English Reformation*, 2d ed. (University Park, Pa., 1989), 278.

17. J. Ketley, ed., *The Two Liturgies, A.D. 1549, and A.D. 1552, with Other Documents Set Forth by Authority in the Reign of King Edward VI* (Cambridge, Eng., 1844), 97–99; 282–83.

18. Ibid., 157.

19. D. MacCulloch, "The Myth of the English Reformation," *JBS* 30, no.1 (Jan. 1991): 1–19.

20. Dickens, *English Reformation*, 359. In addition, this open-ended interpretation of communion was aided by the 1559 words of institu-

tion, which simply combined the 1549 and 1552 formulae, thereby avoiding the exact sense of either.

21. John Jewel to Peter Martyr, April 1559, in *The Zurich Letters* (Cambridge, Eng., 1842), 28–30; Babbage, *Puritanism and Richard Bancroft*, 1–43; N. Jones, *Faith by Statute: Parliament and the Settlement of Religion 1559* (London, 1982), 134–36. See also King James's very similar opinion as expressed in BASILIKON DORON, in *The Political Works of James I*, ed. C. H. McIlwain (1918; rpt., New York, 1965), 17.

22. See Babbage, *Puritanism and Richard Bancroft*, 166–67, for one example, that of John Burges.

23. Fincham, *Prelate*, 212–47.

24. T. Bilson, *A Sermon Preached before the King and Queenes Majesties, at their Coronations on Saint James his Day, being the xxv. of July. 1603* (London, 1604). Bilson was an Elizabethan bishop, having been appointed to the see of Winchester in 1597. He held the post until his death in 1616 and was also a privy councilor (Wood, 1: 124; *DNB*).

25. On the coronation ceremony of which this sermon was a part, see Nichols, *Progresses*, 229–34. And see R. T. Kendall, *Calvin and English Calvinism to 1649* (Oxford, 1979), 85–89, on the relation of outward behavior and inner conviction to Calvinist theology.

26. A full transcript of the Millenary Petition is contained in J. Kenyon, *The Stuart Constitution* (Cambridge, Eng., 1986), 117–19. See also Babbage, *Puritanism and Richard Bancroft*, 43–73; Tyacke, *Anti-Calvinists*, 9–28. A specific complaint about kneeling is not included in the general objections to ceremony in the petition, although this argues for its potential for controversy; Kenyon states that kneeling was "perhaps the only significant point" in the puritan program at the beginning of James's reign (*Stuart Constitution*, 111).

27. Fincham and Lake, "Ecclesiastical Policy of James I," 169–207; Fincham, *Prelate*, 214, 227.

28. *An Abridgement of that Book which the ministers of Lincoln Diocese delivered to his Majesty. Being the first part of an apology for themselves and their brethren that refuse the subscription, and conformity which is required* (London, 1605). The tract was printed by the notorious Puritan clandestine publisher William Jones, who finally fell afoul of the law in 1609, much to James's satisfaction: M. Curtis, "William Jones, Puritan Printer and Propagandist," *The Library*, 5th ser., 19 (1964): 38–66.

29. To cite a few of the many examples, see T. Hutton, *Reasons for Refusal of Subscription to the Book of Common Prayer* (1605); T. Sparke, *A Brotherly Persuasion to Unity and Uniformity* (1607); G. Powel, *A Consideration of the Deprived and Silenced Ministers Arguments* (1606); W. Brad-

shaw, *Twelve General Arguments proving that the ceremonies . . . are unlawful* (1605); S. Hieron, *A Defense of the Ministers Reasons for Refusal of Subscription* (1607); these and other works are also cited in G. Cragg, *Reason and Authority: A Study of English Thought in the Early Seventeenth Century* (Philadelphia, 1975), 127–58.

30. T. Craig, *De Unione Regnorum Britanniae Tractatus* (rpt., Edinburgh, 1909), 137; N. R. N. Tyacke, "The Legalizing of Dissent, 1571–1719," in *From Persecution to Toleration: The Glorious Revolution and Religion in England,* ed. O. Grell, J. Israel, and N. R. N. Tyacke (Oxford, 1991), 26–27; also see Fincham, *Prelate,* 212–13, 258–60.

31. D. G. Mullan, *Episcopacy in Scotland: The History of an Idea, 1560–1638* (Edinburgh, 1986), 152–62.

32. The other articles required assent to confirmation by bishops, the imposition of holy days (Christmas, Good Friday, Easter, Ascension, and Pentecost), and provisions for private baptism and communion (Calderwood, *Perth Assembly,* 8; Mullan, *Episcopacy in Scotland,* 152).

33. This assembly, held in August 1617, reflected the controversial nature of James's religious settlement in Scotland, where he had introduced a limited form of episcopacy. During its three-day course, presbyterian ministers were pitted against the king's emissaries and James's Scottish bishops in debate. And, as at Hampton Court, the contest favored the king and his episcopate: the articles eventually assented to were subsequently passed by a general assembly at Perth in 1618, and by Parliament in 1621 (Mullan, *Episcopacy in Scotland,* 152).

34. Calderwood, *Perth Assembly,* 1–10.

35. *SP 14/89/67,* arrangements in the Chapel Royal, Scotland, 1617; *SP 14/92/75,* letter of Thomas Murray to Francis Bacon, 28 June 1617.

36. Calderwood feared that Scotland would be made to conform to the English Church; see *A Solution of Doctor Resolutus his Resolutions for Kneeling* (Amsterdam, 1619), 55.

37. T. Cogswell, *The Blessed Revolution* (Cambridge, Eng., 1989), 21–32; S. Adams, "Foreign Policy and the Parliaments of 1621 and 1624," in *Faction and Parliament,* ed. K. Sharpe (New York, 1979), 139–41.

38. On synecdoche, see Vickers, *Defence of Rhetoric,* 498.

39. L. Andrewes, *A Sermon Preached before His Majesty at Whitehall* (London, 1611), 7–8. The occasion had a double import: Accession Day fell at Easter that year.

40. W. Westerman, *Jacob's Well: OR, A Sermon Preached before the Kings Most Excellent Majestie at Saint Albans, in his Summer Progress 1612* (London, 1613), 2.

41. Ibid., 53–54.

42. C. Swale, *Jacob's Vow* (London, 1621), 17.

43. Fincham and Lake, "Ecclesiastical Policies of James I and Charles I," 25–36.

44. Morton, *Defense*, 292.

45. James I, *A Meditation upon the Lord's Prayer* (London, 1619), 5–6.

46. *The Workes of that most High and Mightie Prince James . . . Published by James Bp. of Winton. and Deane of His Majesties Chappell Royall* (London, 1616), 575–78. *A Meditation upon the Lord's Prayer* and *A Pattern for a King's Inauguration* (London, 1620) were appended to the published *Workes* in 1620.

47. A. Maxey, *A Sermon Preached before his Majesty at Bagshot, Sept 1 Anno Dom 1616* (London, 1619), 24.

48. L. Andrewes, *A Sermon Preached on Easter Day Last* (London, 1615), 25: "He will not have us worship Him like Elephants, as if we had no joints in our knees."

49. Morton was forced to write *A Defense of the Innocency of the Three Ceremonies of the Church of England* in order to regain royal favor; the treatise is dedicated to Buckingham (Fincham, *Prelate*, 226–27).

50. Peter Lake's description of Andrewes's position as avant-garde has by now become a commonplace ("*Avant-Garde* Conformity," 133).

51. Fincham and Lake, "Ecclesiastical Policies of James I and Charles I," 62–64.

52. For imitators of Andrewes, see M. Reidy, *Bishop Lancelot Andrewes: Jacobean Court Preacher* (Chicago, 1955), 54–57.

53. Andrewes, *Sermon Preached on Easter Day Last*, 30. I have slightly altered the punctuation of the 1614 published version in order to make the sense of the passage more readily apparent. The original runs: "Sure, heed would be taken, that by taking heed, we prove not superstitious: we slip not into the other extreme, before we be aware."

54. N. Spackman, *A Sermon Preached Before His Majesty at Whitehall the First of May, 1614* (London, 1614), 24–26; 46–47; 58.

55. J. Buckeridge, *A Sermon Preached Before His Majesty at Whitehall, March 22. 1617 being Passion-Sunday, Touching Prostration, and Kneeling in the Worship of God. To Which is Added, A Discourse Concerning Kneeling at Communion* (London, 1618), 5–8.

56. Ibid., 243.

57. Lake, "*Avant-Garde* Conformity," 133.

58. L. Andrewes, *XCVI Sermons by the Right Honorable and Reverend Father in God, Lancelot Andrewes, late Lord Bishop of Winchester* (London, 1629), 548; also quoted to different effect by Fincham, *Prelate*, 235, and Lake, "*Avant-Garde* Conformity," 119.

59. A fuller text for Andrewes's remarks, "Touch me not, for I am

not yet ascended to my father" (John 20:17), supports this reading and may also be a rebuke of Calvinist eucharistic doctrine, which taught that receivers were united with Christ in heaven at the moment of communication (Andrewes, *XCVI Sermons*, 546).

60. James I, *Workes*, 607–8.

61. Andrewes, *XCVI Sermons*, 549. For Andrewes's remark as a rebuke to Calvinist "presumption," see Lake, "*Avant-Garde* Conformity," 117.

Chapter 6

1. J. Morrill, "A British Patriarchy? Ecclesiastical Imperialism Under the Early Stuarts," in *Religion, Culture and Society in Early Modern Britain: Essays in Honour of Patrick Collinson*, ed. A. Fletcher and P. Roberts (Cambridge, Eng., 1994), 216.

2. See Peter McCullough, "Making Dead Men Speak: Laudianism, Print, and the Works of Lancelot Andrewes, 1629–1642" (*JBS*, forthcoming) on the significance of the publication of the *XVCI Sermons* and Andrewes's posthumous legacy to Caroline politics. Many thanks to Dr. McCullough for allowing me to see this essay prior to its publication.

3. L. Andrewes, *The Works of Lancelot Andrewes*, ed. J. P. Wilson and J. Bliss (Oxford, 1841–54), 1: xiii–xix; J. H. Newman, *The Via Media of the Anglican Church*, ed. H. D. Weidner (1836; rpt., Oxford, 1990), 71–74, 393; "Lancelot Andrewes," in T. S. Eliot, *Selected Prose*, ed. F. Kermode (1932; rpt., New York, 1975), 179–88.

4. See, e.g., D. MacCulloch, "The Myth of the English Reformation," *JBS* 30, no.1 (1991): 1–19.

5. While Andrewes was an inspiration to the small group of Jacobean anti-Calvinists who came to power under Charles, he was decidedly anti-controversialist as well, which led other, bolder preachers to speak out explicitly where Andrewes kept a politic silence. See N. R. N. Tyacke, *Anti-Calvinists: The Rise of English Arminianism, c. 1590–1640* (Oxford and New York, 1987; rpt., 1991), 123.

6. K. Fincham, *Prelate as Pastor: The Episcopate of James I* (Oxford and New York, 1990), 212–31. Fincham points out that the degree of indulgence shown to certain nonconforming ministers depended on whose jurisdiction they resided in; nonconformity was judged by James's bishops on a case-by-case basis, which allowed for a fair bit of flexibility on the part both of the bishops and of the nonconforming clergy.

7. P. McCullough, *The Sermon at the Court of Elizabeth I and James I* (forthcoming).

8. Peter McCullough ("Making Dead Men Speak," forthcoming) has finally demonstrated, however, that later Calvinist divines also pointed

to the works of Andrewes for entirely different purposes. McCullough suggests that Caroline Calvinists harvested less fruitful support for their positions from Andrewes than did the Laudians.

9. Tyacke, *Anti-Calvinists*, 166–67.

10. C. Dow, *Innovations Unjustly Charged Upon the Present Church and State* (London, 1638), 196–97.

11. Dow asserts that the Elizabethan genesis of doctrinal puritanism was Calvin's "discipline," not his doctrine (ibid., 193–94).

12. See Wood, 2: 399, for a description of Dow as Laud's "creature" and beneficiary.

13. Dow, *Innovations Unjustly Charged*, 197.

Bibliography

Sermons

Andrewes, Lancelot. *A Sermon Preached Before the Kings Majesty at Hampton Court, concerning the Right and Power of Calling Assemblies, on Sunday the 28 of Sept. ANNO 1606. By the Bishop of Chichester.* London, 1606.

————. *A Sermon Preached Before His Majesty at Whitehall.* London, 1611.

————. *A Sermon Preached on Easter Day Last.* London, 1615.

————. *XCVI Sermons by the Right Honorable and Reverend Father in God, Lancelot Andrewes, late Lord Bishop of Winchester.* London, 1629 [1641].

————. *The Works of Lancelot Andrewes.* Edited by J. P. Wilson and J. Bliss. 11 vols. Oxford, 1841–54.

Bancroft, Richard. *Dangerous Positions and Proceedings, published and practiced within this Island of Britain, under pretense of Reformation and for the Presbyterial Discipline.* London, 1593.

————. *A Sermon Preached at Pauls Crosse the 9 of February, being the first Sunday in the Parliament, anno. 1588.* London, 1636.

Bargrave, Isaac. *A Sermon against Selfe-Policy Preached at White-Hall in Lent 1621.* London, 1624.

Barlow, William. *The Summe and Substance of the conference . . . at Hampton Court.* London, 1604.

————. *One of the Foure Sermons preached before the Kings Majestie, at Hampton Court in September last. This Concerning the Antiquity and Superioritie of Bishops. Sept. 21 1606.* London, 1606.

————. *The Sermon Preached at Paules Crosse the Tenth Day of November, being the Next Sunday after the Discoverie of this Late Horrible Treason.* London, 1606.

————. *A Brand, Titio Erepta.* London, 1607.

Bilson, Thomas. *A Sermon Preached before the King and Queenes Majesties, at their Coronations on Saint James his Day, being the xxv. of July. 1603.* London, 1604.

Blague, Thomas. *A Sermon Preached at the Charterhouse Before the Kings Majestie, on Tuesday, the tenth of May, 1603.* London, 1603.

Boys, John. *An Exposition of the Last Psalme, Delivered in a Sermon at Paules Crosse the 5th of November 1613 which I have joined to the festivals as a short apologie for our holy daies in the Church of England.* London, 1615.

Buckeridge, John. *A Sermon Preached at Hampton Court before the Kings Majestie, on Tuesday the 23. of September, Anno 1606.* London, 1606.

———. *A Sermon Preached before His Majesty at Whitehall, March 22. 1617 being Passion-Sunday, Touching Prostration, and Kneeling in the Worship of God. To which is Added, A Discourse Concerning Kneeling at Communion.* London, 1618.

Burges, John. *A Sermon Preached before the late King James his Majesty, at Greenwich, the 19th of July 1604.* London, 1642.

Cowper, William. *Two Sermons Preached in Scotland before the Kings Majesty.* London, 1618.

Crakanthorpe, Richard. *A Sermon at the Solemnizing of the Happie Inauguration of our most Gracious and Religious Soveraigne KING JAMES.* London, 1609.

Curll, Walter. *A Sermon Preached at Whitehall, on the 28 of April, 1622.* London, 1622.

Donne, John. *The Sermons of John Donne.* Edited by G. R. Potter and E. M. Simpson. 10 vols. Berkeley and Los Angeles, 1953–62.

Downame, George. *A Treatise upon John 8:36 Concerning Christian Libertie. The Chief Points Whereof Were Delivered in a Sermon Preached at Pauls Crosse, November 6, 1608.* London, 1609.

Du Moulin, Pierre. *A Sermon Preached before the Kings Majesty at Greenwich the 15. of June. 1615.* Oxford, 1620.

Field, Richard. *A Learned Sermon Preached before the King at Whitehall, on Friday the 16th of March, by M. Doctor Field: Chaplaine to His Majestie.* London, 1604.

Fotherby, Martin. *Foure Sermons, Lately Preached.* London, 1608.

Goodwin, William. *A Sermon Preached before the Kings Most Excellent Majestie at Woodstocke.* Oxford, 1614.

Gordon, John. *Henotikon, or a Sermon of the Union of Great Brittanie.* London, 1604.

Hacket, John. *A Century of Sermons Upon Several Remarkable Subjects: Preached by the Right Reverend Father in God, John Hacket, Late Lord Bishop of Lichfield and Coventry.* London, 1675.

Hall, Joseph. *Works.* Edited by P. Hall. 12 vols. Oxford, 1837.

Hampton, Christopher. *Two Sermons Preached Before the Kings Most Excellent Majesty in the Church of Beauly in Hampshire.* London, 1609.

Hooke, Henrie. *A Sermon Preached Before the King at White-hall, the eight of May. 1604.* London, 1604.

Hopkins, John. *A Sermon Preached before the Kings Majesty*. London, 1604.

King, John. *The Fourth Sermon preached at Hampton Court on Tuesday the last day of Sept. 1606*. Oxford, 1607.

——. *A Sermon Preached at White-Hall the 5. Day of November ann. 1608*. Oxford, 1608.

——. *Vitis Palatina*. London, 1614.

——. *A Sermon Preached at Paules Crosse on Behalf of Paules Church, March 26, 1620*. London, 1620.

Lake, Arthur. *Sermons with Some Religious and Divine Meditations*. London, 1629.

——. *Ten Sermons upon Severall Occasions, Preached at Saint Pauls Crosse and Elsewhere*. London, 1640.

Laud, William. *A Sermon Preached before His Majesty, on Tuesday the nineteenth of June, at Wansted*. London, 1621.

——. *A Sermon Preached at Whitehall, on the 24. of March, 1621*. London, 1622.

Loe, William. *The Kings Shoe. Made, and Ordained to trample on, and to tread down Edomites Delivered in a Sermon before the King at Theobalds October the ninth 1622*. London, 1623.

Mason, Francis. *Two Sermons Preached at the Kings Court this January, 1620*. London, 1621.

Maxey, Anthony. *Five Sermons Preached before the King*. London, 1614.

——. *Certaine Sermons Preached before the Kings Majestie, and elsewhere*. London, 1616.

——. *A Sermon Preached Before His Majesty at Bagshot, Sept 1 Anno Dom 1616*. London, 1619.

Meredith, Richard. *Two Sermons preached before his Majestie, in his Chappell at Whitehall*. London, 1606.

Meriton, George. *A Sermon of Nobilitie. Preached at Whitehall before the King in February 1606*. London, 1607.

Milward, John. *Jacobs Great Day of Trouble, and Deliverance. A Sermon Preached at Pauls Cross, the fifth of August 1607 upon his Majesties deliverance from the Earl Gowries treason and conspiracie*. London, 1610.

Mosse, Miles. *Scotlands Welcome*. London, 1604.

Parry, Henry. *De Regno Dei et Victoria Christiana, Conciones Duae Auctore D. Henrico Parraeos Theologiae Doctore et Decano Cestrensi*. London, 1606.

Playfere, Thomas. *Caesaris superscriptio. Sive conciuncula, coram duobos Potentissimis Regibus, in superiori atrio splendidae illius domus, Honoratissimi Comitis Sarisburiensis, quae vocatur Theobaldus*. London, 1606.

——. *A Sermon Preached Before the Kings Majestie at Drayton in Northamptonshire the sixt day of August 1605*. Cambridge, 1609.

————. *A Sermon Preached Before the Kings Majestie, that day he entred into Oxford, at Woodstock beeing the 27. of August. 1605.* Cambridge, 1609.

————. *Nine Sermons preached by that eloquent Divine of famous memorie.* Cambridge, 1621.

————. *The whole sermons of that eloquent Divine of famous memorie.* London, 1623.

Price, Daniel. *A Heartie Prayer in a needful time of trouble. The Sermon Preached at Theobalds before his Majestie, and the Lords of the Privie Councell an Houre before the Death of our late Sovereigne King James.* London, 1625.

————. *Lamentations for the Death of the late Illustrious Prince Henry . . . Two Sermons Preached in his Highnesse Chappell at Saint James.* London, 1613.

Prideaux, John. *Certaine Sermons.* Oxford, 1637.

Rawlinson, John. *Vivat Rex.* Oxford, 1619.

————. *Four Lenten Sermons.* Oxford, 1625.

Rudd, Anthony. *A Sermon Preached at the Court at Whitehall before the Kings Majesty, upon Sunday being the 13. of May 1604.* London, 1604.

————. *A Sermon Preached before the Kings Majestie at White Hall upon the ninth of Februarie 1605.* London, 1606.

Scott, Thomas. *Christs Politician and Solomans Puritan. Delivered in Two Sermons preached before the Kings Majestie.* London, 1616.

Smith, William. *The Black-Smith.* London, 1606.

Spackman, Norwich. *A Sermon Preached Before His Majesty at Whitehall the First of May, 1614.* London, 1614.

Stock, Richard. *A Sermon Preached at Pauls Crosse, the second of November, 1606.* London, 1607.

Swale, Christopher. *Jacobs Vow.* London, 1621.

Tynely, Robert. *Two Learned Sermons.* London, 1609.

Ussher, James. *A Brief Declaration of the Universalitie of the Church of Christ and the Unitie of the Catholike Faith professed therein. Delivered in a Sermon before his Majestie the 20th of June 1624 at Wansted.* London, 1624.

Wakeman, Robert. "*Salomons Exaltation: A Sermon Preached before the Kings Majestie at Nonesuch, April. 30. 1605.* Oxford, 1605.

Walsall, Samuel. *The Life and Death of Jesus Christ.* London, 1606.

Warburton, George. *King Melchizedech. A Sermon Preached at the Court at East Hamsted in His Majesties last summer progresse on Tuesday the second of September 1623.* London, 1623.

Westerman, William. *Jacobs Well: OR, A Sermon Preached before the Kings Most Excellent Majestie at Saint Albans, in his Summer Progress 1612.* London, 1613.

White, John. *Two Sermons*. London, 1615.

Wilkinson, Robert. *The Merchant Royall. A Sermon Preached at Whitehall before the Kings Majestie*. London, 1607.

———. *Barwickbridge, or England and Scotland coupled. In a sermon tending to peace and unitie. Preached before the King at Saint Andrewes in Scotland Anno Domini 1617 Jul. 13*. London, 1617.

Williams, John. *A Sermon of Apparell preached before the Kings Majestie and the Prince Highnesse at Theobalds. 22 of February 1619*. London, 1620.

———. *Great Britains Salomon*. London, 1625.

Unpublished Manuscripts

PUBLIC RECORD OFFICE, LONDON

SP 14/3/83: Letter of Bancroft and Whitgift to Cecil, dated 24 September 1603.

SP 14/19/27: Letter of Robert Cecil to the Earl of Mar, 9 March 1606.

SP 14/72/129: Letter of John Chamberlain to Dudley Carleton, 13 May 1613.

SP 14/89/67: Arrangements in the Chapel Royal, Scotland, 1617.

SP 14/92/75: Letter of Thomas Murray to Francis Bacon, 28 June 1617.

SP 14/132/85: "Directions for Preachers," appended to a letter from James I to Archbishop George Abbot.

Primary Sources

Adamson, Patrick. *A Declaration of the Kings Majesties intention toward the lait actis of parliament*. Edinburgh, 1584.

An Abridgement of that Book which the ministers of Lincoln Diocese delivered to His Majesty. Being the First Part of an apology for themselves and their brethren that refuse the subscription, and conformity which is required. London, 1605.

Bacon, Francis. *A Breif Discourse of the Happy Union of the Kingdoms of England and Scotland, with Certain Articles concerning the same*. Reprint. London, 1700.

Bancroft, Richard. *A Sermon Preached at Pauls Cross the 9 of February, being the first Sunday in the Parliament, Anno. 1588. by Richard Bancroft D. of Divinity and Chaplain to the Right Honorable Sir Christopher Hatton Knoght and Lord Chancellor of England*. London, 1588.

———. *Dangerous Positions and Proceedings, published and practiced within this Island of Britain, under pretense of Reformation and for the Presbyteriall Discipline*. London, 1593.

Birch, Thomas. *The Court and Times of James I*. 2 vols. London, 1848.

Buchanan, George. *De Jure Regni apud Scotos*. Edinburgh, 1579.

Calderwood, David. *Perth Assembly*. Leiden, 1619.

———. *A Solution of Doctor Resolutus his Resolutions for Kneeling*. Amsterdam, 1619.

———. *The History of the Kirk of Scotland*. 8 vols. Edited by Thomas Thomson. Edinburgh, 1842–49.

Calendar of State Papers, Domestic Series, for the Reign of James I. 4 vols. for 1603–25. London, 1857.

Calendar of State Papers (Venetian), 1603–7. London, 1900.

Campion, Thomas. *De Puluerea Coniuratione* [On the Gunpowder Plot]. Translated by David Lindley. Leeds, Eng., 1987.

Chamberlain, John. *Letters of Chamberlain*. Edited by N. E. Maclure. 2 vols. Philadelphia, 1939.

Craig, Thomas. *De Unione Regnorum Britanniae Tractatus*. Reprint. Edinburgh, 1909.

Dow, Christopher. *Innovations Unjustly Charged Upon the Present Church and State*. London, 1638.

Firth, C. H., ed. *Stuart Tracts, 1603–1693*. Westminster, 1903.

Fuller, Thomas. *The Church History of Britain*. 6 vols. 1655. Reprint. Edited by J. S. Brewer. 6 vols. Oxford, 1865.

Galloway, Bruce, and Brian Levack, eds. *The Jacobean Union: Six Tracts of 1604*. Edinburgh, 1985.

James I, king of England. *A Fruitful Meditation, Containing a Plaine and Easie Exposition . . . of the 20 Chapter of the Revelation*. Edinburgh, 1588.

———. *The Paraphrase upon the Revelation of Saint John*. Edinburgh, 1588.

———. BASILIKON DORON, *or His Majesties Instructions to his Dearest Sonne, Henry the Prince*. 1599. Reprint. London, 1603.

———. *The Workes of that most High and Mightie Prince James, by the Grace of God King of Great Britain, France and Ireland, Defender of the Faith, &c. Published by James Bp. of Winton. and Deane of His Majesties Chappell Royall*. London, 1616.

———. *A Meditation upon the Lord's Prayer*. London, 1619.

———. *A Pattern for a King's Inauguration*. London, 1620.

———. *The Political Works of James I*. Edited by C. H. McIlwain. 1918. Reprint. New York, 1965.

———. *Letters of King James VI and I*. Edited by G. P. V. Akrigg. Berkeley, Calif., 1984.

———. *King James VI and I: Political Writings*. Edited by Johann P. Sommerville. Cambridge, Eng., and New York, 1994.

Kenyon, J. P., ed. *The Stuart Constitution*. Cambridge, 1986.

Ketley, Joseph, ed. *The Two Liturgies*, A.D. *1549, and* A.D. *1552, with Other Documents Set Forth by Authority in the Reign of King Edward VI*. Cambridge, Eng., 1844.

Larkin, J. F., and P. L. Hughes, eds. *Stuart Royal Proclamations*. 2 vols. Oxford, 1973.

Morris, J., ed. *The Condition of Catholics Under James I: Father Gerard's Narration of the Gunpowder Plot*. London, 1871.

Morton, Thomas. *A Defense of the Innocency of the Three Ceremonies of the Church of England*. London, 1618.

Nichols, J. *The Progresses . . . of James I*. 4 vols. London, 1828.

Pont, Robert. *De Unione Britanniae Seu De Regnorum Angliae et Scotiae*. Edinburgh, 1604.

Rimbault, R. F., ed. *The Old Cheque-Book or Book of Remembrance of the Chapel Royal, 1561–1744*. London, 1872.

Rushworth, John. *Historical collections of private passages of state, weighty matters in law, remarkable proceedings in five Parliaments, beginning the sixteenth year of King James, anno 1618, and ending . . .* [with the death of King Charles I, 1648]. 8 vols. London, 1659–1701.

Venn, John, and J. A. Venn. *Alumni cantabrigienses: A Biographical List of All Known Students, Graduates and Holders of Office at the University of Cambridge, from the Earliest Times to 1900*. 10 vols. Cambridge, Eng., 1922–54.

Weldon, Anthony. *The Court and Character of King James: Written and Taken by Sir A. W.* London, 1650.

Wood, Anthony. *Alumni oxonienses: The Members of the University of Oxford, 1600–1714; Their Parentage, Birthplace, and Year of Birth, with a Record of Their Degrees. Being the Matriculation Register of the University, Alphabetically Arranged, Revised and Annotated*. Edited by Joseph Foster. 4 vols. Oxford and London, 1891–92.

Wotton, Henry. *The Life and Letters of Sir Henry Wotton*. Edited by L. P. Smith. 2 vols. Oxford, 1907.

The Zurich letters, comprising the correspondence of several English bishops and others, with some of the Helvetian reformers, during the early part of the reign of Queen Elizabeth. Edited and translated by Hastings Robinson. Cambridge, Eng., 1842.

Secondary Sources

Adams, Simon. "Spain or the Netherlands? The Dilemma of Early Stuart Foreign Policy." In *Before the Civil War*, ed. H. Tomlinson, 79–102. London, 1983.

———. "Foreign Policy and the Parliaments of 1621 and 1624." In *Faction and Parliament: Essays on Early Stuart History*, ed. K. Sharpe. New York, 1985.

Aiken, Lucy. *Memoirs of James I*. 2 vols. Boston, 1822.

Babbage, S. B. *Puritanism and Richard Bancroft*. London, 1962.

Bellany, Alistair. "A Poem for the Archbishop's Hearse." *Journal of British Studies* 30, no. 2 (1995): 137–64.

Bernard, G.W. "The Church of England c.1529–c.1642." *History* 75, no. 244 (June 1990): 183–206.

Bindoff, S. T. "The Stuarts and Their Style." *English Historical Review* 60 (1945): 192–216.

Bossy, John. "The English Catholic Community 1603–1625." In *The Reign of James VI and I*, ed. A. G. R. Smith. New York, 1973.

———. *The English Catholic Community 1570–1850*. London, 1975.

Cardwell, E. *History of Conferences . . . from the Year 1558 to the year 1690*. Oxford, 1840.

Chandos, John. *In God's Name: Examples of Preaching in England from the Act of Supremacy to the Act of Uniformity, 1534–1662*. Indianapolis, 1971.

Clifton, Robin. "Fear of Popery." In *The Origins of the English Civil War*, ed. C. Russell, 144–67. London, 1973.

Cogswell, Thomas. *The Blessed Revolution*. Cambridge, Eng., 1989.

Collinson, Patrick. *The Elizabethan Puritan Movement*. London, 1967. Reprint. Oxford, 1990.

———. *Archbishop Grindal: The Struggle for a Reformed Church*. Berkeley, Calif., 1979.

———. *The Religion of Protestants*. Oxford, 1982.

———. *Godly People*. London, 1983.

———. "The Jacobean Religious Settlement: The Hampton Court Conference." In *Before the Civil War*, ed. Howard Tomlinson, 27–51. New York, 1983.

———. "England and International Calvinism, 1558–1640." In *International Calvinism*, ed. M. Prestwich, 197–223. Oxford, 1985.

———. *The Birthpangs of Protestant England: Religious and Cultural Change in the Sixteenth and Seventeenth Centuries*. New York, 1988.

———. "The Cohabitation of the Faithful with the Unfaithful." In *From Persecution to Toleration: The Glorious Revolution and Religion in England*, ed. O. Grell, J. Israel, and N. Tyacke, 51–76. Oxford, 1991.

———. "The Theatre Constructs Puritanism." In *The Theatrical City: Culture, Theatre, and Politics in England, 1576–1649*, ed. D. Smith, R. Strier, and D. Bevington, 157–69. Cambridge, Eng., 1995.

Coolidge, John S. *The Pauline Renaissance in England: Puritanism and the Bible*. Oxford, 1970.

Cowan, Samuel. *The Gowrie Conspiracy and Its Official Narrative*. London, 1902.

Cragg, Gerald. *Reason and Authority: A Study of English Thought in the Early Seventeenth Century*. Philadelphia, 1975.

Cressy, David. *Bonfires and Bells: National Memory and the Protestant Calendar in Elizabethan and Stuart England*. Berkeley, Calif., 1989.

Cuddy, Neil. "The Revival of the Entourage: The Bedchamber of James I, 1603–1625." In *The English Court*, ed. D. Starkey, 173–225. London and New York, 1987.

Curtis, M. H. "The Hampton Court Conference and Its Aftermath." *History* 46 (1961): 1–16.

Cust, Richard, and Ann Hughes, eds. *Conflict in Early Stuart England*. London, 1989.

Daiches, David. *Scotland and the Union*. London, 1977.

Davies, Horton. *Like Angels from a Cloud*. New York, 1986.

Dickens, A. G. *The English Reformation*. New York, 1964. 2d ed. London, 1989.

Donaldson, Gordon. "The Attitude of Bancroft and Whitgift to the Scottish Church." *Transactions of the Royal Historical Society*, 4th ser., 24 (1942): 95–115.

———. *Scotland: The Shaping of a Nation*. London, 1974.

———. *All the Queen's Men*. London, 1983.

Duchein, Michel. *Jacques 1ᵉʳ Stuart: Le roi de la paix*. Paris, 1985.

Enright, M. J. "King James and His Island: An Archaic Kingship Belief?" *Scottish Historical Review* 55, nos. 159–60 (1975): 29–42.

Facey, Jane. "John Foxe and the Definition of the English Church." In *Protestantism and the National Church*, ed. P. Lake and M. Dowling, 162–92. London, 1987.

Ferguson, W. *Scotland's Relations with England to 1707*. Edinburgh, 1977.

Ferrell, Lori Anne. "Donne and His Master's Voice, 1615–1625." *John Donne Journal* 11, nos. 1–2 (1992): 59–70.

———. "Kneeling and the Body Politic." In *Religion, Literature and Politics in Post-Reformation England, 1540–1688*, ed. D. Hamilton and R. Strier, 70–92. Cambridge, Eng., 1995.

Fincham, Kenneth. *Prelate as Pastor: The Episcopate of James I*. Oxford and New York, 1990.

———, ed. *The Early Stuart Church, 1603–1642*. Stanford, 1993.

Fincham, Kenneth, and Peter Lake. "The Ecclesiastical Policy of King James I." *Journal of British Studies* 24, no. 2 (April 1985): 173–92.

———. "The Ecclesiastical Policies of James I and Charles I." In *The Early Stuart Church*, ed. K. Fincham. Stanford, 1993.

Fletcher, Anthony, and Peter Roberts, eds. *Religion, Culture and Society in Early Modern Britain: Essays in Honour of Patrick Collinson*. Cambridge, Eng., 1994.

Galloway, Bruce. *The Union of England and Scotland 1603–1608*. Edinburgh, 1986.

Gardiner, Samuel Rawson. *The History of England from the Accession of James I to the Outbreak of the Civil War, 1603–1642*. 10 vols. London and New York, 1894–96.

Grayson, C. "James I and the Religious Crisis in the United Provinces, 1613–19." In *Reform and Reformation: England and the Continent, c. 1500–c. 1750*, ed. D. Baker, 195–219. Studies in Church History, Subsidia 2. Oxford, 1979.

Grell, Ole, Jonathan Israel, and N. R. N. Tyacke, eds. *From Persecution to Toleration: The Glorious Revolution and Religion in England*. Oxford, 1991.

Haigh, Christopher. "The Recent Historiography of the English Reformation." *Historical Journal* 25, no. 4 (Dec. 1982): 995–1007.

Hamilton, Donna, and Richard Strier, eds. *Religion, Literature and Politics in Post-Reformation England, 1540–1688*. Cambridge, Eng., 1995.

Harrison, A. W. *The Beginnings of Arminianism*. London, 1926.

Hill, J. E. C. *Economic Problems of the Church, from Archbishop Whitgift to the Long Parliament*. 1956. Reprint. Oxford, 1968.

Hurstfield, Joel. *Freedom, Corruption and Government in Elizabethan England*. London, 1973.

———. "Gunpowder Plot and the Politics of Dissent." In *Early Stuart Studies*, ed. H. Reinmuth. Minneapolis, 1976.

Jones, Norman. *Faith by Statute: Parliament and the Settlement of Religion 1559*. London, 1982.

Kendall, R. T. *Calvin and English Calvinism to 1649*. Oxford, 1979.

Kirk, James. "The Polities of the Best Reformed Kirks: Scottish Achievements and English Aspirations in Church Government After the Reformation." *Scottish Historical Review* 59 (1980): 25–53.

Lake, Peter. *Moderate Puritans and the Elizabethan Church*. Cambridge, Eng., 1982.

———. "Calvinism and the English Church, 1560–1640." *Past and Present* 114 (Feb. 1987): 32–76.

———. *Anglicans and Puritans? Presbyterianism and English Conformist Thought from Whitgift to Hooker*. London and Boston, 1988.

———. "Anti-Popery: The Structure of a Prejudice." In *Conflict in Early Stuart England*, ed. R. Cust and A. Hughes, 72–107. London, 1989.

———. "Lancelot Andrewes, John Buckeridge, and *Avant-Garde* Conformity at the Jacobean Court." In *The Mental World of the Jacobean Court*, ed. L. Peck. Cambridge, Eng., 1991.

———. "The Laudian Style." In *The Early Stuart Church*, ed. K. Fincham. Stanford, 1993.

Lee, Maurice, Jr. *James I and Henry IV: An Essay in English Foreign Policy.* Urbana, Ill., 1971.

———. *Government by Pen: Scotland Under James VI and I.* Urbana, Ill., 1980.

———. *Great Britain's Solomon: James VI and I in His Three Kingdoms.* Chicago, 1990.

Levack, Brian. *The Formation of the British State: England, Scotland and the Union 1603–1707.* Oxford, 1987.

Lindley, David. "Campion's Lord Hay's Masque and Anglo-Scottish Union." *Huntington Library Quarterly* 43, no. 1 (1979): 1–11.

———. "Who Paid for Campion's Lord Hay Masque?" *Notes and Queries* 26, no. 2 (1979): 144–45.

———. *Thomas Campion.* Leiden, 1986.

Long, A. *James VI and the Gowrie Mystery.* London, 1902.

Lossky, Nicholas. *Lancelot Andrewes the Preacher, 1555–1626.* Oxford, 1979.

Lythe, S. G. E. "The Union of the Crowns in 1603 and the Debate on Economic Integration." *Scottish Journal of Political Economy* 5 (1958): 219–28.

MacCulloch, Diarmid. "The Myth of the English Reformation." *Journal of British Studies* 30, no.1 (January 1991): 1–19.

McCullough, P. "Making Dead Men Speak: Laudianism, Print, and the Works of Lancelot Andrewes, 1629–1642." *Historical Journal*, forthcoming.

———. *The Sermon at the Court of Elizabeth I and James I.* Cambridge, Eng., forthcoming.

MacLure, M. *The Paul's Cross Sermons, 1534–1642.* Toronto, 1958.

McGee, S. *The Godly Man in Stuart England.* New Haven, Conn., 1976.

———. "William Laud and the Outward Face of Religion." In *Leaders of the Reformation,* ed. R. DeMolen, 318–44. Selinsgrove, Pa., 1984.

Mason, Roger, ed. *Scots and Britons: Scottish Political Thought and the Union of 1603.* Cambridge, Eng., 1994.

———. "George Buchanan, James VI and the Presbyterians." In *Scots and Britons,* ed. id.

Milton, Anthony. *Catholic and Reformed: The Roman and Protestant Churches in English Protestant Thought, 1600–1640.* Cambridge, Eng., 1995.

Mitchell, W. Fraser. *English Pulpit Oratory from Andrewes to Tillotson.* London, 1932.

Morrill, John. "The Religious Context of the British Civil War." *Transactions of the Royal Historical Society,* 5th ser., 34 (1984).

———. *The Scottish National Covenant in Its British Context.* Edinburgh, 1991.

————. "A British Patriarchy? Ecclesiastical Imperialism Under the Early Stuarts." In *Religion, Culture and Society in Early Modern Britain: Essays in Honour of Patrick Collinson*, ed. A. Fletcher and P. Roberts. Cambridge, Eng., 1994.

Morrill, John, Paul Slack, and Daniel Woolf, eds. *Public Duty and Private Conscience in Seventeenth-Century England*. Oxford, 1993.

Mullan, David George. *Episcopacy in Scotland: The History of an Idea*. Edinburgh, 1986.

Nicholls, Mark. *Investigating the Gunpowder Plot*. Manchester, 1991.

Nobbs, D. *England and Scotland, 1560–1707*. London, 1952.

Norman, E. *Roman Catholicism in England*. Oxford, 1985.

Omond, G. W. T. *The Early History of the Scottish Union Question*. Edinburgh, 1897.

Patterson, W. Brown. "King James I's Call for an Ecumenical Council." In *Councils and Assemblies: Papers Read at the Eighth Summer Meeting and the Ninth Winter Meeting of the Ecclesiastical History Society*, ed. G. J. Cuming and Derek Baker. Studies in Church History, No. 7. Cambridge, Eng., 1971.

————. "James I and the Huguenot Synod of Tonneins of 1614." *Harvard Theological Review* 65, no. 2 (1972): 241–70.

————. "The Synod of Dort and the Early Stuart Church." In *This Sacred History*, ed. D. S. Armentrout. Cambridge, Mass., 1990.

Peck, Linda, ed. *The Mental World of the Jacobean Court*. Cambridge, Eng., 1991.

Quintrell, B. "The Royal Hunt and the Puritans, 1604–1605." *Journal of British Studies* 31 (1980): 41–58.

Reidy, Maurice. *Bishop Lancelot Andrewes: Jacobean Court Preacher*. Chicago, 1955.

Reynolds, E. E. *The Roman Catholic Church in England and Wales: A Short History*. Wheathampstead, Eng., 1973.

Roughead, W. N. *The Riddle of the Ruthvens and Other Studies*. London, 1919.

Russell, Conrad. *The Causes of the English Civil War*. Oxford, 1990.

————. *The Fall of the British Monarchies, 1637–1642: The Ford Lectures Delivered in the University of Oxford, 1987–8*. Oxford, 1991.

————. "The Anglo-Scottish Union, 1603–1643: A Success?" In *Religion, Culture and Society in Early Modern Britain: Essays in Honour of Patrick Collinson*, ed. A. Fletcher and P. Roberts. Cambridge, Eng., 1994.

————, ed. *The Origins of the English Civil War*. London, 1973.

Schwartz, M. "James I and the Historians: Toward a Reconsideration." *Journal of British Studies* 13 (1974): 114–34.

Shami, Jeanne. "Introduction: Reading Donne's Sermons," *John Donne Journal* 11 (1992): 2–24.

Sharpe, Kevin. *Criticism and Compliment: The Politics of Literature in the England of Charles I.* Cambridge, Eng., 1987.

———. *Politics and Ideas in Early Stuart England: Essays and Studies.* London, 1989.

———. *The Personal Rule of Charles I.* New Haven, 1993.

———. "Private Conscience and Public Duty in the Writings of King James VI and I." In *Public Duty and Private Conscience in Seventeenth-Century England*, ed. J. Morrill, P. Slack, and D. Woolf. Oxford, 1993.

———. "The King's Writ: Royal Authors and Royal Authority in Early Modern England." In *Problems in Focus: Culture and Politics in Early Stuart England*, ed. K. Sharpe and P. Lake. London, 1994.

———. "Religion, Rhetoric, and Revolution in Seventeenth-Century England." *Huntington Library Quarterly* 58, no. 3 (July 1995): 255–58.

———, ed. *Faction and Parliament: Essays on Early Stuart History.* New York, 1985.

Shriver, F. "Hampton Court Revisited: James I and the Puritans." *Journal of Ecclesiastical History* 33 (1982): 48–71.

———. "Orthodoxy and Diplomacy: The Vorstius Affair." *English Historical Review* 336 (July 1970): 449–74.

Smith, D., R. Strier, and D. Bevington, eds. *The Theatrical City: Culture, Theatre, and Politics in England, 1576–1649.* Cambridge, Eng., 1995.

Smuts, M. *Court Culture and the Origins of a Royalist Tradition in Early Stuart England.* Philadelphia, 1987.

Sommerville, J. P. *Politics and Ideology in England, 1603–1640.* New York, 1986.

Spedding, J. *The Life and Times of Francis Bacon.* London, 1878.

Strier, R. "Donne and the Politics of Devotion." In *Religion, Literature and Politics in Post-Reformation England, 1540–1688*, ed. D. Hamilton and R. Strier. Cambridge, Eng., 1995.

Todd, Margo. "Introduction." In *Reformation to Revolution: Politics and Religion in Early Modern England*, ed. id. London, 1995.

Trevor-Roper, Hugh. "The Union of Britain in the Seventeenth Century." In id., *Religion, the Reformation and Social Change*, 445–67. London, 1967.

Tyacke, N. R. N. "Puritanism, Arminianism and Counter-Revolution." In *The Origins of the English Civil War*, ed. Conrad Russell, 119–43. London, 1973

———. "The Rise of Arminianism Reconsidered." *Past and Present* 115 (1987): 201–16.

————. *The Fortunes of English Puritanism, 1603–1640.* London, 1989.

————. *Anti-Calvinists: The Rise of English Arminianism, c. 1590–1640.* Oxford and New York, 1987. Reprint, 1991.

————. "The Legalizing of Dissent, 1571–1719." In *From Persecution to Toleration: The Glorious Revolution and Religion in England,* ed. O. Grell, J. Israel, and N. Tyacke. Oxford, 1991.

Underdown, David. *A Freeborn People: Politics and the Nation in Seventeenth-Century England.* Oxford, 1996.

Vickers, Brian. *The Defence of Rhetoric.* Oxford, 1988.

Walsham, Alexandra. *Church Papists.* London, 1994.

Wedgwood, C. V. "Anglo-Scottish Relations, 1603–1640." *Transactions of the Royal Historical Society* 32 (1950): 31–48.

Weiner, Carol. "The Beleaguered Isle: A Study of Elizabethan and Early Jacobean Anti-Catholicism." *Past and Present* 51 (May 1971): 27–62.

Welsby, Paul. *Lancelot Andrewes, 1555–1626.* London, 1958.

White, Paul. "The Rise of Arminianism Reconsidered: A Rejoinder." *Past and Present* 101 (1983): 217–29.

————. *Predestination, Policy and Polemic: Conflict and Consensus in the English Church from the Reformation to the Civil War.* Cambridge, Eng., 1992.

————. "The *Via Media* in the Early Stuart Church." In *The Early Stuart Church, 1603–1642,* ed. K. Fincham. Stanford, 1993.

Williamson, Arthur. *Scottish National Consciousness in the Age of James VI.* Edinburgh, 1979.

Willson, D. H. "James I and His Literary Assistants." *Huntington Library Quarterly* 8, no. 1 (1944–45): 35–57.

Wormald, Jenny. *Court, Kirk and Community: Scotland, 1470–1625.* London, 1981.

————. "James VI and I: Two Kings or One?" *History* 68 (1983): 187–209.

————. "Gunpowder, Treason and Scots." *Journal of British Studies* 24 (April 1985): 141–68.

————. "The Union of 1603." In *Scots and Britons: Scottish Political Thought and the Union of 1603,* ed. R. Mason. Cambridge, Eng., 1994.

Wright, L. "Propaganda Against James I's 'appeasement' of Spain." *Huntington Library Quarterly* 6, no. 2 (1942–43): 149–72.

Index

In this index an "f" after a number indicates a separate reference on the next page, and an "ff" indicates a separate reference on the next two pages. A continuous discussion over two or more pages is indicated by a span of page numbers, e.g., "57–59." *Passim* is used for a cluster of references in close but not consecutive sequence.

Library of Congress Cataloging-in-Publication Data

Ferrell, Lori Anne
    Government by polemic : James I, the king's preachers, and
the rhetorics of conformity, 1603–1625 / Lori Anne Ferrell.
        p.   cm.
    Includes bibliographical references and index.
    ISBN 0-8047-3221-3 (alk. paper).
        1. Great Britain—Politics and government—1603–1625.
2. Rhetoric—Political aspects—Great Britain—History—17th
century.   3. Christianity and politics—Great Britain—
History—17th century.   4. Dissenters, religious—England—
History—17th century.   5. Christianity and politics—Church
of England.   6. Sermons, English—History and criticism.
7. James I, King of England, 1566–1625   8. England—Church
history—17th century.   9. Church of England—History.
10. Conformity   11. Polemics.   I. Title.

DA391.F47   1998
941.06'1—dc21   98-3771
                                                           CIP

This book is printed on acid-free, recycled paper.

Original printing 1998
Last figure below indicates year of this printing:
07   06   05   04   03   02   01   00   99   98